YOUR
HAPPIER LIFE
TOOLBOX

HOW A DATA-DRIVEN DAD CRACKED THE CODE ON HAPPINESS (AND HOW YOU CAN TOO)

BY BILLY MARSHALL

CONTENTS

YOUR INNER GAME
SECTION ONE

CHAPTER 1:
FROM NEGATIVITY BIAS TO INTENTIONAL JOY

CHAPTER 2:
BECOMING THE CEO OF YOUR OWN MIND

CHAPTER 3:
BUILDING UNSHAKEABLE INNER STRENGTH

CHAPTER 4:
FINDING YOUR SOMETHING BIGGER

YOUR SUCCESS SYSTEMS
SECTION TWO

CHAPTER 5:
OPTIMIZING YOUR HUMAN OPERATING SYSTEM

CHAPTER 6:
DESIGNING A LIFE THAT ACTUALLY WORKS

CHAPTER 7:
THE ART OF SUSTAINABLE LIVING

CONNECTION THAT MATTERS
SECTION THREE

CHAPTER 8:
TRANSFORMING SURFACE CONNECTIONS INTO SOUL CONNECTIONS

INTRODUCTION

It was about 2 a.m., phone glowing on my face. I typed four words that would change everything: *"how to be happy."*

I should've been asleep. By every external measure, life was good. Loving wife, Suzy, asleep beside me? Check. Five great kids and five grandbabies? Check. Good friends, a boat, a home near the ocean? Check. Every box on the "life is okay" checklist was ticked. And still I lay there, eyes open, stuck on a question my degrees and decades hadn't answered.

I spent my career designing technical frameworks and data tools to help business leaders make smart decisions. So I did the only thing that made sense. I pointed that lens inward. Could the lessons of happiness be turned into something clear, usable, and repeatable?

My mind wasn't broken; it had just been handed a problem it wasn't trained to solve.

That late-night question became a project: to apply my data-driven methods to the messier puzzle of my own head.

I had read shelves of self-help books, but the truth is I couldn't even remember which ones I'd read, let alone many of their takeaways. So I went back to the search bar with a more specific question. Could happiness be boiled down to a science? I wasn't looking for a quick fix. I was looking for rules I could count on.

Scrolling for something concrete, I found Dr. Laurie Santos and her podcast, *The Happiness Lab*. The next morning, with Yeti, our golden retriever, chasing waves beside me, I started collecting insights. I eventually devoured more than 200 episodes. The science was fascinating, but I hit a familiar wall. The information was falling out of my head almost as fast as it was going in. I needed a system.

So I did what any data-obsessed dad would do. I built a spreadsheet. What began as a simple tracking tool quickly grew into a full-on research project. I cross-referenced podcast insights with dozens of books spanning decades, used technology to dive deeper, and organized everything by category with clear action steps.

My poor kids, bless their patience, humored me by reading that spreadsheet as I dug up new "treasures." Suzy would joke about my disappearing acts, but she also saw that it was working. I was becoming calmer, more present, and happier.

Then I started noticing the same quiet struggle everywhere. My kids, now adults, facing their own challenges. Friends scrolling anxiously on their phones. You know the look, the glazed-over, thumb-scrolling trance we all pretend we don't do. Coworkers burned out despite hitting every marker of the American Dream. I realized this project wasn't just for me anymore.

Emailing my cluttered spreadsheet to the people I cared about felt as personal as sending a carrier pigeon with a pie chart. That's when the feeling arrived. Not a tidy thought, but an absurd, terrifying, undeniable prompting from the heart: *this needs to be a book*. Me? The guy who considers listening to a book on Audible "reading"? It felt like being signed up for a marathon I didn't know I'd entered. But I laced up my shoes and decided to run anyway.

You're holding the book that didn't exist at 2 a.m., the one I desperately needed. A research-backed toolbox of daily happiness practices you can actually use. Each tool is grounded in science, tested in real life, and simple enough to use when your brain is running on fumes. I'm not a happiness guru. I'm a stubborn, data-driven dad who refused to quit until this book included only tools with solid evidence of real-world impact.

You'll notice this book is called *Your Happier Life Toolbox*, not *Your Happy Life Toolbox*. That's intentional. Chasing "happy" as a final destination is a trap. **Becoming happier is a journey we can all start today.**

That 2 a.m. search didn't give me an answer; it started the right journey. Now it's your turn.

Your happiness is not a solo project; it's a public service. In a world starving for connection and drowning in anxiety, your calm is contagious. Your patience can de-escalate a conflict. Your vulnerability gives others permission to be real.

This isn't just about feeling better; it's about being better. It is about calming your own home, strengthening your workplace, and healing your small corner of the world. This is how we change our world. Not through grand gestures, but through the cumulative impact of ordinary people committing to the radical act of choosing joy.

And if a weird, data-driven, spreadsheet-building dad from Jersey can figure this out, trust me. You've got this.

I've already built your first tool: an online hub with resources, guided practices, and a community of fellow builders at www.yourhappier.life.

For now, let's get to work.

HOW TO USE
THIS BOOK

Whether you devour this book from start to finish or sample it like a happiness buffet, you'll find tools you can use right away to start building a life you love. To help you navigate, here's what you'll find inside:

What You'll Find Inside

The book is built on a simple framework with three parts:

- **Your Inner Game:** Tools to transform your mental patterns from enemy to ally
- **Your Success Systems:** Habits that ignite lasting energy and purpose
- **Your Connections:** Strategies to create relationships and community that sustain you

Throughout the three parts, you'll find 42 scientifically proven tools. While the world of happiness research is vast, these are the ones that truly **move the needle**. They represent the foundational principles you need to build a happier life. Each tool follows the same simple recipe:

- **Why It Matters** (no fluff, just real talk)
- **The Science Behind It** (research from the smart people)

- **My Journey** (my messy attempts, failures included)
- **Reflecting On** (a prompt to make it personal)
- **Action Steps** (from easy to stretch goals)

There's also a **myth-busting Appendix** that clears away what doesn't work. If you're feeling stuck despite 'doing everything right,' I suggest starting there to pinpoint the faulty happiness theories holding you back.

In fact, I'll spoil two of the biggest lies for you right now, because dismantling them right out of the gate is important.

- Happiness Is Fixed by Genetics
- Happiness Requires No Effort; It Just Happens

The truth is, your happiness isn't fixed, but changing it takes intentional effort: which is why the key isn't just to read this book, but to **do it**. Here's how to put it all into practice:

- **Start small:** Pick ONE tool and try the easiest version for a week
- **Keep it visible:** Dog-ear pages, highlight passages, leave the book where you'll see it
- **Lower the bar when stuck:** Cut any action step in half (then half again) until it feels doable
- **View this as a lifelong companion:** This toolbox is meant to be revisited as your life changes, because the tool you need today might be different from the one you need next year
- **Focus on generating momentum:** A clumsy, five-second attempt is the small effort that delivers a huge return: and it's far better than the perfect session you keep putting off

This isn't a test. There's no deadline for transforming your life. Just grab a highlighter, pick something that speaks to you, and actually try it.

Let's figure this happiness thing out together.

YOUR INNER GAME
SECTION ONE

On a perfect spring day, I launched my boat feeling like the king of the world—right up until I heard the locked-up trailer wheel. *"No big deal,"* I told myself. *"Just keep driving and it'll work itself loose."*

While fixating on that screaming wheel, I completely forgot I was pulling a trailer and swung wide, introducing it to a telephone pole. While making a left-hand turn nonetheless! As I returned home, I noticed my wife and neighbor were standing with front-row seats to my spectacular display of absentmindedness.

I was furious with myself. *"How could you forget you're pulling a trailer? What kind of idiot are you?"*

But something interesting happened on that five-minute drive home: Between the self-flagellation and colorful language, I caught myself. I took a deep breath and started talking to myself differently: "Hey Billy, stuff happens. Nobody got hurt. The trailer can be fixed. Let it go, Billy. Just breathe and let it go."

By the time I returned, the transformation wasn't complete, but it had started. I looked at Suzy, shrugged my shoulders, and said, "Oops. Hopefully I won't do that again."

That moment taught me something valuable about the voice in my head. We all have two possible voices when we mess up. The drill sergeant who berates us for every mistake, or the compassionate friend who says, "That stinks, but you'll figure it out." For too long, I defaulted to the drill sergeant. Now I'm practicing calling on my friend.

Because here's the truth: The telephone pole doesn't care whether I beat myself up or not. *But my heart sure does.* The trailer doesn't get fixed any faster if I'm busy listing all my character flaws. But I sure feel a lot better when I give myself the grace I'd give anyone else.

That five-minute drive home became my masterclass in self-compassion.

And that's what this entire section is about. Learning to be the friend to yourself that you'd be to anyone else, whether you're dealing with wayward boat trailers or any of life's thousand other curveballs.

But before we can own the Inner Game of our own minds, we have to fire the fraudulent consultants who have been giving us bad advice. For years, I operated on a set of damaging myths about how our minds are supposed to work: and chances are, you have too. Let's bust five of the biggest right now:

- Negative Emotions Signal Something Is Wrong
- Happiness Means Feeling Good All the Time
- I Can't Be Happy During Adversity
- Perfectionism Leads to Excellence
- Stress Must Be Eliminated

These beliefs aren't just wrong; they're roadblocks that keep us stuck in cycles of anxiety and self-criticism. In the following chapters, we're going to build the toolkit to smash right through them. (And if you're eager to see more about the lies we're dismantling, you can jump and read the science behind all 37 myths in the Appendix at any time.)

Obviously, I'm not sitting cross-legged on a mountain somewhere, dispensing wisdom between bites of organic kale. I'm just a regular guy who's spent six decades stumbling my way, learning, forgetting what I learned, and then relearning it all over again. My journey with the "Inner Game" has been about as graceful as my attempts at dancing the "electric slide": which, for the record, Suzy and I consider a success if I don't hurt anyone on the dance floor! But you know what? Just like those wedding reception dance floors, I keep showing up, laughing at myself, and giving it another go. Because sometimes the best stories, and the best growth, come from those moments when we're willing to look a little foolish in pursuit of something that brings us joy.

But this stuff matters deeply. Managing your inner game isn't about achieving perfection. It's about conducting the chaos. You might look at it as a symphony orchestra. Without a conductor, it'll play whatever notes come along, usually producing more chaos than a middle school band practice. The tools in this section are about becoming the intentional conductor of your own mental music.

All of this really, really matters. Because when you get down to it, **the quality of your life depends less on doing everything right and more on what's happening between your ears.** These tools won't make you perfect. They'll make you peaceful with your imperfection. You can have everything society says you're supposed to want and still feel empty inside. Or you can face genuine challenges and still find moments of jaw-dropping joy and peace. The difference is finding the way to Master Your Inner Game with the tools you've got in your psychological toolbox.

If you're ready to stop being your own worst enemy, let's dive in. Think of this section as your foundational toolkit for mental and emotional well-being. We'll explore science-backed strategies to help you weather storms, celebrate sunshine, and find beauty in ordinary Tuesdays.

THESE TOOLS ARE ORGANIZED INTO FOUR CORE AREAS OF MASTERY:

CHAPTER 1: FROM NEGATIVITY BIAS TO INTENTIONAL JOY

- Practicing Daily Gratitude: Training your brain to notice and appreciate what's good
- Practicing Optimism: Maintaining hope while facing reality head-on
- Reframing Negativity Positively: Challenging automatic negative interpretations
- Savoring Positive Experiences: Stretching and deepening moments of joy
- Cultivating Humor & Laughter: Finding lightness even in difficult times

CHAPTER 2: BECOMING THE CEO OF YOUR OWN MIND

- Practicing Mindfulness Meditation: Gently training your attention to stay present
- Using Deep Breathing to Relax: Activating your body's natural calm-down system
- Labeling Your Emotions: Naming feelings to reduce their power over you
- Placing Yourself in Awe & Wonder: Connecting to something larger than yourself

CHAPTER 3: BUILDING UNSHAKEABLE INNER STRENGTH

- Practicing Self-Compassion: Treating yourself with the kindness you'd offer a friend

- Leveraging Character Strengths: Using your natural gifts more intentionally
- Embracing a Growth Mindset: Viewing challenges as opportunities to develop
- Accepting What You Can't Control: Focusing energy where it truly makes a difference

CHAPTER 4: FINDING YOUR SOMETHING BIGGER: CONNECTING TO SOMETHING GREATER THAN YOURSELF

These aren't discrete techniques. They're instruments in your mental orchestra. And like any good symphony, the magic happens when they all play together, each one supporting and enhancing the others.

These tools won't make your life perfect. Lord knows mine isn't, with regrets that keep me up at night and a highlight reel of mess-ups that's still recording. My promise is this: these practical, science-backed strategies won't change what life tosses your way, but **they will fundamentally transform how you experience life**. They'll help you find islands of calm in your personal hurricane and genuine belly laughs in the middle of your mistakes.

The beautiful truth is that happiness isn't some distant destination you reach after you've checked all the right boxes. It's available right now. Even with a damaged boat trailer and a bruised ego.

So grab a comfortable seat and maybe your favorite beverage. We're about to dive into the most important journey you'll ever take. The one between your ears. And I promise, we'll have some fun along the way.

CHAPTER 1:

FROM NEGATIVITY BIAS TO INTENTIONAL JOY

For much of my life, I drifted along, unconsciously tethered to the whims of my own thoughts. Reacting rather than directing, consumed rather than in control. It wasn't until later in life that I realized something profound: I had the power to influence and manage my own mindset. I'm not saying I've mastered it, not even close, but I have learned how to step in, take the reins, and gently tame the inner beast when it starts running wild.

The other night, I climbed into bed battling wild negativity. Finally, I challenged the voice in my head: "Who put you in charge of what we're thinking?" Realizing I accidentally said it out loud, I chuckled. Suzy rolled over: "Who are you talking to?" "Myself," I admitted. Without missing a beat, she sighed, "That's cool. Can you tell whoever's 'in charge' to dial it down a notch?" We both laughed. Guess even my inner demons need to use their inside voices.

As amusing as it was, that moment captured an essential truth: **happiness isn't determined by what happens to us, but by how we talk to ourselves about it.**

Your mindset isn't just some fluffy concept. It's the control panel for your entire life experience. And the best part? You can rewire it. Not overnight, and not perfectly, but reliably and meaningfully. In this chapter, we'll explore five science-backed tools that can transform your mental landscape from a battlefield to a garden:

- How to use gratitude to shift your brain's default setting from "what's wrong" to "what's right"
- Why optimism is less about blind positivity and more about resilient thinking
- How to reframe negative thoughts without suppressing your authentic feelings
- The underrated power of savoring good moments (and why we're so bad at it)
- Why laughter might be the most undervalued mental health tool in your arsenal

These aren't quick fixes or magic pills. They're tools that when used have pulled me back from the edge more times than I can count. Let's dig in.

PRACTICING DAILY GRATITUDE
WHY GRATITUDE MATTERS

Your brain is a threat-detection machine. It evolved to find dangers, not joy, which is why it's so good at cataloging every annoyance from work stress to spilled coffee. This survival wiring is making us miserable. Gratitude isn't fluffy nonsense. It's the software upgrade you need to run a happier operating system.

When you deliberately practice gratitude, you're essentially giving those toxic emotions, anger, envy, resentment, less space in your mental apartment. They don't disappear completely (wouldn't that be nice?), but they do get downgraded from the master bedroom to the closet under the stairs.

Gratitude also works wonders for your relationships. Think about it: when someone genuinely appreciates you, doesn't that strengthen your connection? The same works in reverse. People who regularly express gratitude report feeling less lonely and more supported, even when life gets rough.

Speaking of rough patches, gratitude builds emotional resilience like nothing else. It's like having a mental emergency fund when life throws an unexpected expense your way. **Those who practice gratitude consistently recover faster from setbacks and maintain their balance during storms that would knock others flat.**

Your body responds to gratitude, too. Regular gratitude practice reduces cortisol, leading to better sleep, lower blood pressure, and a stronger immune system. Not bad for something that costs absolutely nothing, right?

THE SCIENCE BEHIND GRATITUDE

Remember when your mom told you to count your blessings? Turns out, she was onto something scientifically solid. In 2005, Dr. Martin Seligman (the godfather of positive psychology) ran what he called a "gratitude intervention" study.[1] Participants who wrote down three things they were grateful for each day showed significant increases in happiness and decreases in depression, not just during the experiment but for months afterward. Even more impressive? The folks who stuck with it for just one week were still experiencing benefits six months later. Talk about getting your money's worth!

Think of gratitude like wiping a dirty windshield. Suddenly you notice the good stuff that was always there, hidden in your mental blind spots. Without gratitude, your brain defaults to spotting dangers and annoyances (thanks, evolution!). With it, you start catching the positive moments you'd normally miss.

Take a look under the hood: gratitude practice actually reduces cortisol (that nasty stress hormone) and boosts serotonin and dopamine (the feel-good chemicals). You're essentially giving yourself a natural mood enhancer without the prescription. The more you practice, the more automatic this positive focus becomes, until your brain starts taking the scenic route without you having to redirect it.

The bottom line? Three minutes of gratitude journaling can create six months of increased happiness. If that's not the best mental health bargain out there, I don't know what is.

MY JOURNEY TOWARD GRATITUDE

One day, driving home with a flimsy paper plate of chicken wraps that Suzy had shoved into my hands as I was running out the door, I decided to practice gratitude. **Not the polite "thanks honey" kind, but the brain-rewiring kind I'd been learning about.** While driving to my destination, I paused to really appreciate her small kindness. A funny thing happened. Suddenly she seemed more awesome. This wasn't about manners anymore; this was brain chemistry in action. I realized if I kept doing this, she'd become harder NOT to appreciate. Gratitude glasses don't change the person, but they sure soften your gaze, making loving others a whole lot easier.

REFLECTING ON GRATITUDE

Before we jump into some practical ways to grow your gratitude muscles, take a moment to reflect on this: What's one small, ordinary thing in your life that you'd deeply miss if it suddenly disappeared tomorrow? And how often do you pause to appreciate that very thing while it's right in front of you?

ACTION STEPS TOWARD GRATITUDE

Ready to flex that gratitude muscle? Here are six simple ways to get started:

- **Morning Coffee Gratitude**: Pair gratitude with your first sip of coffee each day, immediately making it enjoyable and effortless.
- **Gratitude text**: Write out a real thank-you text to someone. You know, the kind where you actually say why they matter. You can keep it as your own gratitude moment or hit send and probably make someone cry happy tears.
- **Gratitude Snapshots**: Take a daily photo of something you're thankful for, turning gratitude into a playful, creative activity.
- **Gratitude Buddy**: Exchange daily gratitude messages with a friend, making accountability social, enjoyable, and easy.
- **Three Good Things**: Quickly note three positives before bed, rewarding yourself with a relaxing night time ritual afterward.

- **Gratitude Game**: Challenge yourself daily to find hidden positives in tough situations, rewarding each success with immediate small celebrations.

MOVING ON FROM GRATITUDE

Now that we've explored how gratitude can shine a light on what's already good in your world, let's flip the script and talk about how optimism can help you face what lies ahead. Because while gratitude anchors you joyfully in the present, optimism lights the path forward, giving you the courage to step confidently into your future.

PRACTICING OPTIMISM
WHY OPTIMISM MATTERS

L et's get something straight. Optimism isn't about slapping a smiley face sticker over your problems or pretending life is all rainbows and unicorns. That's delusion, not optimism. **Real optimism is about maintaining hope while facing reality head-on.**

This kind of grounded optimism is like having good shock absorbers for life's inevitable bumps. When you hit a pothole, whether it's a work setback, relationship hiccup, or global pandemic, optimistic thinking helps you rebound faster instead of getting stuck in the ditch of despair.

Beyond just feeling better, the benefits run deep. Optimistic people consistently show better cardiovascular health, stronger immune systems, and even live longer. Their brains literally process stress differently, preventing the kind of chronic fight-or-flight response that wears your body down over time.

Perhaps most importantly, optimism is contagious in the best possible way. Your hopeful outlook ripples outward, strengthening bonds with the people around you. You become the person others want to be around when times get tough. Not because you're blindly positive, but because you can see both the reality of the situation and the possibilities within it.

THE SCIENCE BEHIND OPTIMISM

Ever wonder why some people recover from setbacks while others get stuck in a downward spiral? Researchers have been curious about this, too. A groundbreaking study by Dr. Lee and colleagues found that optimistic folks don't just feel better.[2] They actually live longer, healthier lives than their pessimistic counterparts.

Separately, other research shows that optimism creates what scientists call a "challenge response" rather than a "threat response" to stress.[3] While pessimists experience stress as threatening (triggering fight-or-flight), optimists experience that same stress as challenging (triggering focus and problem-solving). Same event, completely different physical and mental response.

This isn't just about being born lucky with a sunny disposition. Studies show that optimism is more like a muscle than an inborn trait. The more you practice optimistic thinking patterns, the stronger and more automatic they become.

MY JOURNEY TOWARD OPTIMISM

Growing up, my life felt like a never-ending round of musical chairs. I never quite knew where I'd land when the music stopped. Strangely enough, this constant chaos strengthened me instead of breaking me down. Each time I survived another storm, I found myself thinking, "Hey, if I got through that mess, I can handle whatever's next!"

Later on, I discovered there was a fancy term for this attitude: learned optimism. Instead of always bracing myself for disaster, I began flipping the script and asking, "What's the best thing that could happen here?" Sure, life still tosses curveballs, but now I carry optimism like a flashlight in a dark tunnel. I might not see the end yet, but I trust it's there.

REFLECTING ON OPTIMISM

What story do you tell yourself when things go sideways? Do you automatically jump to "Just my luck" or "Nothing ever works out for me," or can you spot that this setback is just temporary and specific to this situation? I've discovered that tweaking your explanatory style, even just a little, can transform not only how you feel in that moment, but what actions you decide to take next. Instead of retreating, you might find yourself reaching for another possibility.

And let's be honest about something we rarely acknowledge: **how often do things actually turn out better than we feared?** Our mental scorecard highlights the disasters while conveniently forgetting all those times when what we dreaded either never happened or somehow turned into something unexpectedly good.

ACTION STEPS TOWARD OPTIMISM

Alright, let's roll up our sleeves and plant some optimism seeds:

- **Your "Future You" Headline:** Imagine yourself 1 year from now, absolutely crushing it. What's the best headline describing your life? Write it down, then list three reasons why. This reverse-engineers your optimism, giving you a clear, inspiring direction.
- **Talk Back to Your Inner Grump:** When negativity strikes, acknowledge it, then gently challenge the story it's telling you. Don't let that ol' voice run the whole show!
- **Optimism Buddy**: Stuck in a negative loop? Grab a friend for an Optimism Reframe! Weekly, discuss a challenge. Your buddy helps you gently reframe it with questions like, "What's the lesson?" It's a mental workout for optimistic thinking.
- **"Yet" Trick**: Shift "I can't" thoughts to "I can't yet," immediately reframing setbacks into optimistic opportunities.
- **Role Model Inspiration**: Reflect on a hopeful role model's journey during moments of doubt, making optimism feel accessible.

- **Celebrate Learning**: Immediately reward yourself after successfully reframing a setback as a valuable learning moment, reinforcing this powerful tool.

MOVING ON FROM OPTIMISM

Now that we've explored how optimism can transform your relationship with the future, let's turn to a skill that changes how you handle the inevitable bumps along the way. **Because while optimism helps you believe in good outcomes, reframing gives you the tools to handle whatever actually shows up.**

REFRAMING NEGATIVITY POSITIVELY

WHY REFRAMING NEGATIVITY POSITIVELY MATTERS

We all have that friend who can find the storm cloud in every silver lining. Maybe sometimes that friend is you. No judgment. Our brains are literally wired to spot dangers and dwell on threats. It's like we're walking around with a built-in negativity magnet, constantly collecting evidence that life is hard and people can't be trusted.

The problem? This mental tool keeps your body in a low-grade stress response all day long. Your heart beats a little faster, your muscles stay tensed, and stress hormones like cortisol flood your system. No wonder you're exhausted by dinnertime!

Reframing isn't about pretending everything's great when it isn't. **It's about challenging the automatic catastrophic interpretations your brain loves to generate.** It's catching yourself right as you're about to mentally escalate a minor paper cut into an emotional amputation.

This mental flexibility does more than just improve your mood. It changes your brain's functions. Regular reframing practice reduces activity in your amygdala (your brain's panic button) and strengthens your prefrontal cortex (your brain's wise counselor). Over time, you spend less energy ruminating on problems and more energy solving them.

Perhaps most importantly, reframing creates space between stimulus and response. What psychologist Viktor Frankl called "the gap." In that gap lies your freedom to choose how you respond rather than simply react.

THE SCIENCE BEHIND REFRAMING NEGATIVITY POSITIVELY

Remember that sweaty-palmed feeling before giving a presentation? Turns out, how you interpret those physical sensations makes all the difference. In a fascinating study, Dr. Jamieson found that people taught to view pre-performance jitters as helpful energy (rather than harmful anxiety) performed better and showed healthier cardiovascular responses.[4]

It's like your body is giving you the same ingredients, racing heart, butterflies in stomach, but your interpretation determines whether you cook up a stress meltdown or peak performance. The physical sensations don't change, but the meaning you attach to them changes everything.

Scientists call this "cognitive reappraisal," and it's like having a mental gear shift that lets you downgrade threats to challenges. Your brain actually processes the same events differently when you reframe them. Less alarm bell, more "let's figure this out" mode.

MY JOURNEY TOWARD REFRAMING NEGATIVITY POSITIVELY

I need to manage this loud, unruly committee in my head. Negative voices that act like harsh critics, pointing out every misstep. I hold myself to very high standards, and the voice driving me forward isn't always friendly.

I knew I needed to dial it back, maybe talk to myself like I'd talk to a friend. So I tried a goofy trick: addressing myself by name with a genuine sense of curiosity. *Alright, Billy, let's see what we've got here.* At first, it felt absurd, but oddly enough, it worked! Creating that bit of distance helped me see myself as a supportive coach rather than my toughest critic.

Now, when negativity sneaks in with a gloomy whisper like "You're doomed," I respond, "Relax, Billy, you're just trying something new." **Funny how naming my inner critic took away its power. Truth is, when you introduce yourself to your demons, they're much less scary over coffee.**

REFLECTING ON REFRAMING NEGATIVITY POSITIVELY

Think about the last time something went sideways on you. What story did you tell yourself about why it happened? Was it permanent ("This is just how it always goes for me"), personal ("I'm the common denominator in all my disasters"), and pervasive ("Now everything's ruined")? What if you rewrote that same story, but made it temporary ("Today didn't go as planned"), specific ("This presentation needed more work"), and partial ("This affects this project, not my entire career")? All without sugarcoating what actually happened?

ACTION STEPS TOWARD REFRAMING NEGATIVITY POSITIVELY

Time to get our hands dirty: here's how you make this happen:

- **Rewrite the Nasty Headline:** That sour thought? Question it! "Is that the *only* truth here?" Find a kinder angle, pal.
- **Friend Talk:** Next time you mess up, pause and ask: "What would I say to my best friend right now?" Then say exactly that to yourself, using your own name. But here's the kicker. **Get genuinely curious about what you're feeling.** Like, "Hey Billy, what's really going on here? Why's this hitting so hard?" Turns out, combining self-compassion with honest curiosity about your emotions works way better than the usual inner beatdown.

- **"At Least" Technique**: Combat negativity by stating "At least..." to soften disappointments, instantly reducing stress.
- **Humor Spin**: Mentally transform frustrating situations into humorous scenarios, immediately defusing stress through laughter.
- **Worry Delay**: Distract yourself for 10 minutes before revisiting a negative thought, immediately reducing emotional intensity.
- **Gratitude Add-on**: Balance negative thoughts by adding "and I'm grateful for...," instantly shifting your emotional tone.

MOVING ON FROM REFRAMING NEGATIVITY POSITIVELY

Now that we've explored how to handle life's inevitable curveballs, let's talk about making the most of the good stuff when it comes your way. Because while reframing helps you manage the downs, savoring helps you amplify the ups: and that's where some real magic happens.

SAVORING POSITIVE EXPERIENCES
WHY SAVORING POSITIVE EXPERIENCES MATTERS

L et me ask you something: How many amazing moments have slipped through your fingers because you were too busy planning the next thing or worrying about something else? If you're like most people, the answer is "way too many." **We've become experts at rushing through life, rarely stopping to actually taste the metaphorical (or literal) ice cream before it melts.**

Savoring is the art of stretching positive experiences, squeezing every drop of goodness from them instead of gulping them down and moving on. It's about being fully present when something good happens, whether it's a major achievement or just a perfect cup of coffee, and letting it sink all the way in.

The practice flips on your brain's reward center and releases a surge of dopamine and serotonin. The more you deliberately savor positive moments, the stronger these neural pathways become, gradually rewiring your brain to notice and appreciate the good more automatically.

The beauty of savoring is that it doesn't require more positive experiences. Just more awareness of the ones you're already having. It's about quality over quantity, depth over breadth. And perhaps most powerfully, savoring shared experiences strengthens bonds with others, creating meaningful connections that buffer against life's inevitable hard times.

THE SCIENCE BEHIND SAVORING POSITIVE EXPERIENCES

Ever wonder why some people can take one small positive experience, like a perfect cup of coffee or a sunny afternoon, and truly bask in it, while others let major wins pass by without a second thought? Scientists have discovered the first group has discovered something powerful for their happiness, and it's a learnable skill.

Paul Jose, Bee T. Lim, and savoring researcher Fred Bryant conducted a daily diary study in 2012 that revealed this phenomenon.[5] Participants tracked their positive experiences and how much they savored them each day. The results were remarkable: people who deliberately savored good moments reported consistently higher happiness levels. Most importantly, this savoring skill was especially beneficial on days when positive experiences were scarce

In fact, these smart researchers found that savoring was most beneficial for people who had fewer daily pleasures to begin with. It was like this skill helped them "wring out" every last drop of joy from each good experience, boosting their mood and overall life satisfaction like crazy. It wasn't about how many good things happened, but how much they milked the good things that did happen!

The research makes it clear that savoring, the deliberate act of appreciating positive moments, isn't just a nice-to-have. It's a powerhouse tool that counteracts stress and cranks up your well-being. **Instead of letting good moments zip by, you learn to grab hold, stretch them out, and let the goodness sink in. You're not just experiencing joy; you're investing in it!**

MY JOURNEY TOWARD SAVORING POSITIVE EXPERIENCES

I live in New Jersey, near the picturesque Manasquan River, where Suzy and I dock our pontoon boat. Summers are magnificent. We've been blessed with wonderful friends at the marina and family who eagerly join our aquatic adventures during those four glorious months of the year.

One evening remains etched in my memory: We were cruising along the river, mesmerized by nature's spectacular show as the sunset transformed everything with its perfect palette of colors. I'd enjoyed a few beverages. Nothing irresponsible, just enough to feel pleasantly unwound.

Without warning, I cut the engine, scanned my friends' faces with sudden seriousness, and then gazed at the sky and proclaimed, "Hey y'all, where the heck are we?! (long pause) How the heck did we get here?" My cautious buddy, remembering I'd had a few drinks, immediately stiffened, genuinely concerned I'd lost all navigational awareness. His genuine panic made the moment priceless! We all cracked up, then paused to absorb our surroundings and savor the experience. The poor guy actually thought I was hopelessly lost, when in reality, I just wanted everyone to appreciate how fortunate we were to be precisely where we were. Something we frequently miss when constantly rushing toward whatever comes next.

REFLECTING ON SAVORING POSITIVE EXPERIENCES

When was the last time you fully immersed yourself in a positive experience without simultaneously thinking about what's next or checking your phone? What small pleasures happen in your everyday life that you might be rushing past without really tasting, feeling, or appreciating? What's one moment from today that you could revisit right now and savor more fully?

ACTION STEPS TOWARD SAVORING POSITIVE EXPERIENCES

Let's cut to the chase. Here are 6 easy ways to jump in:

- **Micro Celebrations**: Do a quick joyful gesture for tiny wins (fist pump, dance), instantly reinforcing joy.
- **Savor Ritual**: Take 30 extra seconds savoring everyday pleasures (coffee, sunsets), turning routine into enjoyable rituals.
- **Highlight Replay**: Briefly relive one daily highlight in detail each evening, deepening its emotional impact immediately.
- **Joy Album**: Capture happy moments in photos to create a visual collection that instantly boosts mood on tougher days.
- **Weekly Awe Walk**: Commit 15 distraction-free minutes each week to discovering and savoring awe-inspiring details around you, deepening appreciation and joy.
- **Share Joy Actively**: *Tell someone about a positive experience immediately, amplifying happiness through social connection.*

MOVING ON FROM SAVORING POSITIVE EXPERIENCES

Now that we've learned the upside of squeezing every drop of goodness from life's positive moments, let's explore something that can create those moments out of thin air, even on the toughest days: humor. **Because while savoring helps us appreciate what's already good, laughter helps us find lightness even when things seem heavy.**

CULTIVATING HUMOR & LAUGHTER

WHY CULTIVATING HUMOR & LAUGHTER MATTERS

Remember the last time you laughed so hard your face hurt? That full-body, can't-catch-your-breath kind of laughter that makes everything else temporarily disappear? That wasn't just fun. It was medicine. Powerful, free, side-effect-free medicine that your body and brain desperately need.

Laughter sets off a mini fireworks display in your body. Endorphins explode like tiny, joyous sparks, chasing away stress and pain, lowering stress hormones, and boosting your immune system. One good belly laugh can instantly shift your emotional state from stressed to relieved, creating a mental reset button you can press anytime.

But humor isn't just about finding things funny. It's about developing a lens to spot the absurdity, irony, and unexpected connections in everyday life. This perspective is like emotional armor during tough times, creating distance between you and your problems without denying they exist.

Perhaps most powerfully, shared laughter creates instant bonds. It dissolves tension, builds trust, and creates a sense of "we're in this together" that few other experiences can match. In a world where loneliness has become an epidemic, humor creates bridges between people faster than almost anything else.

Even during life's darkest chapters, humor provides perspective and relief. **It's not about laughing off serious problems. It's about finding moments of lightness that make the heaviness more bearable. Think of humor as the pressure-release valve on life's pressure cooker.**

THE SCIENCE BEHIND CULTIVATING HUMOR & LAUGHTER

Ever wonder why a hearty laugh feels like potent medicine? Science totally backs it up! It's not just a mood lift, folks. It's your biology doing something awesome.

Get this: Lee Berk's team (Berk et al., 1989) ran a cool trial.[6] One group watched a funny video (the real belly-laugh kind!), another didn't. They tracked stress hormones like cortisol and adrenaline. The laughs? Bam! Their levels of these key "stress-o-meter" hormones nosedived compared to the no-laugh crew. This "high-spirited laughter" actually reversed the body's typical stress response. Think powering down the internal stress factory!

The takeaway? It's solid biological proof, my friends! Humor and laughter literally calm your body and slash stress. How cool is that for a happiness habit?!

MY JOURNEY TOWARD CULTIVATING HUMOR & LAUGHTER

About five years ago, I was dragging my sorry self home after the kind of workday that makes you question your career choices and possibly your entire life path. I didn't want to walk through my front door trailing dark clouds like some cartoon character, so I tried something that seemed almost too simple. I made myself laugh. Not a polite chuckle or a sarcastic snort, but an actual, genuine laugh.

And wouldn't you know it? The darn thing worked. My mood shifted like someone had flipped a switch. I was so thrilled with this accidental discovery that I immediately thought, "This is it! My contribution to humanity!" With the zeal of someone who's found the secret to world peace in their glove compartment, I rushed to register makeyourselflaugh.com.

Fast forward to today, and that website remains as empty as my promises to start meal prepping on Sundays. Turns out, writing "Step 1: Laugh" doesn't quite cut it as groundbreaking self-help content. So somewhere in the digital graveyard, makeyourselflaugh.com sits abandoned. Probably having a good laugh at my expense. But what I did learn from that failed digital venture is that some brilliant ideas are best left between you and your steering wheel. You get the point.

REFLECTING ON CULTIVATING HUMOR & LAUGHTER

When was the last time you laughed until your sides hurt? What situations, people, or types of humor reliably bring you joy? And more importantly, how might you build more intentional laughter into your daily routine, especially when life feels heavy or overwhelming?

ACTION STEPS TOWARD CULTIVATING HUMOR & LAUGHTER

Time to put rubber to the road with these 6 helpers for bringing more laughter into your life, even during those days when humor feels miles away:

- **Humor Treasure Hunt:** Unearth an old comedy favorite. Revisit what makes *you* genuinely laugh. It's pure gold.
- **Humor Journal:** Briefly note daily funny moments, immediately boosting mood and creating a personalized humor archive.
- **Laughter Yoga Trial:** Spend a minute laughing intentionally, even if forced, to spark real laughter and immediate relaxation.
- **Comedy Swap:** Exchange funny memes or jokes daily with friends, instantly enhancing social connection through humor.
- **Laugh at Yourself:** Turn embarrassing moments into

humorous stories immediately, reframing awkwardness positively.

- **Silly Minute Daily:** Give yourself permission for brief daily silliness, releasing stress instantly with playful behavior.

WRAPPING UP THE CHAPTER

N ow that we've explored these five powerful mindset tools, from gratitude to optimism, reframing to savoring, and finally to humor, it's time to see how they all work together. While each tool is powerful on its own, the real magic happens when they start to reinforce and amplify each other, creating a positive mindset greater than the sum of its parts.

Think of your mindset as a garden. The five tools we've explored, gratitude, optimism, reframing, savoring, and humor, aren't separate plants but an interconnected ecosystem. *Gratitude prepares the soil, making it rich and receptive. Optimism plants seeds of possibility that grow toward the future. Reframing acts as a protective fence, keeping destructive pests of negativity at bay. Savoring is the act of stopping to smell the roses you've grown, absorbing their beauty and fragrance fully. And humor? It's the unexpected wildflowers that pop up even in challenging seasons, reminding you that beauty can emerge anywhere.*

These tools create a powerful synergy when used together. The more grateful you become, the easier it is to be optimistic. The better you get at reframing, the more naturally you'll spot opportunities for humor. And as you savor more deeply, your capacity for gratitude expands.

Remember that boat ride I mentioned earlier? That moment captured this interconnection perfectly. The gratitude for being on the water led to savoring the sunset, which created an opportunity for humor that we still laugh about today. One practice naturally flowed into another, creating a moment none of us will forget.

YOUR BRAIN'S AMAZING ABILITY TO CHANGE

These five mindset tools literally change your brain through what scientists call neuroplasticity. I think of it more like creating pathways in the snow. The first time you walk a new path, it's tough going. The twentieth time? You've got a clear trail that's easy to follow.

Each time you practice gratitude, optimism, reframing, savoring, or humor, you're stomping down that snow a little more, creating clearer, stronger neural pathways. But let's be honest about what this journey actually looks like in real life.

Think of it like training a puppy. At first, your brain will wander off, chasing negative thoughts like squirrels. That's normal! Just gently redirect it back to the path you want to follow. Over time, with consistent training, your brain learns the new routes you want it to take.

The transformation is both mental and physical. New connections form, stress centers calm down, and pleasure centers activate more easily. You're rebuilding your brain's operating system from the ground up. Now, when life inevitably gets messy, you'll have a reliable system to fall back on

YOUR POSITIVE MINDSET CHEAT SHEET

When life gets messy (and it will), keep this quick reference guide handy:

- **Shift from "Why me?" to "What for?"**: Every setback contains a lesson or opportunity if you're willing to look for it.
- **Choose your mental neighborhood wisely**: You become like the thoughts you hang around with most often.
- **Stop treating joy like a reward for finishing your to-do list**: *Happiness isn't the destination; it's the vehicle that gets you there.*

- **Play the long game with your brain**: Small daily mindset tools compound like interest, creating massive change over time.
- **Remember that gratitude turns what you have into enough**: The secret to having it all is recognizing you already do.
- **Treat your attention like your most valuable currency**: Whatever you focus on will grow, so choose carefully what you feed with your focus.
- **Be as kind to yourself as you would be to a friend**: These principles might seem overwhelming at first, but remember you don't have to master them all at once.

THE CHOICE IS ALWAYS YOURS

As we wrap up this chapter, I want to leave you with something I've learned through years of stumbling, forgetting, remembering, and trying again: Developing a positive mindset is less about feeling good all the time and more about having tools to work with whatever life throws your way. These five tools aren't magic spells that make problems disappear. They're more like reliable friends who help you navigate the storms with a bit more grace and a lot less suffering.

Your mindset isn't something you have. It's something you practice, like learning to play the guitar or perfecting your grandma's lasagna recipe. Some days your practice will be beautiful, and some days it'll sound like a cat with its tail caught in a door. That's not failure: that's just being human.

The real power isn't in working with these tools perfectly. **It's in the moment of awareness when you realize you have a choice about how to respond to life.** It's in that split-second pause when you decide whether to water your mental garden with gratitude or let it go thirsty, whether to put on your optimism gloves or handle sharp situations bare-handed, and whether to sit on your savoring bench or rush past the beauty without noticing.

Your mindset is built one choice at a time. And my friend, that changes everything.

CHAPTER 2:

BECOMING THE CEO OF YOUR OWN MIND

Have you ever been deep in an important task when your brain suddenly decides it's urgent to replay that embarrassing thing you said in 2003, or rehearse conversations that will probably never happen? (*Just me? Okay then.*)

Practicing mindfulness and emotional management has been surprisingly eye-opening. Growing up, nobody handed me an instruction manual on handling what's happening inside my head. Discovering I could pause and step back felt revolutionary. I could examine my thoughts. It's almost like I stumbled onto a secret superpower: Emotional X-ray vision. *I often wish science would invent an internal warning system, my own mental "Check Engine" light that blinks when it's time to pop the emotional hood and investigate.* Until technology catches up, though, I've learned the joy of regularly peeking under my own mental hood. It's definitely made life's drive smoother.

The mental tools in this chapter aren't complicated neuroscience experiments requiring lab coats and safety goggles. They're practical daily tools, like mindfulness meditation, deep breathing, emotion labeling, and finding moments of awe, that can transform your relationship with that fascinating, frustrating three-pound universe between your ears.

Ready to make friends with your mind? Let's dive in. We'll start with the foundation. Learning to observe your thoughts without getting swept away by them.

PRACTICING MINDFULNESS MEDITATION

WHY MINDFULNESS MEDITATION MATTERS

L et's be honest. Our minds are like overexcited puppies, running in circles, chasing squirrels, and occasionally tracking muddy paws all over the metaphorical carpet of our peace. Studies show we spend about half of our waking hours with our minds wandering away from whatever we're supposed to be doing. No wonder we're exhausted by dinnertime!

When you practice mindfulness regularly, your brain changes. The areas involved in emotion regulation get stronger, which means you're less likely to fly off the handle when your kid spills juice on your laptop or your boss springs a last-minute deadline on you. Your resilience muscles grow, making it easier to bounce back from life's inevitable gut punches.

The science is clear: mindfulness lowers depression symptoms, reduces anxiety, and helps you stay focused on what truly matters. It's like giving your mental immune system a daily vitamin. You're building protection against the constant barrage of stressors that come with modern life. And maybe most importantly, it helps you to be present for the good stuff, instead of missing it because you're mentally rehearsing tomorrow's meeting.

THE SCIENCE BEHIND MINDFULNESS MEDITATION

What's really happening in your brain when you meditate? Researchers at the University of Wisconsin (Davidson et al., 2003) found something fascinating. Mindfulness doesn't just make you feel better in the moment; it creates lasting changes in your brain and body.[7]

Think of your brain like a muscle. When you meditate, you're essentially doing push-ups for your prefrontal cortex. The part that helps you stay calm when your buttons get pushed. Over time, this area gets stronger and can better regulate your emotional responses. It's like upgrading your brain's operating system from "Reactionary Hothead 1.0" to "Thoughtful Response 3.0."

But the benefits go beyond your brain. That same study found that mindfulness improves your immune system too. It's like your body and brain are having this conversation: "Hey, we're not constantly stressed and on high alert anymore, so maybe we can divert some resources to actually fighting off that cold." The result? You get sick less often and recover faster when you do.

These changes start happening after just eight weeks of regular practice. **Your brain is literally rebuilding itself to be more resilient and less reactive. All because you decided to sit still and pay attention to your breath for a few minutes each day.**

MY JOURNEY TOWARD MINDFULNESS MEDITATION

Every January brings fresh hope and another mindfulness app download, accompanied by that familiar conviction: this year will be different. By mid-month, the practice inevitably gets abandoned, another casualty of a mind that prefers chasing figurative chickens to sitting still. Living as an unmedicated ADHD adult means my mind loves spontaneous detours, making traditional meditation particularly tough.

Ironically, these failed attempts have taught valuable lessons about slowing down. Complete zone-outs have become less frequent, replaced by something approaching presence during crucial conversations: or at least present-adjacent awareness. Sure, the restlessness remains, but glimpsing mindfulness's magic keeps the door open for another try, another attempt to focus on breath rather than those crazy chickens.

REFLECTING ON MINDFULNESS MEDITATION

When was the last time you felt truly present. Not planning, worrying, or rehashing, but simply experiencing the moment you were in? And what would your day feel like if you could bring that quality of attention to even the most ordinary activities, like drinking your morning coffee or listening to a friend?

ACTION STEPS TOWARD MINDFULNESS MEDITATION

Ready to tame those wild mental chickens? Here are six ways to start without losing your mind:

- **Two-Minute Starter**: Begin with just two minutes of focusing on your breath. Seriously, anyone can do anything for two minutes. Even sitting still with your own thoughts.
- **Forget perfection:** Mind wandered off to plan dinner? Awesome. Gently bring it back. That is the practice, not a mistake!
- **Mindful Movement**: If sitting meditation makes you want to climb the walls, try walking meditation instead. Same benefits, less torture, and you get some movement too.
- **Brain Spa Ritual**: Create a comfy meditation spot with a candle or something nice to look at. Your brain deserves a little ambiance for this important work.
- **Group Meditation**: Join a class or online group. When your mind wanders, at least you'll be comfortable knowing everyone else's probably did too.

- **Curiosity Experiment**: Approach meditation with playful curiosity instead of grim determination. "Hmm, what's happening in my mind right now?" feels way better than "Focus, you undisciplined potato!"

MOVING ON FROM MINDFULNESS MEDITATION

Now that we've explored how to sit still with our thoughts, let's talk about something you can actually use when life hits the fan. Because while meditation is great when you've got time and a quiet spot, sometimes you need instant calm in the middle of absolute chaos. Enter deep breathing, your portable peace button.

USING DEEP BREATHING TO RELAX
WHY USING DEEP BREATHING MATTERS

While mindfulness trains you for the mental marathon, deep breathing serves as your emotional first aid kit. Always available, incredibly effective, and thankfully, impossible to forget at home. Life's inevitable curveballs transform your breath into an instant reset button.

Deep breathing activates your vagus nerve, flipping your internal 'calm down' switch from panic mode to peace. **Imagine your nervous system like a car alarm stuck blaring. Deep breathing quietly turns the alarm off, letting your body relax again.** Within seconds, your body shifts from fight-or-flight panic to rest-and-digest calm. Your blood pressure drops, your racing heart slows, and your mind stops spinning disaster scenarios like a Vegas roulette wheel.

Beyond these immediate benefits, regular deep breathing actually improves your mood by naturally boosting serotonin levels. The same feel-good brain chemical targeted by many antidepressants. It's like having a happiness booster built right into your body, accessible anytime.

The beauty of breathing techniques is how they build emotional resilience over time. Each deep breath you take doesn't just help in the moment. It's training your nervous system to recover more quickly from future stress. Plus, the anxiety reduction is cumulative, creating a gradually calmer baseline for your everyday emotional state.

THE SCIENCE BEHIND USING DEEP BREATHING

Lowering your stress hormones without fancy supplements or expensive therapies might be simpler than you think. Just breathe differently. Science backs this up: Perciavalle and his research team found that deep breathing techniques can significantly decrease cortisol, your body's main stress hormone, and lower your heart rate.[8]

These powerful techniques often involve diaphragmatic breathing, where you breathe deeply into your belly, typically at a slow pace of around 6 breaths per minute. Making your exhale longer than your inhale is key, as this helps activate the parasympathetic nervous system, your body's built-in calm-down switch.

Think of stress like revving your car engine in neutral. You're burning fuel but going nowhere. Deep breathing is like shifting back into gear so your body can operate efficiently again. Indeed, researchers, including Perciavalle's team with their findings on lowered heart rates, have observed how just a few minutes of controlled breathing can begin to ease the body's stress response. Many studies also show these types of breathing techniques can reduce blood pressure, essentially turning down the body's alarm system.

What's most remarkable is how this simple physical action creates a cascade of positive emotional effects. The work by Perciavalle's team, for instance, showed that the breathing technique directly improved participants' mood states. It's a powerful reminder that sometimes the fastest way to change your feelings is through your lungs, not just your thoughts.

MY JOURNEY TOWARD DEEP BREATHING

Breathing always seemed obvious. Inhale, exhale, maybe hold your breath underwater to impress friends at the pool. Then life taught me otherwise. The hidden power only revealed itself during a moment of genuine panic: late for a critical meeting, trapped in traffic, stress mounting like a pressure cooker. Suddenly, "five seconds in, five seconds out, move your belly" transformed from basic biology into an emotional lifeline.

Unlike meditation, which remains mostly an annual January failure, deep breathing actually stuck. Now, when overwhelm creeps in, that little internal voice kicks in: *Deep belly breath, Billy. Five seconds in, five seconds out. Walk it off.* Remarkably, it works! Those abandoned mindfulness apps? Maybe not a total waste after all. Just expensive admission tickets to the free show of conscious breathing.

REFLECTING ON DEEP BREATHING

Think about the last time you felt anxious or overwhelmed. Did your breathing change? Did it get shallow, quick, or did you even hold your breath without realizing it? What might change if you could catch that breathing pattern early and use it as your signal to reset?

ACTION STEPS TOWARD DEEP BREATHING

Let's get practical with some breathing tactics that won't have you hyperventilating into a paper bag:

- **Try the 4-6 Breath for Instant Calm:** Breathe into your belly for a 4-count and exhale for a 6-count. The longer exhale is your body's emergency brake for stress.
- **For engaging playfully:** Make breathing a game. Try to exhale as slowly as you can, pretend to blow bubbles underwater, or inflate a balloon in your stomach that slowly releases air. Playful breathing circumvents the stress response and accesses your creative consciousness.
- **The "Hold Your Horses" Breath:** Feeling your temper about to blow its stack? Take one slow, deliberate breath before you say a word. Buys you a moment, might save you an apology.
- **For Mental Focus:** Use patterned rhythms like 'square breathing'. Equal counts of 4 for inhale, hold, exhale, hold. This

mathematical approach gives your logical mind something to focus on while your body relaxes of its own accord.

MOVING ON FROM DEEP BREATHING

Now that we've got our breathing functioning as nature intended, let's build on this foundation with another powerful practice. Sometimes the first step to handling an emotion is giving it a name tag rather than letting it crash your mental party incognito.

LABELING YOUR EMOTIONS

WHY LABELING YOUR EMOTIONS MATTERS

That funk you can't quite identify, or the moment you snapped at your partner over dirty dishes when work stress was the real culprit. Welcome to the confusing world of unlabeled emotions, where feelings go incognito and cause trouble.

Naming your emotions isn't just psychological busywork. It's like turning on a light in a dark room. When you accurately label your feelings, you activate your brain's prefrontal cortex, which helps regulate those emotions instead of being hijacked by them. **It's the difference between being swept away by a current or standing on the shore observing the water.**

This simple practice dramatically enhances your emotional intelligence and self-awareness. Instead of vague discomfort, you recognize specific feelings, disappointment, frustration, embarrassment, which makes them much easier to manage. Plus, labeling actually reduces the intensity of negative emotions, like turning down the volume on an overly loud speaker.

Perhaps most importantly, emotion labeling transforms how you communicate. Instead of expecting others to read your mind (a strategy with a stunning 0% success rate), you can clearly express what's happening internally, leading to deeper connections and fewer misunderstandings.

THE SCIENCE BEHIND LABELING YOUR EMOTIONS

Science confirms what folklore has long suggested: naming things gives you power over them. Research by Dr. Matthew Lieberman and colleagues shows that labeling emotions significantly reduces psychological distress and contributes to higher overall well-being when practiced regularly.[9]

Think of your emotions like pop-up notifications on your mental desktop. Ignoring them doesn't make them disappear. They just stack up and slow down your system. Researchers found that simply naming the emotion creates enough mental space to process it. It's like clicking "acknowledge" on those notifications so your brain can regain regular functioning.

What's particularly interesting is that this verbal labeling activates your rational brain while simultaneously calming your emotional brain. It's like having an internal translator that converts raw emotional data into language your thinking brain can actually use.

MY JOURNEY TOWARD LABELING EMOTIONS

Each of this book's 42 tools demanded its own personal story. Some practically wrote themselves. This one fought me like a cat getting a bath.

I sat for hours trying to conjure up some solid tale about labeling emotions. Nothing. My frustration went from "mildly annoyed" to "want to throw my laptop through the window" in thirty minutes.

Head in hands, ready to delete the whole chapter, it hit me. Wait, I'm literally writing about labeling emotions WHILE having an emotional meltdown. Maybe I should practice what I'm preaching?

So I asked: "Billy, what exactly are you feeling?"

The answer punched me in the gut: "Poser."

There it was. I felt like a complete fraud. Who was I to write about happiness when I couldn't even come up with a decent story without having a breakdown?

But then I laughed at the irony. I'd just given myself the perfect example. I have the story.

The added bonus. Naming my imposter syndrome became my secret weapon for the rest of the book. Every time the "you're not qualified" voice started yapping, I'd label it: "Oh, hello Imposter Syndrome. Thanks for visiting, but I've got a book to write."

The irony isn't lost on me. I discovered the value of labeling emotions by having a meltdown about labeling emotions. Classic.

REFLECTING ON LABELING YOUR EMOTIONS

When was the last time an emotion caught you off guard or led to a reaction you later regretted? If you had paused to name that feeling before responding, how might the situation have unfolded differently?

ACTION STEPS TOWARD LABELING YOUR EMOTIONS

Ready to name those emotional visitors? Here's your emotional vocabulary cheat sheet:

- **Name and Tame**: When emotion strikes, simply say its name aloud like you're introducing it at a dinner party: "This is anxiety" or "I'm feeling disappointed." Naming it immediately reduces its power over you.
- **Emoji Express**: If finding words feels hard, start with emoji labels. Try a 😟 or 😔 to help you recognize your feelings before finding the words.
- **One-Line Feelings Journal**: Keep a tiny feelings log: "Today I felt _____ when _____." No need for paragraphs. Just connect the dots between events and emotions.
- **Color Your Mood**: Assign colors to common emotions and check in with yourself: "I'm feeling very orange (frustrated)

right now." Sometimes visual labels work better than verbal ones.

- **Emotion Gauge Check:** Little peeved or full-blown furious? Mildly miffed or majorly melancholy? Naming the volume helps you know if you need a whisper or a shout.
- **Compassionate Labels**: Add kindness to your labeling: "I'm feeling anxious, and that's okay." Combining accuracy with self-compassion is emotional intelligence gold.

MOVING ON FROM LABELING YOUR EMOTIONS

With breathing and emotion-labeling in your toolbox, you've got powerful ways to manage your inner landscape. Now let's expand our view outward to find something that shifts our perspective entirely. The transformative experience of awe.

PLACING YOURSELF IN AWE & WONDER

WHY PLACING YOURSELF IN AWE & WONDER MATTERS

Between the constant selling, fixing, and reminding us we're not enough, our days blur together. Wake up, scroll, work, scroll, sleep, repeat. Somewhere in this routine, we forget that we're actually living on a giant rock spinning through space at 1,000 miles per hour.

That feeling, that drop-in-your-stomach, catch-your-breath moment of pure awe, is more than just a nice experience. It's like hitting a psychological reset button. When you stand at the edge of the Grand Canyon or look up at a sky full of stars, something shifts inside you. **Suddenly, your daily worries seem smaller, more manageable. Not because they've disappeared, but because they've been right-sized by something greater.**

Beyond the physical benefits, awe expands your perception of time. People report having more time available when they experience awe regularly. In our chronically rushed culture, that's practically a superpower. Awe also increases feelings of connectedness, gratitude, and life satisfaction. All key ingredients in the recipe for lasting happiness.

The best part? You don't need a vacation to Yosemite or a telescope to access this state. Awe is available in ordinary moments if you train yourself to notice it.

THE SCIENCE BEHIND PLACING YOURSELF IN AWE & WONDER

Want to feel like you've got all the time in the world? Experience more awe. Melanie Rudd and her research team discovered that awe-inducing experiences create a perception of time expansion. Making you feel less rushed and more present.[10]

Think of awe as your brain's way of hitting the refresh button. When study participants experienced awe, whether from nature, art, or extraordinary human achievements, their mental state shifted dramatically. Researchers observed increases in happiness, generosity, and what they termed "time affluence". The sense of having abundant time rather than scarcity.

What's fascinating is how this momentary feeling can create lasting changes in behavior. People who regularly experienced awe reported greater life satisfaction and showed measurably more generous behaviors toward others. It's as if glimpsing something vast and wonderful helps shift our focus toward connection rather than competition.

Additionally, studies show that experiencing awe can help lower stress hormones in your body. It's like your nervous system gets a chance to recalibrate: this powerful emotion can contribute to a calmer physiological state, potentially influencing your heart rate to stabilize or slow and promoting deeper breathing as your body relaxes. That constant background anxiety often quiets down. The beauty is that this isn't just a temporary high. Regular doses of awe and wonder can create lasting changes in your emotional baseline.

MY JOURNEY TOWARD PLACING MYSELF IN AWE & WONDER

One frigid, 20-degree night, after finally getting our gifted hot tub working, the moment seemed right for a test soak. As a first-time hot tub owner, a test soak seemed essential. Sinking beneath the stars, breath steaming in the chilly air, something unexpected happened. That quiet moment, gazing upward into an impossibly vast universe, triggered an internal shift. A gentle, humbling reminder of life's beauty and the joy found in recognizing our cosmic insignificance.

Our yard isn't exactly private, so neighbors strolling by might've glimpsed a grown man, teary-eyed, half-submerged, contemplating life's mysteries. In the midst of this cosmic hot tub revelation, surrounded by the gentle bubbling and winter silence, I experienced a flash of clarity. Well, almost clarity, since I'm still trying to figure out what I want to be when I grow up. My heart somehow heard something that my mind just can't handle. These moments of connection to something larger than ourselves often occur when we least expect them and in the most unlikely settings.

That night became a turning point in my journey of self-discovery, a stepping stone toward the person I was meant to become. Clearly, starry skies and hot tubs help, though my neighbors probably debated whether to call the police or a priest. I'm pretty sure one of them took a photo. If I ever run for office, that's definitely going to surface.

REFLECTING ON: PLACING YOURSELF IN AWE & WONDER

When was the last time you experienced genuine awe: that feeling of being small in the presence of something vast? What triggers that sensation for you personally: nature, music, art, human achievement, or something entirely different?

ACTION STEPS TOWARD PLACING YOURSELF IN AWE & WONDER

Grab a pencil or just your good intentions. It's wonder-hunting time:

- **Schedule a Weekly Awe Date:** Block it on your calendar like a critical appointment. Visit a scenic overlook, watch a stunning nature documentary, or go to a museum.
- **Everyday Awe Journaling**: Keep a tiny "moments of wonder" journal where you jot down daily encounters with the

amazing. A perfect spider web, a child's laughter, a mathematical concept that blows your mind.

- **Beginner's Mind:** Try experiencing familiar things as if for the first time. Eat an orange slowly with full attention, or walk your neighborhood looking for details you've never noticed before.
- **Child's Perspective:** Borrow a kid's eye view (or an actual kid) for an hour. Lie on the grass watching clouds, examine bugs with fascination, or ask "why" questions about ordinary objects.
- **Virtual Awe Playlist**: Create a collection of awe-inspiring videos, images, or music for quick wonder boosts. Think stunning natural phenomena, space photography, or whatever makes your jaw drop.
- **Daily Music Medicine**: Make intentional music listening part of your day. Choose tunes that move your soul. Whether you're cooking, commuting, or just need a mood boost, let the music work its magic. Bonus points if you dance like nobody's watching. Research shows music reduces stress hormones instantly.
- **Philosophical Awe Moments**: Ponder mind-bending concepts like infinity, quantum physics, or the unfathomable number of cells working together to make your body function right now. Intellectual awe counts too

WRAPPING UP THE CHAPTER:

THE BRAIN SCIENCE BEHIND OWNING YOUR MIND

E very time you work with these mindfulness and emotional management tools, you're rewiring your brain. Your brain is like my garage workshop. Constantly being reorganized based on which tools you actually use. And just like in my garage, the tools you reach for most often end up in the easiest-to-access spots. The neural pathways you exercise get stronger, while the ones you ignore gradually weaken.

When you consistently practice mindfulness, your prefrontal cortex, the brain's wise CEO, gets stronger and better connected. Meanwhile, your amygdala, the jumpy security guard always looking for trouble, finds itself taking more coffee breaks, not screaming 'wolf!' quite so often. It's happening because your brain builds new neural pathways whether you're meditating on a fancy cushion or just taking mindful breaths while waiting in the grocery line.

This neuroplasticity means that small, consistent practices can create profound changes over time. Every mindful moment, every deep breath, every accurately labeled emotion, and every experience of awe is like adding another drop of water to the stream that eventually carves a new path through the landscape of your mind. But what does this transformation actually look like in daily life? Let me paint you a picture of the journey ahead.

YOUR MIND MASTERY TIMELINE: THE JOURNEY AHEAD

How do you know these tools are working? Simple: that constant mental chatter starts having longer commercial breaks.

Picture yourself stepping onto a path, not some mythical hero's journey with dragons and magic swords, but a real, everyday path toward mental peace. I want to show you what the journey looks like when you actually use these four tools to work. Not the Instagram-perfect version, but the messy, beautiful, real-life transformation that unfolds.

First Week: The Awakening You're thinking, "Wait, my thoughts aren't facts?" This becomes your first revelation. Like discovering your mental shoelaces have been tied together all this time. You catch yourself mid-spiral once or twice, thinking, "Huh, that's interesting," instead of being swept away. Your emotions: Brief moments of surprising calm appear between the usual chaos: like finding unexpected $20 bills in random coat pockets. Your daily life: You notice the taste of your morning coffee for perhaps the first time. Your partner comments that you seem "weirdly present" during at least one conversation.

By Month One: The Awareness Shift Your thinking: The space between trigger and reaction grows from microscopic to noticeable. Like upgrading from dial-up to high-speed internet, your mental processing feels less jumpy. Your emotions: You start labeling feelings instead of drowning in them. "Hello Anxiety, is that you again?" becomes a familiar internal conversation. Your daily life: Arguments defuse faster. You catch yourself taking that deep breath before responding to that email that would've normally sent you into orbit.

Three Months In: The Integration Phase Your thinking: Your aforementioned "mental chickens" still run wild occasionally, but you've learned to herd them back into the coop without drama. Your emotions: Emotional waves still come, but you've learned to surf instead of getting pummeled. Even family holidays feel marginally less like psychological warfare. Your daily life: People start asking if something's different about you. "New haircut?" they guess. Nope, just your new relationship with your mind.

Six Months Later: The New Normal Your thinking: Self-compassion replaces self-criticism as your default setting. Your internal dialogue sounds more like a supportive friend than a drill sergeant with anger issues. Your emotions: You experience the full spectrum of emotions but aren't held hostage by them. Even intense feelings become valuable data rather than dictators of your day. Your daily life: Your capacity to stay present during both celebrations and challenges has fundamentally changed. You find yourself regularly pausing to experience moments of genuine awe in ordinary life.

The Full Transformation: Not Perfection, But Freedom Here's the truth about transformation that nobody tells you: it's not about reaching some mythical state of perpetual zen. I still have days where my mind resembles a hamster on espresso. **The real change happens when you stop expecting perfection and start embracing progress: when the path itself becomes home, not just the destination.**

Remember that transformation isn't a straight line; it's more like my attempts at drawing a circle. Well-intentioned but wobbly. Some days you'll feel like a mindfulness master, and others you'll wonder if your brain has been replaced with a pinball machine. That's not failure: that's being human. And *learning to embrace that messy, imperfect journey might be the greatest transformation of all.*

YOUR MIND MASTERY CHEAT SHEET

Here's your quick reference guide for those moments when life feels overwhelming:

- **Two Minutes is Better Than None**: Even the shortest mindfulness practice counts. Don't wait for the "perfect" 30-minute window that never arrives.

- **Name It to Tame It**: When emotions run high, labeling them out loud instantly reduces their power over you.
- **Your Breath is Portable Therapy**: No matter where you are, five deep breaths can reset your nervous system faster than any pep talk.
- **Small Moments of Awe Count**: You don't need the Grand Canyon; a perfect sunset or starry night can deliver the same perspective shift.
- **Progress, Not Perfection**: Every time you catch your mind wandering and gently bring it back, you're building mental muscle. That's the workout, not the interruption.
- **Emotions are Weather, Not Climate**: Just as you wouldn't define the climate by today's weather, don't mistake temporary emotional states for your overall mental health.
- **Compassion Beats Criticism**: When you notice yourself struggling, try speaking to yourself like you would a good friend. It changes everything.

YOUR EMOTIONAL TOOLKIT IS ALWAYS WITHIN REACH

Pay attention to the following tips for when life gets messy: these tools aren't luxuries for perfect days when you already feel good. They're emergency tools for your worst moments. You don't need special equipment, perfect circumstances, or even much time. Your breath is always with you. Your ability to name feelings is always available. Moments of awe are hiding in plain sight, waiting to be noticed.

The gap between feeling overwhelmed and finding your center isn't filled with more information. It's bridged by these simple tools that reconnect you with yourself and the present moment. They work not because they're complicated or exotic, but because they align with how your brain and body naturally function best.

So the next time your thoughts are racing, your emotions are spiraling, **or the world feels too much, remember: you're carrying an entire emotional toolkit inside you. These tools aren't about becoming**

someone different; they're about accessing the calm, clarity, and connection that have been within you all along. All you need to do is reach for the right tool and use it, however imperfectly, with whatever time you have.

And that, my friend, makes all the difference.

CHAPTER 3:
BUILDING UNSHAKEABLE INNER STRENGTH

Ever notice, when the world is quiet and your defenses are down, whose voice echoes loudest in your head. Your harshest critic or your kindest friend? *Yeah, that one. The inner critic that somehow manages to catch every single mistake you make while completely missing the seventeen things you did right.* We've all got that voice. Mine sounds suspiciously like my first mean boss who never let us rest and made us drive a broken-down car with a chained German Shepherd that was used as a security guard at night. Yours probably has its own equally charming origin story.

For me, this chapter on building resilience and practicing self-compassion is where we get to the heart of what it takes to master your inner game. My sense of peace has often hung by a thread, sustained only by resilience and self-compassion, stumbling forward in all my messy humanness.

Yet somehow, pressing forward taught me something powerful: **learning to love myself through all the broken pieces has been my saving grace.** Thanks to the wisdom and kindness generously shared by others, I've been able to piece together a version of myself I genuinely like. I'm not claiming I've cracked life's code, but choosing compassion amid chaos turned out to be my best decision yet. As it turns out, I'm surprisingly happier.

In this chapter, you'll discover five science-backed tools that will help you:

- Build unshakable resilience that bounces back from life's inevitable face-plants
- Transform your harshest inner critic into your most compassionate ally
- Find strength in your unique character traits (even the quirky ones)
- Embrace growth even when progress feels messier than a toddler with spaghetti
- Learn when to push forward and when to simply accept what is

Ready to turn down the volume on that inner critic and crank up the self-compassion? Let's dive in.

PRACTICING SELF-COMPASSION
WHY PRACTICING SELF-COMPASSION MATTERS

F ar from being some fluffy concept for people with too much time on their hands, self-compassion is the difference between drowning in stress and building genuine resilience. When you replace that mental drill sergeant with a voice of understanding, your entire nervous system shifts. Your body literally calms down. Heart rate steadies, blood pressure drops, and those stress hormones that have been wreaking havoc finally take a coffee break.

But what really matters is that self-compassion makes you stronger, not weaker. Scientists have discovered that people who practice it bounce back faster from setbacks, take more healthy risks, and ironically, achieve more of their goals. They're not afraid of failing because they know failure won't define them or trigger an internal beatdown.

Self-compassion dramatically boosts your overall life satisfaction. That constant background voice of not-good-enough finally quiets down. You start experiencing genuine emotional balance instead of ricocheting between perfectionism and self-criticism. Your optimism grows because setbacks become less daunting when you're not piling on extra punishment.

And the best part? Anyone can learn this skill. Yes, even you, especially you, with your lifetime membership to the Self-Critics Club. I was the president of that club, and if I can learn to talk to myself with kindness, there's hope for everyone.

THE SCIENCE BEHIND SELF-COMPASSION

Some people can just dust themselves off after failure while others spiral into shame? Scientists were curious too. In a fascinating study, researchers Breines and Chen discovered something game-changing: how you talk to yourself after a face-plant actually determines how quickly you get back up.[11]

They found that people who showed themselves compassion after blowing it (rather than beating themselves up) bounced back faster and showed more motivation to improve. It's like your brain has two possible recovery paths: the shame spiral or the growth rebound. Self-compassion literally activates different neural pathways. The ones that say "Hey, mistakes happen to everyone," instead of "You're a hopeless case."

Think of self-criticism as trying to motivate a scared kid by yelling at them. It might work short-term, but that kid's just going to hide next time. Self-compassion is like putting an arm around that kid's shoulder instead, creating safety that builds genuine confidence.

MY JOURNEY TOWARD SELF-COMPASSION

It's strange, isn't it? You'd think being kind to ourselves would come naturally. After all, who willingly chooses a life spent yelling insults at themselves? Sounds pretty ridiculous from this angle, yet there I was, doing exactly that. Often.

Parenting mistakes are especially tough. That's when I realized I needed to talk to myself like I would to a friend. Friends mess up, sometimes frequently, and I never scold them for being absolute mess-ups. I comfort them, remind them to be kind to themselves, and encourage them to just "do the next right thing." I love that line; it makes mistakes manageable, even hopeful.

Ironically, when I discovered the science-backed benefits of self-compassion, I initially got angry at myself for not adopting it sooner. Talk about self-sabotage! Eventually, I reined in that irony, making peace with Billy's inevitable slip-ups. **Being kind to myself isn't just smart. It's necessary. It's even kinda fun, like finally letting the class clown out of detention after decades of unnecessary punishment.**

REFLECTING ON SELF-COMPASSION

Take a moment and think about your best friend calling you after a rough day where they really messed up. What words naturally come out of your mouth? When was the last time you spoke to yourself with that same gentleness after a similar mistake? What would change if you became your own best friend instead of your harshest critic?

ACTION STEPS TOWARD SELF-COMPASSION

Alright, let's get practical. Here are six ways to start treating yourself like someone who actually deserves some basic human kindness:

- **Friend Self-Talk**: Next time you mess up, pause and ask: "What would I say to my friend right now?" Then say exactly that to yourself.
- **Mistake Comfort**: After a setback, give yourself a small comfort. A cup of tea, a walk, or even just a deep breath. Small kindness, big impact.
- **Letter of Compassion**: Write yourself a supportive note during tough times. Feel weird? Imagine writing to your best friend, then address it to yourself.
- **Encouraging Mantras**: Create a go-to phrase for rough moments: "This is hard, but I'm doing my best" or my personal favorite, "Well, that was educational."
- **Celebrate Small Wins**: Did you get out of bed today? Answer an email? Not yell at someone annoying? That's a win. Acknowledge it, friend.

- **Imagine Advising Another**: When stuck in self-criticism, imagine someone else in your exact situation. What advice would you give them? Now take it yourself.

MOVING ON FROM SELF-COMPASSION

Now that we've learned to silence our inner drill sergeant, let's focus on bringing our natural strengths into the spotlight. **Because once you've stopped beating yourself up for what you lack, you can finally appreciate the unique gifts you already have, like discovering a treasure chest in your own backyard that you've been walking past for years.**

LEVERAGING CHARACTER STRENGTHS

WHY CHARACTER STRENGTHS MATTER

We've all got that friend who's always chasing the next self-improvement fix. Reading books about their weaknesses, taking courses on things they're terrible at, and basically treating their life like a never-ending home renovation project. But what if they're looking at the whole thing backwards?

Imagine focusing on the things you're naturally good at instead of obsessing over your shortcomings. That's what leveraging character strengths is all about. **It's like finally noticing you've been trying to write with your non-dominant hand for decades when you could've just switched to the other one.**

Something magical happens when you deliberately use your natural strengths. Whether it's your wicked sense of humor, your knack for solving puzzles, or your ability to make strangers feel instantly comfortable. Your satisfaction skyrockets. Your confidence grows. Your relationships deepen. And most surprisingly, your depression and anxiety often pack their bags and move to a less hospitable neighborhood.

This isn't about ignoring areas for growth. It's about recognizing that watering the flowers in your mental garden works better than constantly yanking at the weeds. And the research backs this up: people who regularly use their character strengths report higher levels of happiness, better relationships, and a deeper sense of purpose. Not bad for simply doing more of what you're already naturally good at.

THE SCIENCE BEHIND LEVERAGING CHARACTER STRENGTHS

Ever wonder why some activities leave you energized while others drain your life force faster than my phone battery? The answer lies in the science of character strengths. In a groundbreaking study, Seligman and his team discovered that when folks identify and regularly use their unique character strengths, their happiness doesn't just nudge up a little. It takes a significant leap.[1]

Think of your character strengths like your psychological superpower pack. Some people have creativity that makes MacGyver look unimaginative. Others have kindness that would make Mother Teresa say, "Take it down a notch, you're making me look bad." When you tap into these innate powers daily, your brain serves up a cocktail of feel-good chemicals that no artificial happiness hack can match. The participants in Seligman's study who used their signature strengths in new ways every day for just one week showed significant increases in happiness and decreases in depression for up to six months afterward. **Six months of improved well-being from one week of effort. That's a return on investment that would make Wall Street jealous! It's like finally using the right tool for the job after years of hammering screws with a banana.**

MY JOURNEY TOWARD CHARACTER STRENGTH

Let me start with what I'm terrible at: being orderly and dealing with bureaucracy. So naturally, 20 years ago I started my own CPA firm. Because nothing says "genius" like building a business around your biggest weakness.

Here's the kicker: my own taxes hadn't been filed in three years. The IRS owed ME money, and I still didn't file them. Oh, and it's illegal to prepare taxes professionally when yours aren't current. My business card should've read "Billy Marshall, CPA: Do as I Say, Not as I Do."

When I finally filed under threat of losing my license, I got thousands back. Money I desperately needed, sitting there because I hated paperwork more than I loved money.

The only part I enjoyed was the "creative" side. Finding gray areas. Spoiler alert: the IRS doesn't appreciate creativity.

After that disaster, I embraced my actual strengths: winging it, not filing it. Show me something that requires making sense of total chaos through data, and I come alive. Like this huge work project I was assigned. It was like building the plane while flying it, except all the parts were scattered across the sky and we had to catch them mid-flight. My team pulled it off. It was chaos, terrifying, and the most work fun I've had in years.

The lesson? Stop fixing what you're bad at. I'll never be organized. But the guy who builds wings while falling? That's exactly who I needed to be.

REFLECTING ON LEVERAGING CHARACTER STRENGTHS

When did you last lose track of time doing something that felt natural to you? What particular strength were you using at that moment? And here's the million-dollar question: how might you intentionally create more opportunities to use that strength in your daily life, both for your own enjoyment and to contribute something meaningful to others?

ACTION STEPS TOWARD LEVERAGING CHARACTER STRENGTHS

Time to put rubber to the road! Here are six ways to start flexing those natural strength muscles:

- **Strength Quiz Fun**: Take The VIA Character Strengths Survey. It's quick, fun, and reveals your unique superpowers.
- **Weekly Strength Challenge**: Pick one strength each week and find a new way to use it. Great at spotting humor? Keep a daily funny moment journal.
- **Buddy Strength Challenge**: Team up with a friend and assign each other playful "strength missions."
- **Strengths in Action**: Stuck on a problem? Tackle it using your top strength instead of the "normal" approach. Amazing how creativity can solve what logic can't.
- **Strength Storyboard**: Create a quick list of times your natural strengths saved the day. This becomes your personal highlight reel for low-confidence moments.
- **Daily Strength Intention**: Each morning, pick one strength you'll deliberately use that day. "Today I'll use my appreciation of beauty to notice three amazing things on my commute."

MOVING ON FROM LEVERAGING CHARACTER STRENGTHS

As powerful as embracing your natural strengths, the real game-changer comes when you pair that awareness with a growth mindset. **Because, look, some skills are just plain gifts, no doubt about it. But true fulfillment, the kind that really makes your heart happy-dance, well, that blooms when we trust we can grow anywhere we choose to put in good, honest effort and practice.**

EMBRACING A GROWTH MINDSET
WHY EMBRACING A GROWTH MINDSET MATTERS

Have you ever watched a kid trying to learn something new? They fall, laugh, get up, fall again, and somehow keep going with that infectious determination. Then, somewhere along the way to adulthood, many of us develop a brittle relationship with failure. We start dividing the world into "things I'm good at" and "things I'm bad at". Case closed, no appeals process.

But what if that's all just a story we've been telling ourselves? What if our abilities aren't carved in stone but more like clay waiting to be shaped? That's the essence of a growth mindset. The belief that your talents and abilities can be developed through effort, good strategies, and input from others.

This mental shift is like discovering you've been driving with the emergency brake on for years. Suddenly everything moves a whole lot easier. Suddenly, failure isn't a judgment on your worth but simply information about what to try next. **Challenges become invitations rather than threats. And your focus shifts from "proving I'm smart enough" to "getting smarter through effort."**

The beauty of embracing a growth mindset isn't just academic. It fundamentally changes how you experience life. Your fear of failure diminishes because setbacks become temporary teachers rather than permanent labels. Your resilience skyrockets because you know that struggle is just part of the growth process. And perhaps most importantly, your innate optimism gets a major boost because artificial limitations no longer trap you.

THE SCIENCE BEHIND EMBRACING A GROWTH MINDSET

Isn't it weird how some folks handle stress like they're swatting away mosquitoes, while others get completely derailed? Fascinating research on mindset gives us a clue. Schroder and his research team discovered that people with a growth mindset don't just perform better. They stress better too.[12]

When facing challenges, the fixed-mindset brain lights up with threat responses, throwing an internal temper tantrum. But the growth-mindset brain? It calmly activates problem-solving networks instead. **It's like the difference between your computer freezing completely versus running a helpful troubleshooting program. Same external problem, dramatically different internal experience.**

The coolest part? This mindset shift doesn't just change how you feel. It literally rewires how your brain processes setbacks. It's like installing a mental operating system upgrade that transforms error messages from "Fatal System Failure" to "Helpful Debugging Information."

MY JOURNEY TOWARD GROWTH MINDSET

Embracing a growth mindset is core to who I am. Not by choice, but by necessity, given my talent for creating chaos every time I aim to grow. My projects rarely unfold as smoothly as planned; just ask anyone who tours the camper van Suzy and I built. I'm no craftsman. I've got crooked shelves and plumbing held together by sheer optimism. Our van is more like a climate controlled fort on wheels than a real camper van. Each feature proudly took me at least three tries. But that's exactly the point: growth means fully expecting and accepting the inevitable screw-ups along the way.

Suzy captured this perfectly when she gave me a shirt that reads: 'It's not easy being me, and I'm not good at it yet.' That 'yet' is crucial, capturing the essence of persistence and stubborn optimism that keeps me returning for another glorious try. **Not to mention it is way more fun to try new things instead of fearing failure. When you embrace the power of "yet," life becomes an adventure of possibilities rather than a minefield of potential mistakes.**

REFLECTING ON EMBRACING A GROWTH MINDSET

Think about something you've always believed you "just can't do" or aren't "naturally good at." What would change if you added the word "yet" to the end of that sentence? How might your approach to challenges shift if you viewed your abilities as constantly evolving rather than fixed traits? Where might you be in a year if you embraced the power of "not good at it...Yet"?

ACTION STEPS TOWARD EMBRACING A GROWTH MINDSET

Let's roll up our sleeves and rewire that beautiful brain of yours with these six practical steps:

- **Celebrate Mistakes**: Next time you mess up, actually high-five yourself and say, "Great! Now I know one way that doesn't work." Feel ridiculous? Good. That's growth happening.
- **Add "Yet" Statements**: Catch yourself saying "I can't do this"? Simply add "yet" to the end. That three-letter word packs a psychological punch that keeps possibilities open.
- **New Skill Fun**: Pick something you're comically bad at and spend 15 minutes trying it purely for laughs. Terrible drawing? Awful dancing? Embrace the beautiful disaster of learning.
- **Effort Rewards**: After doing something challenging, give yourself a small reward. Not for the outcome but for the sheer effort. I treat myself to fancy coffee after difficult writing sessions.

- **Growth Stories**: Share your most spectacular failures-turned-successes with friends. My camper van tales have become legendary dinner party material.
- **Visual Growth Cues**: Post sticky notes with growth reminders where you'll see them daily.

MOVING ON FROM EMBRACING A GROWTH MINDSET

Now that we've embraced the power of growth and "yet," let's tackle perhaps the most challenging mindset shift of all. Learning to accept what we genuinely can't control. **Because sometimes the greatest strength comes not from changing reality, but from making peace with it exactly as it is. Like finding the wisdom to know the difference between what you can change and what you need to accept.**

ACCEPTING WHAT YOU CAN'T CONTROL

WHY ACCEPTING WHAT YOU CAN'T CONTROL MATTERS

Have you ever noticed how much energy we waste fighting battles we can't possibly win? We rage against traffic, argue with weather forecasts, and get frustrated when other people (stubbornly) refuse to become the improved versions we've designed for them in our heads.

This constant resistance to reality isn't just exhausting. It's the psychological equivalent of repeatedly running into a brick wall and then filing a complaint about the wall's poor placement. **Acceptance doesn't mean resignation or giving up. It means stopping the pointless fight with what already is, so you can direct your precious energy toward what can actually be changed.**

The shift from resistance to acceptance is like putting down a heavy backpack you didn't even realize you were carrying. Your stress levels drop dramatically once you stop fighting the unchangeable. Your anxiety decreases because you're no longer constantly scanning for things that aren't going "according to plan." And perhaps most importantly, your overall emotional balance improves because you're no longer living in a perpetual state of frustrated expectations.

This wisdom isn't new. Stoic philosophers have been preaching it for centuries. But modern psychology confirms what they intuited: peace comes not from controlling the uncontrollable but from focusing your energy solely on your true sphere of influence. Everything else? You simply let it be.

THE SCIENCE BEHIND ACCEPTING WHAT YOU CAN'T CONTROL

Ever wonder why fighting against reality feels so utterly exhausting? Science has figured that out, too. In a groundbreaking study on chronic pain, McCracken and Eccleston discovered something counterintuitive. People who psychologically accepted their pain actually suffered less and reported better daily functioning than those who fought it.[13]

Think about that for a second. By accepting something difficult, they experienced less difficulty. **It's like life's great paradox. Struggling against the stream exhausts you, while flowing with it conserves your energy for the swimming that actually matters.** When you stop resisting what you can't change, your brain literally calms down. Less stress hormones, lower blood pressure, decreased anxiety.

This isn't just feel-good philosophy; it's neurological reality. Your brain on acceptance is fundamentally different from your brain on resistance. One conserves precious mental resources; the other burns through them like my nephew goes through a bag of chips. Quickly and with nothing to show for it afterward.

MY JOURNEY TOWARD ACCEPTING WHAT I COULDN'T CONTROL

About 30 years ago, Stephen Covey's *Seven Habits of Highly Effective People* flipped a switch in my brain, especially the difference between my "circle of influence" versus the larger "circle of concern." It freed me, allowing me to pour my energy into things I could actually change rather than stressing over what was beyond my reach.

And amazingly, as promised, that approach slowly expanded my circle of influence. I wish I could say I've mastered it, but I'm far from perfect. It remains my anchor, especially when life's storms hit hardest, like watching a child struggle.

Those moments are tough; your heart breaks, and the impulse to fix everything is overwhelming. "Why can't I just stop their pain?" or "Why can't someone do things differently?" becomes a draining refrain. But Covey's lesson reminds me to step back, take a breath, and focus only where I have real power, giving me sanity when I need it most. It's not always easy, but it's always worth it.

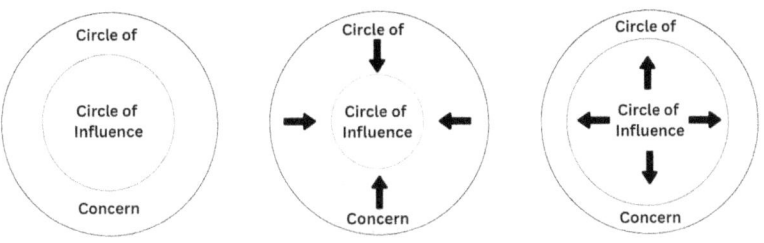

REFLECTING ON ACCEPTING WHAT YOU CAN'T CONTROL

Think about something you've been fighting against that simply won't budge, no matter how much energy you pour into changing it. How would your daily experience shift if you fully accepted this reality exactly as it is right now? What mental and emotional resources might become available to you if you stopped this particular battle? Where could you redirect that energy in ways that might actually make a difference?

ACTION STEPS TOWARD ACCEPTING WHAT YOU CAN'T CONTROL

Ready to put down some of those heavy mental burdens? Here are six practical ways to practice acceptance:

- **Control List**: Grab a paper, draw a line down the middle, and sort your current stressors into "Can Control" and "Can't

Control." Then commit to focusing exclusively on the first column.

- **Symbolic Release Ritual**: Write down something you can't control on a leaf or paper boat, then release it into moving water. Sounds woo-woo until you feel the tangible relief.
- **Acceptance Mantra**: Develop a short phrase that helps you let go. Mine is simple. "Let it go... Let it go, Billy."
- **Worst-Case Scenario Check**: Ask yourself: "If this worst-case scenario happens, will I still be okay eventually?" The answer is almost always yes, bringing immediate perspective.
- **"Circle of Influence" Reminder**: Draw two circles on an index card. A small inner circle **(what you influence)** and a larger outer circle (what concerns you. Ignore them if outside of the circle of influence). Keep it handy for overwhelming moments.
- **Gratitude Refocus**: When ruminating on what you can't change, immediately list three things you're grateful for in your control. Mental pattern interrupt at its finest.

WRAPPING UP THE CHAPTER:

WHAT'S HAPPENING IN YOUR BRAIN

Every time you practice self-compassion instead of self-criticism, you're once again laying down new neural pathways. Each time you use your strengths or embrace a growth opportunity, you're strengthening specific connections, making them your brain's go-to response. The transformation happens gradually through these resilience-building tools, creating lasting changes in how you process challenges and emotions. **These *small, consistent* efforts compound over time, literally changing your default settings and making resilience your natural state, even during life's inevitable storms.**

The really cool part? With enough repetition using self-compassion, strengths, growth mindset, and acceptance, these new approaches become your default settings. The pathways for resilience get stronger while the old ruts of rumination and self-doubt gradually fade from disuse.

LIFE-CHANGING CONTRASTS

Before & After: The Resilience Revolution

Before: The Morning Mistake Your alarm didn't go off. You oversleep, rush around like a caffeinated squirrel, and spill coffee down your shirt. As you change clothes, your inner critic launches its morning broadcast. "Way to go, genius. Late again. Everyone at work knows you can't get it together. This whole day is ruined before it even started." Your shoulders tense, your jaw clenches, and you carry that heavy cloud of self-directed anger into everything that follows.

After: The Morning Mistake Your alarm doesn't go off. You oversleep and immediately notice the familiar tightness in your chest. But instead of letting the critical tirade begin, you take a breath and think, "If my friend overslept, what would I say to them?" You remind yourself that everyone has mornings like this. You quickly prioritize what actually needs doing, use your natural strength of adaptability, and text your boss with a realistic arrival time. The day isn't perfect, but it's no longer poisoned by self-criticism either.

Before: The Project Setback Your big idea at work hits an unexpected roadblock. Immediately, your mind fills with evidence of your inadequacy: "I should have seen this coming. I'm not cut out for this level of responsibility. Everyone else would have handled this better." You avoid talking about the problem, hoping it will somehow resolve itself, while stress builds like pressure in a shaken soda can.

After: The Project Setback Your big idea hits the same roadblock, but your response is fundamentally different. You think, "This is challenging, but challenges help me grow." You draw your circle of influence, focusing only on what you can actually impact. You tap into your character strength of creativity to brainstorm alternatives. Most importantly, you reach out for input instead of hiding the problem. The obstacle hasn't changed, but your relationship to it has transformed completely. And perhaps most importantly, here's how these tools help with life's deeper questions:

Before: The Deeper Questions Late at night, those existential questions creep in: "What's the point of all this anyway?" But instead of exploring them, you reach for your phone, scrolling mindlessly to escape the discomfort. You wake feeling oddly empty, disconnected from any sense of meaning, wondering why happiness always seems just out of reach.

After: The Deeper Questions The same late-night questions arise, but now you recognize them as invitations rather than threats. You spend a few minutes in reflection, connecting to what truly matters to you. Whether through prayer, meditation, or simply watching the stars, you allow yourself to experience the mystery of being human without needing perfect answers. You fall asleep with a sense of being part of something larger than yourself, and wake with purpose that transcends daily tasks.

These aren't just different reactions. *They're completely different experiences of being alive.* The circumstances haven't changed, but you've transformed your internal landscape from a battlefield into a garden by practicing self-compassion, using your strengths, embracing growth, accepting what you can't control, and connecting to deeper meaning. And that, my friend, changes everything.

YOUR RESILIENCE & SELF-COMPASSION CHEAT SHEET

Here's your pocket guide to resilience and self-compassion. Clip it, save it, heck, tattoo it somewhere if you're feeling dramatic:

- **Talk to yourself like you're talking to a friend**. Your brain doesn't know the difference, but your heart sure does.
- **Use your strengths daily, even in small ways**. They're the emotional equivalent of compound interest.
- **Add "yet" to your "I can't" statements**. Three letters that transform dead ends into doorways.
- **Draw your circle of influence regularly**. Then pour your energy only inside that line.
- **Connect to something bigger than yourself daily**: because perspective is the antidote to most suffering.
- **Celebrate mistakes as growth moments**. They're tuition you've already paid, so might as well reap the benefit of the lesson.
- **Remember that hard times introduce you to parts of yourself you didn't know existed**. Often the best parts.

THE BOTTOM LINE

Life's going to knock you down. That's not pessimism. It's just the price of admission for being human. But resilience isn't about avoiding the falls; it's about how you get back up afterward.

These four tools, self-compassion, leveraging strengths, embracing growth and accepting what you can't control, aren't quick fixes or trendy techniques. They're timeless tools that have helped people weather life's storms for generations. The science just helps us understand why they work so well.

I'm still learning them myself, pressing *forward* with all my messy imperfections. Some days I nail it; other days, not so much. But that's exactly the point: **this journey isn't about perfection. It's about progress, purpose, and finding unexpected joy along the way, even when the path gets rocky.**

Pay attention to this: resilience isn't something you're born with or without. It's something you build, one small choice at a time. And the wonderful thing? You can start right now, exactly where you are. And that's the most beautiful part of this whole journey. It begins with a single, imperfect step.

CHAPTER 4:

FINDING YOUR SOMETHING BIGGER

At 3 a.m., when the world is quiet and your defenses are down, a question rises like smoke: *"Is this all there is?"*

It's a question that can surface even when everything else is going right. Here we are, friends. We've learned how to wrangle our runaway thoughts, navigate life's sudden turns, and be kinder to ourselves when we mess up. We've built a solid toolbox for our inner game, but that question still finds us in the quiet moments.

In our crazy-busy, notification-obsessed world, we've somehow managed to make our lives incredibly full and strangely empty at the same time. We're checking boxes, crushing goals, staying "productive". Yet many of us still find ourselves wrestling with that same restless question. And that restless feeling isn't a glitch in your system. It's your soul knocking on the door, asking to be invited to the party.

Think of this chapter as the final tool for your inner-game toolbox. If learning to manage your thoughts is like upgrading your brain's operating system, and mindfulness is like learning to actually use that system without constantly crashing it, then "Finding Your Something Bigger" is like figuring out where you're actually trying to go and why the journey matters in the first place.

Now, before you start worrying that I'm about to get all preachy on you. Don't be. That's not what this is about. This isn't about joining any particular religion or becoming the type of person who posts sunrise meditation quotes every morning (though if that's your jam, more power to you!). This is about carving out space to connect with something bigger than your grocery list and credit card balance. Whatever that "something bigger" looks like for you.

WHY FINDING YOUR SOMETHING BIGGER MATTERS

I've learned the hard way that you can win at everything society keeps score on and still feel like you're losing at life. Because success without meaning is just expensive emptiness.

Discovering your "bigger Why" feeds a deeper hunger we all carry. It's that sense of connection that quiets the noise. This sense of connection doesn't require a specific label or path. It can be found in a moment of awe in nature, a shared purpose with others, or the quiet clarity of scientific truth. The goal is simply to anchor your daily grind to something more meaningful. And if words like 'spiritual' make you itchy, stay with me: this is about finding what gives your life meaning, whatever that looks like for you.

And if you're tempted to think this is just feel-good fluff, the research is pretty compelling. People who regularly engage in some form of deeper connection don't just report feeling better. They demonstrate measurably greater emotional resilience when life delivers an unexpected blow. They show higher life satisfaction scores, a stronger sense of purpose, less isolation, and more genuine community connections. Crucially, they also show a greater ability to find meaning in life's inevitable suffering, transforming difficult circumstances into opportunities for growth. Most fascinating of all? They maintain more optimism during tough times. It's not because they're in denial, but because they have a broader perspective. This is the perspective of awe, that feeling of being part of something vast, which has the powerful effect of shrinking our personal worries and reminding us what truly matters.

Rather than forcing yourself into spiritual practices that feel fake or uncomfortable, this is about intentionally creating space to connect with something larger than yourself. However you define that. Because when your everyday actions get rooted in deeper meaning, even ordinary moments can become extraordinarily fulfilling.

THE SCIENCE BEHIND FINDING YOUR SOMETHING BIGGER

The journey to "Finding Our Something Bigger" has been around for thousands of years across virtually every human culture for good reason. There's solid science backing up their staying power. Researchers, including prominent figures like Harold G. Koenig, have extensively documented that individuals who regularly engage in some form of spiritual practices consistently show measurably lower rates of depression and higher life satisfaction over the long term, extending beyond temporary mood boosts.[14]

Think of your pursuit of deeper meaning as cross-training for your psyche. Just like mixing up your workouts prevents injury and builds overall fitness, spiritual practices strengthen mental muscles you might not otherwise exercise. They light up brain regions associated with compassion, perspective-taking, and emotional regulation. Basically building a more robust psychological immune system capable of handling life's inevitable shocks and stresses with greater calm and clarity.

These benefits are not tied to specific beliefs. Profoundly, clinical research shows substances like psilocybin can induce mystical experiences of lasting significance. In a groundbreaking 2006 Johns Hopkins study, participants reported these events, marked by intense feelings of unity, sacredness, and transcendence of time and space, as among the most meaningful of their lives.[15] The enduring positive impact reveals something profound about our design: our brains aren't just capable of finding meaning, they are actively wired to seek it out. The value here is knowing that the hunger for "something bigger" is not a personal flaw, but a fundamental part of being human.

This same sense of connection is also at the heart of awe. The practical value of this is immense. Research shows that the experience of awe literally quiets our noisy inner critic and fosters what scientists call a "small self". A fundamental perspective shift from "I" to "we."[16] This feeling of being part of something vast and interconnected is the antidote to feeling isolated and overwhelmed, connecting us back to our communities and a shared sense of humanity.

Science also shows us that spiritual beliefs powerfully shape how we understand mortality and aging, generally reducing anxiety and increasing acceptance of life's natural rhythms. Perhaps most profound of all, spiritual contemplation helps us make meaning out of suffering, potentially transforming traumatic experiences into opportunities for personal growth.[17] This ability to find purpose even in difficult circumstances is one of spirituality's most robust contributions to human well-being. But enough about the research. Let me tell you how this played out in my own messy journey.

MY JOURNEY TOWARD FINDING MY SOMETHING BIGGER

Years ago, my spiritual life wasn't just part of my world. It was my entire world. I ran a Christian bookstore and coffee shop called Holy Grounds (yes, the pun was absolutely intentional, and yes, I'm still proud of it) where we held worship gatherings twice a week. The singing, praying, reflecting, connecting with something infinitely bigger than myself. It all felt deeply, authentically real. All this while going to church EVERY day.

Then life threw me one of its famous curveballs, and everything I thought I knew shattered like a dropped coffee mug. The certainty of faith that I'd wrapped myself in unraveled, leaving me with questions instead of answers: and maybe that's exactly what I needed.

Today, I'm anchored in love, beauty, and what I can only describe as a curious wonder toward something greater than myself. Sometimes I catch glimpses of profound awe. Moments that remind me exactly who I am, or at least who I'm aiming to become. I still "hear" that voice pushing me forward with love and strength. I just can't give the voice a name. I've come to the point that when I strip away all the theological complexity and doctrinal debates, **love always gets the last word**. Not as some cheesy greeting card sentiment, but as the truest thing I know about why any of us are here in the first place. And finding my version of that truth? That's been the most transformative discovery of my entire journey. Maybe even more important than all the other tools I've shared in this book.

REFLECTING ON FINDING YOUR SOMETHING BIGGER

When was the last time you experienced a moment of genuine awe. One of those times when everything seemed to slow down and you felt connected to something infinitely larger than yourself? What created that moment? And what's one small, practical step you could take to invite more of those experiences into your regular routine?

ACTION STEPS TOWARD FINDING YOUR SOMETHING BIGGER

Let's get practical with six straightforward approaches to finding your "something bigger":

- **Brief Daily Reflection**: Set aside 5 quiet minutes each morning or evening to contemplate what gives your life meaning. No special equipment required. Just you and your thoughts.
- **Write Your Future Eulogy (The Uplifting Version)**: This isn't morbid; it's a powerful tool for clarity. Set a timer for 15 minutes and write a short speech that you would want a loved one to give about you at the end of a long and fulfilling life. What did you contribute? What were you passionate about? How did you make people feel? Don't focus on career accomplishments, but on character and connection. This exercise cuts through the noise and reveals what truly matters to you.

- **Nature as Sanctuary**: Make regular dates with the natural world. Walk in a park, watch a sunset, or simply sit under a tree. Nature has a way of right-sizing our problems instantly.
- **Meaningful Texts Ritual**: Regularly read something that inspires you to tap into some higher purpose. Could be ancient wisdom, poetry, philosophy. Whatever speaks to your deeper questions.
- **Community Reflection**: Find a group that discusses meaningful topics. One of the reasons I wrote this book, for example, was to use it for a "Beer & Big Questions" meet-up at my barn that tackles life's mysteries without taking itself too seriously.
- **Acts of Service**: Do something kind without expectation of return or recognition. Nothing connects you to purpose faster than genuine contribution to others' well-being.

The beautiful thing about finding "your something bigger" is its flexibility. Nature lovers might find transcendence hiking trails or watching sunsets. Creative types often discover it through art, music, or poetry. Service-oriented people find meaning through volunteering. Analytical minds might prefer structured contemplative practices. You get to experiment until you find what truly fits your unique nature.

But, after all my searching, finding your "something bigger" isn't a luxury or an add-on to a happier life. Rather, it's the foundation that helps give everything else meaning. **Those moments when you touch something vast and mysterious, whether through prayer or poetry, service or stargazing? They're not just nice experiences. They're reminders of why all the other tools in this book matter.**

Because when you're anchored to something greater than your daily worries, every gratitude practice becomes deeper, every moment of mindfulness more profound, every act of self-compassion more natural. **You're not just managing your inner game anymore. You're** playing for something that matters. And that, my friend, changes everything.

WRAPPING UP YOUR INNER GAME:

S o here we are. Four chapters, fourteen science-backed tools, and **one fundamental truth: mastering your inner game isn't about perfection, it's about practice**. From that first moment of gratitude to finding your something bigger, we've completed our journey through "Mastering Your Inner Game."

When I think about everything we've covered in this mental and emotional well-being toolbox, I'm reminded of my Uncle Bob's actual toolbox. A battered metal case with decades of dings and paint splatters. As a kid, I'd watch him sort through those tools with absolute certainty about which one he needed for each job. Monkey wrench for the plumbing, Phillips head for the cabinet hinges, hammer for... well, pretty much anything if you're stubborn enough.

Each chapter has given you a different set of tools for your inner workshop:

- Chapter 1's five mindset shifters (gratitude through humor) that transform how you see everything.
- Chapter 2's four awareness builders (mindfulness through awe) that help you become the CEO of your own mind.
- Chapter 3's four resilience makers (self-compassion through acceptance) that turn stumbles into strength.

- Chapter 4's spiritual compass that points toward meaning when everything else feels empty.

Some days you'll need them all. Other days, just one will do the trick.

That's exactly what we've been building here. Not just random tools tossed in a box, but a carefully curated collection that works together. Some days you need gratitude to adjust your perspective, other days deep breathing keeps you from saying something you'll regret, and sometimes self-compassion is the only thing that will get you off the couch after an epic fail. The beauty is having options when life inevitably throws you a curveball or a flat tire or, in my case, a boat trailer meeting a telephone pole.

Over time, I've noticed something important: these practices work better together than they do on their own. Mindfulness makes gratitude deeper. Self-compassion makes growth possible. Humor makes it all bearable. It's like they're having a continuous conversation with each other inside your head, gradually replacing that critical drill sergeant with a whole committee of more helpful voices.

And let's be real. We're all works in progress. I still have days when my thoughts race faster than a squirrel running from Yeti, moments when I ruminate on a minor embarrassment from 2006, and times I forget every single one of these tools and temporarily revert to the emotional resilience of a two-year-old.

But here's the difference: I now recognize the drift before I'm halfway down the river. I catch myself quicker. I bounce back faster. And most importantly, I've learned to laugh at the whole messy process rather than beating myself up for not being "enlightened enough." **Turns out, enlightenment might just be accepting that you'll never be fully enlightened, and being perfectly okay with that beautiful mess.**

Mastering your inner game isn't about achieving some perfect state of perpetual bliss. These tools help you build a life where you can hold both the heartache and the joy, the failures and the victories, the certainty and the doubt. All without being crushed or inflated by any of it. They're about creating enough inner spaciousness to host all of your experiences without being defined by any single one of them.

If I could go back in time and tell my younger self one thing about this journey, it would be this: start sooner, expect less perfection, and enjoy the ride more. Beneath the noise and distraction lies your inherent wholeness, which these tools help you uncover rather than fixing perceived brokenness.

My hope for you isn't that you master these tools perfectly. Far from it. My hope is that you give yourself permission to start messy. Just remember to:

- **Start small.** Progress, not perfection, is the goal. Don't try to master fourteen tools overnight.
- **Let one tool be enough.** Even a single consistent practice, like gratitude, can shift your entire outlook.
- **Take what works for you.** Let the rest wait in the toolbox. You can always come back for them when you need them.
- **Trust the process of gradual change.** My hope is that six months or six years from now, you'll find yourself automatically taking that deep breath before responding to your angry teenager, laughing at yourself when you make a mistake, or noticing sunset colors even on a difficult day.
- **Look for the subtle shifts.** Eventually, you'll realize that something has changed inside you. Not dramatically, but fundamentally.

Because that's how real change happens. Not in giant leaps of perfection, but in tiny moments of showing up differently, over and over again, until one day the new path is the obvious one.

Now, I promised you a complete happiness toolbox, and we're just getting started. See, all this inner work we've been doing? It's like having a perfectly tuned engine with no gas in the tank if we ignore the physical foundation. Your mind might be ready to soar, but if your body's stuck in the park, you're not going anywhere.

So let's shift gears. Time to explore how your physical habits either fuel or sabotage everything we've just built. Because even the best inner game can't overcome a body running on fumes.

Now let's keep going. We've got a whole lifetime to practice, and we're going to need it!

YOUR SUCCESS SYSTEMS
SECTION TWO

Take my short-lived career as a 'biker dude'. A midlife crisis without training wheels. I convinced myself buying a motorcycle was financially brilliant, despite having no idea how to operate one. My maiden voyage home was a disaster: zigzagging through the neighborhood, getting caught in a downpour, and running out of gas on the highway. That beautiful machine eventually found a new home with someone who actually knew what they were doing.

Sound familiar? Maybe not the motorcycle part specifically, but I bet you've had your own version of chasing happiness down a road that turned out to be a dead end. We all have. And that's exactly what this section is about. Not the motorcycle mishaps, but the deeper truth they reveal.

So what are these dead-end roads we keep taking? Most of them are well-lit, popular highways our culture tells us lead directly to the good life. We've been handed a faulty map, full of myths about what success and a well-built life actually look like. Before we lay the foundation for what does work, let's tear down five of the biggest lies that keep us on the hamster wheel:

- More Money Will Make You Happier
- Material Possessions Bring Lasting Happiness
- Achieving Goals Creates Lasting Happiness
- Keeping Busy Will Make You Happy
- More Free Time = More Happiness

Chasing these myths is like my motorcycle adventure. A lot of noise and effort that ultimately leaves you stranded. They keep us building our lives on shaky ground, wondering why we feel so wobbly. The tools in the following chapters are about building on solid rock instead. (And as always, if you want to see the full list of faulty blueprints, you can find all 37 myths we're demolishing in the Appendix.)

I've learned this the hard way: You can have the most enlightened mind in the world, but if you're powering it with four hours of sleep, drive-thru meals, and a body that hasn't moved since the dial-up era, you're just a genius driving a car with no wheels. Good luck with that spiritual awakening, friend.

It's like trying to build a gorgeous dream house on a foundation of Jell-O. Doesn't matter how fancy your mental furniture is or how stylish your emotional décor. If the foundation's wobbly, you're just decorating tomorrow's sinkhole. Your physical habits aren't separate from your happiness. They're the launching pad.

I've been my own guinea pig in this department, stumbling through enough embarrassing experiments to write a book called "What Not To Do." Like the time I convinced myself I could function just fine with five hours of sleep every night. *I absolutely could not.* Or my brief home brewing stint, where I thought I could contain myself with two sixtels of great beer at my fingertips. *Again, I absolutely could not.*

What all these stumbles taught me is that happiness isn't some mystical state that descends on the worthy few. It's way more practical than that. It naturally bubbles up when your daily habits align with how your body and brain work. Revolutionary, I know! In the chapters ahead, we'll dig into three areas that form your happiness foundation:

CHAPTER 5: OPTIMIZING YOUR HUMAN OPERATING SYSTEM

- Prioritizing sleep
- Exercising regularly
- Mindful Nutrition
- Connecting with nature

CHAPTER 6: DESIGNING A LIFE THAT ACTUALLY WORKS

- Setting meaningful goals
- Taking proactive steps towards goals
- Engaging in lifelong learning
- Practicing Financial Well-Being
- Managing Your Schedule for "Time Affluence"

CHAPTER 7: THE ART OF SUSTAINABLE LIVING

- Taking breaks & vacations
- Strengthening digital resilience
- Decluttering
- Engaging in hobbies & flow activities
- Choosing experiences over possessions

These aren't just nice ideas plucked from self-help books. Each chapter blends solid research (without getting all textbook-y), stories from my own messy journey, and concrete steps you can actually take today. Not in some distant future when the stars align and you magically have more time.

The coolest part? These tools work together like old friends. When you move your body regularly, you sleep better. When you sleep better, you make smarter food choices. When you eat well, you have more energy for things that matter. Focusing on what matters makes you less likely to burn out. When you take real breaks, your creativity gets a jumpstart. It's this beautiful upward spiral instead of the downward one many of us know too well.

So consider this section your invitation to stop overthinking happiness and embody it through daily tools that work with your brain's wiring, not against it. Because your body already knows how to be happy, it just needs your daily habits to stop throwing wrenches in the machinery.

Ready to build that foundation together? Let's roll up our sleeves and get started. I promise it'll be at least a tad bit smarter than my motor-cycle adventure. And significantly less likely to end with you soaking wet on the wrong highway.

CHAPTER 5:

OPTIMIZING YOUR HUMAN OPERATING SYSTEM

The biggest lie we tell ourselves about energy is that it's something we lose. The truth is, we don't lose it. We sabotage it. We trade it away for cheap comforts and bad habits in a thousand tiny transactions every day. I was the master of the energy heist, pulling off the 'work hard, play hard' con on myself for decades. This is the story of how I learned to stop being a master thief and started becoming a savvy investor in my own well-being.

On one side, I'm disciplined enough to average 10,000 steps daily for over a year straight and can crank out more pushups than most twenty-somethings. But then there's my shadow side: for far too long, I treated alcohol like a basic food group, convincing myself that my "work hard, play hard" lifestyle was sustainable despite mounting evidence to the contrary.

This wasn't just an occasional celebration gone sideways. It was my standard operating procedure. A ritual as reliable as my morning coffee. The most revealing part? I didn't drink to numb emotional pain (at least that's what I told myself). I drank because somehow I'd internalized the idea that enjoying life meant pouring another round, even as recovery times stretched longer and morning mental clarity became increasingly rare.

As I've crossed deep into midlife, the consequences have become impossible to ignore. That morning brain fog doesn't politely exit after breakfast anymore. It lingers like an unwelcome houseguest. My sleep quality, energy levels, and productivity all take measurable hits. Most importantly, it's just plain unfair to the people who matter most in my life. They deserve a fully present husband, father, and friend, not someone operating at 70% capacity because of a few bad choices. And that realization was my wake-up call.

But here's where this story takes a turn that surprised even me. After years of this pattern, I've recently discovered the growing world of quality non-alcoholic options. I'm actually sipping an Athletic Brew as I write this, and I have to admit. Waking up clear-headed is a game-changer for my energy and mood. Writing this down for a book that others might read makes me uncomfortable, but that's precisely why it needs to be said. Our energy levels aren't just about exercise and sleep. They're about the subtle ways we sabotage ourselves while wondering why we're always running on empty.

This chapter isn't about perfection. It's about momentum. It's about identifying the habits that either fuel your energy or drain it unnecessarily. My journey back from that 70% version of myself wasn't about willpower; it was about building a better system. I realized that my energy wasn't just being drained by one bad habit. It was being undermined by a faulty foundation. That realization led me to the four pillars of what I now call my Human Operating System. The non-negotiable, science-backed tools that transformed not just my energy levels but my entire approach to well-being:

- Prioritizing quality sleep (the foundation everything else depends on)
- Moving your body consistently (even when your couch has gravitational superpowers)
- Mindful Nutrition (fueling rather than fighting your body's natural systems)

- Connecting with nature (with some help from my four-legged personal trainer)

These surprisingly simple practices are the key to finding your sweet spot of sustainable energy and genuine happiness. Let's get started. No perfection required. Only progress.

PRIORITIZING SLEEP
WHY PRIORITIZING SLEEP MATTERS

Sleep is that thing we all claim to love but treat like an optional luxury when life gets busy. I get it. There's always one more email to answer, one more video to watch, one more project to finish. Sleep is one thing we can compromise on when time gets tight.

But here's the hard truth I learned the painful way: Skimping on sleep isn't just making you tired. It's making you a less functional human being. When you're sleep-deprived, your emotional responses go haywire. That minor annoyance from your coworker? Suddenly, it feels like a personal attack. That small setback on a project? Now it seems like the end of the world.

Quality sleep is the foundation that supports everything else in your life. It restores your emotional balance and enhances your thinking ability. Most importantly, it acts as a buffer against life's inevitable stresses. Without it, your resilience crumbles. Funny how problems that seemed insurmountable at midnight often look manageable after a good night's sleep. That's not a coincidence. That's your brain chemistry at work. When properly rested, you can access parts of your brain that handle complex problem-solving and emotional regulation. When exhausted, those parts go offline, leaving you with your cranky lizard brain in charge.

THE SCIENCE BEHIND PRIORITIZING SLEEP

Remember how your mom always said things would look better after a good night's sleep? It turns out that she was dropping some serious neuroscience truth bombs. The study by Ben Simon and Walker in 2019 discovered that even one night of poor sleep jacks up anxiety levels by nearly 30%.[18] That's not just feeling a little on edge. Moving your base-line emotional state from "I got this" to "everything is terrible."

What's happening behind the scenes is fascinating. Think of it like this: during quality sleep, your brain processes and regulates the day's emotional experiences, much like a nightly reset for your emotional operating system. Scientific studies show that deep sleep, in particular, helps restore activity in the medial prefrontal cortex, a brain region crucial for keeping anxiety in check. Without this, emotional reactivity can significantly increase.

Think of sleep as your brain's emotional reset button. Skip pressing it, and you're essentially trying to run today's programs on yesterday's overheated, glitchy operating system. No wonder everything crashes.

MY JOURNEY TOWARD PRIORITIZING SLEEP

Twenty years ago, I was the poster child for sleep deprivation heroism. Fresh out of a divorce that felt like emotional whiplash, juggling more jobs than a circus performer, and raising kids who worked as hard as I did, I wore my exhaustion like some twisted badge of honor. "Sleep?" I'd scoff. "I'll sleep when I'm dead. Or when I get the right job, which-ever comes first."

Then came the intervention from an older friend with laugh lines around his eyes who seemed perpetually at peace. After listening to my problems for a while, his first question wasn't about my feelings or parenting strategies. He simply asked, "Are you getting enough sleep?"

I stared at him like he'd suggested breathing underwater. Sleep? That optional activity I'd been skipping for years? What could that possibly have to do with my life falling apart?

Everything, as it turns out.

These days, sleep and I have developed a mature relationship. I've become that guy who tracks sleep cycles on his Fitbit with scientific dedication. Each month, the app assigns me an animal sleep personality. Currently, I'm a tortoise (frankly, a personal attack). Last month? A parrot. Bright and energetic.

But two decades of stubborn learning taught me that this wise man wasn't just being thoughtful. He was tossing me a life preserver when I was too busy drowning to notice I was in water.

REFLECTING ON PRIORITIZING SLEEP

When you think about your typical day, what activities are you prioritizing over sleep? Are those late-night scrolling sessions or extra work hours truly more valuable than waking up refreshed and emotionally balanced? What small adjustment to your evening routine could you make tonight that would improve your sleep quality?

ACTION STEPS TOWARD PRIORITIZING SLEEP

Ready to transform your relationship with sleep? Let's get practical:

- **Reframe downtime**: Think sleep is unproductive? Quality rest actually boosts focus, mood, and health. Consider those 7-8 hours essential recovery time for your brain and body.
- **Create a wind-down ritual**: Mind racing at night? Establish a calming pre-sleep routine with dim lights and maybe some journaling. Your brain needs transition time between day and night modes.
- **Break up with blue light:** Late-night screen habit? Swap your phone for a book 30 minutes before bed. Blue light blocks melatonin production: that's not just wellness fluff, it's basic biology.
- **Stick to a schedule**: No set bedtime? Keep sleep timing

consistent, even on weekends. Regular rhythms train your body for deeper, more restorative sleep cycles.

- **Track your progress**: Our tech gadgets are game-changers. Just strapping on a watch that monitors your sleep gives you real data to work with. When you measure something, you're naturally more motivated to improve it.
- **Optimize your cave**: Poor sleep environment? Make your bedroom cool, dark, and quiet. Cut evening caffeine too. These simple tweaks significantly improve sleep quality.

MOVING ON FROM PRIORITIZING SLEEP

Once you start getting quality sleep, you'll notice something amazing: you have more energy. Now, let's talk about the best way to invest it.

EXERCISING REGULARLY
WHY EXERCISING REGULARLY MATTERS

I f sleep is your body's foundation, then exercise is the electricity that powers the whole system. Yet for most of us, between work deadlines, family drama, and the siren call of the couch, the power is perpetually off. The problem is that your body and brain silently keep score of those missed connections.

When you move your body regularly, you're essentially flooding your brain with mood-enhancing endorphins. Nature's own anxiety and depression fighters. No prescription required. That runner's high isn't just a myth; it's your neurochemistry throwing a little party in your honor.

Beyond the chemical boost, exercise builds something equally powerful: self-esteem. Hitting that new personal record or simply showing up when you didn't want to create a sense of mastery that spills over into every corner of your life. You start thinking, "If I can do those extra ten push-ups, maybe I can also tackle that work project I've been avoiding."

Your brain becomes sharper too. That mental fog that's been following you around? Regular movement helps clear it away, improving memory, focus, and creative thinking. Ever notice how your best ideas often come during or right after a walk? That's not a coincidence. It's your brain operating at full capacity.

The benefits extend to your bedroom too (and I'm talking about sleep, folks). Regular exercise helps you fall asleep faster and dive deeper into those restorative sleep cycles, which indirectly supercharges your mood the next day. It's a gift that keeps on giving.

Perhaps most importantly, consistent movement, whether structured exercise routines or playful activity, acts as a stress vaccine, reducing the hormones that make you feel frazzled and overwhelmed. Your emotional resilience gets a serious upgrade, helping you weather life's inevitable storms more gracefully.

THE SCIENCE BEHIND EXERCISING REGULARLY

Ever wonder if that post-workout glow is all in your head? Turns out science has your back on this one. In a groundbreaking study, Babyak and his colleagues found something that should make pharmaceutical companies nervous. Exercise matched antidepressant medication for effectiveness in treating depression.[19] Crucially, the exercise group had significantly lower relapse rates.

Think about that for a second. Moving your body isn't just temporarily boosting your mood; it's creating lasting changes in your brain that help prevent you from sliding back into the darkness. It's like the difference between taking a pain pill for your bad back versus fixing the underlying issue through physical therapy.

When you exercise, your body becomes its medicine cabinet, dispensing exactly what your brain needs, when it needs it. Unlike a pill that might give you a laundry list of side effects (including the always popular "call your doctor if your happiness lasts more than four hours"), the only side effects of this natural remedy are better sleep, improved focus, and maybe some pleasantly sore muscles. Speaking of sore muscles, let me tell you about my complicated relationship with the gym.

MY JOURNEY TOWARD EXERCISING REGULARLY

Exercise and I have what you might call a "committed but compli-cated" relationship. While I've never managed consistent gratitude journaling, I've somehow maintained a meticulous spreadsheet of every workout for the past seven years. This digital diary tells no lies: when I'm on, I'm Captain America. When I'm off, I'm a bear in full hibernation. Sometimes vanishing from fitness for 100+ days.

Once, during an extended slump, I vented to my seriously athletic son-in-law, nearly waving the white flag on fitness due to age and frustra-tion. Instead of agreeing with my pity party, he calmly shrugged, "That's what's good about you. You'll start again soon." Nine simple words that hit harder than any motivational poster.

What he didn't see was the internal battle before every restart. That pre-workout anxiety hits me like clockwork. Racing heart, sweaty palms, brain screaming, *DANGER!* as if the gym were a burning building instead of a place with elliptical machines and bad music. I've learned this fight-or-flight response is just my body's confused attempt at protection. *We're middle-aged and out of shape*, it warns, *This could go badly!* But what you must understand is that **when I push through that false alarm, it proves my anxiety is a terrible fortune teller.** Every time five minutes in, I'm always fine. Ten minutes in, I remember why I came.

REFLECTING ON EXERCISING REGULARLY

Before we dive into how to make this habit stick, take a moment to consider your own relationship with movement. When was the last time you finished a workout and thought, "Wow, I regret doing that"? And what stories are you telling yourself about exercise that might not actually be true?

ACTION STEPS TOWARD EXERCISING REGULARLY

Alright, folks, enough with the excuses: here's how to actually make this happen:

- **Take tiny steps**: Not athletic? Skeptical? Start with a 5-minute daily walk. Even light movement elevates mood and confidence, no gym required.
- **Work through anxious thoughts:** Since your body anticipates activity, it triggers your fight-or-flight response. I feel this as anxiety. The "not smart" shortcut is avoiding the workout entirely. Press through. The feeling disappears on its own.
- **Find your fun**: Hate traditional workouts? Discover an activity you enjoy or recruit an exercise buddy. When it's fun, you'll actually show up.
- **Start at home**: Gym intimidation real? Begin with simple home routines or neighborhood walks. Comfort builds confidence. Science confirms that self-efficacy fuels habit formation.
- **Track your progress:** Similar to the gratitude journaling we explored earlier in Chapter 1, consider buying a tracking device or log your progress (and mishaps) manually
- **Make it non-negotiable**: Struggle with consistency? Treat exercise like a must-attend meeting. Track small wins (distance, reps) to trigger motivation.

MOVING ON FROM EXERCISING REGULARLY

Now that we've tuned our sleep cycles and kickstarted our metabolism with consistent movement, it's time to look at the fuel we put in the tank. Because quality fuel makes all the difference in how your body and mind function throughout the day, let's explore how mindful eating and drinking can take your energy levels from sputtering to supercharged.

MINDFUL NUTRITION
WHY MINDFUL NUTRITION MATTERS

F ood isn't just fuel. It's information. Every bite you take sends chemical messages throughout your body and brain, influencing everything from your energy levels to your mood. That midday crash after a carb-heavy lunch? That's not just in your head. It's your blood sugar taking a nosedive, dragging your focus and mood along with it.

The connection between gut and brain health has become one of the most fascinating research areas in recent years. Scientists have discovered that your gut produces many of the same neurotransmitters that regulate your mood, including about 90% of your serotonin, a feel-good chemical we all need more. It's like having a second brain in your belly, one that's constantly chatting with the one in your head.

Eating mindfully isn't just about what you eat. It's about how you eat it. When you slow down and actually pay attention to your food rather than inhaling it while staring at a screen, you not only enjoy it more, but you're also more likely to notice when you're satisfied before reaching the overstuffed, regret-filled stage we all know too well. And those subtle feelings of satisfaction and appreciation create ripples that affect your entire day.

THE SCIENCE BEHIND MINDFUL NUTRITION

Research in the field of mindful eating (with notable contributions from researchers like Jean Kristeller and others around the early 2010s) has shown that mindful eating doesn't just change what you eat. It can transform your entire relationship with food and your body.[20]

The science is pretty wild: when you eat on autopilot, your brain barely registers the experience, leaving you unsatisfied no matter how much you consume. It's like your brain is saying, *Did we just eat? I must have missed it. Better keep looking for food!* But when you slow down and engage all your senses, your brain gets the message loud and clear, triggering satisfaction signals that actually last.

Think of mindful eating like switching from watching a movie in black and white on a tiny screen to experiencing it in full IMAX color. Same movie, completely different experience: and you don't need to eat more to feel satisfied.

Let me toss in another science fact, one that'll probably make you nod knowingly. **Diets flat-out don't work.** I'm not just saying this as someone who's tried every food fad since the grapefruit craze of '88. Wing and Phelan did this eye-opening study back in 2005 where they tracked folks who actually kept significant weight off long-term. Know what they found? The successful ones weren't jumping from diet to diet like I used to jump from channel to channel before Netflix.[21] Nope, they made honest-to-goodness lifestyle changes. Moving their bodies regularly, eating with some rhyme and reason, and keeping tabs on themselves. Meanwhile, those temporary "cabbage-soup-for-two-weeks" diets? About as effective as mopping the floor while the sink is still overflowing. You end up right back where you started, maybe with a few extra pounds for your trouble.

MY JOURNEY TOWARD MINDFUL NUTRITION

Evolution didn't exactly equip me for a world where chocolate-covered almonds are so readily available. As an ordinary human, I approach unlimited food access with all the self-control of a golden retriever at an all-you-can-eat buffet.

My most effective strategy turned out to be simple: keep temptations out of sight. It's amazing how much easier it is to resist what you can't see. I discovered that if I couldn't see the chips, I somehow forgot we owned them.

On a positive note, Suzy and I have found unexpected joy in our haphazard health journey. Our latest obsession? Dehydrating anything that doesn't move fast enough. We've transformed perfectly respectable bananas into oddly addictive chips and have almost convinced ourselves that kale becomes edible when properly dried.

The progress is glacially slow but surprisingly sustainable. As long as I keep hiding temptations from myself (sometimes forgetting where I put them), there might be hope for this middle-aged work in progress.

REFLECTING ON MINDFUL NUTRITION

Think about your last truly satisfying meal. What made it special? Was it the food, company, setting, or simply that you were fully present for the experience? And when you reach for comfort foods during stressful times, what would happen if you paused for just 30 seconds to check in with what your body needs in that moment?

ACTION STEPS TOWARD MINDFUL NUTRITION

Let's turn these insights into practical steps you can actually use:

- **Set yourself up for success**: No time for healthy eating? Batch-cook on Sundays or prep grab-and-go meals. Planning beats willpower whenever hunger strikes.
- **Retrain your taste buds**: Think healthy food is bland? Gradually swap processed foods for well-seasoned whole foods. Your palate adapts faster than you think. Science shows taste preferences change in just a few weeks.

- **Choose what you see**: Keep fruits and healthy snacks within your line of sight. Hide all unhealthy items that have the power to lead you toward making poor decisions.
- **Plan for social eating**: Events derailing your intentions? Eat a healthy snack beforehand and choose smaller portions of indulgences. This prevents hunger-driven decisions without sacrificing enjoyment.
- **Create a pause button**: Stress triggering snack attacks? Wait just 5 minutes and take a few deep breaths or a short walk. This mindful delay helps distinguish emotional hunger from physical hunger.
- **Connect the dots**: Doubt food affects mood? Notice how balanced meals keep your energy steady while sugar crashes drive irritability. The mood-food connection isn't just theory. It's biochemistry in action.

MOVING ON FROM MINDFUL NUTRITION

But optimizing your energy isn't just about what you consume; it's about your environment. That brings us to the most overlooked and freely available energy source there is: the natural world. Nature has an almost magical way of recharging our mental and physical batteries, yet many of us spend 90% of our lives indoors. Let's explore how reconnecting with the natural world might be the missing piece in your energy puzzle.

CONNECTING WITH NATURE

WHY CONNECTING WITH NATURE MATTERS

We evolved in the great outdoors for thousands of generations, yet most of us now spend over 90% of our lives inside artificial environments. Our bodies and brains know something's off, even if we don't consciously register it. That low-level tension that builds during a day of fluorescent lighting and recycled air? It's not your imagination. It's your system craving what it was designed for.

Nature exposure isn't just a nice-to-have luxury for weekend hikes. It's a fundamental human need that impacts everything from stress to creativity. When you step outside, your blood pressure drops, your stress hormones decrease, and your brain shifts into a different mode of attention that actually allows it to rest and recover from the constant focus modern life demands.

The irony is that most of us sacrifice time in nature because we're "too busy". Yet even brief exposure to nature makes us more productive, creative, and emotionally resilient when we return to our tasks. It's like we're skipping the very thing that would make everything else easier. Plus, something about being in natural spaces reminds us we're part of something larger than our daily worries, offering a perspective shift that can instantly make problems seem more manageable.

THE SCIENCE BEHIND CONNECTING WITH NATURE

Remember how focusing on detailed work all day leaves your brain feeling like overcooked pasta? Researchers Berman and colleagues discovered why back in 2008. They found that urban environments demand what's called "directed attention". A limited mental resource that gets depleted as you force yourself to focus and ignore distractions. It's like running your phone with multiple apps open. Battery drain is inevitable.[22]

On the other hand, nature engages what scientists call "soft fascination". An effortless type of attention that restores your mental batteries instead of draining them. Those gently moving leaves, the patterns of light on water, the distant horizon: these natural elements hold your attention without requiring effort.

The research showed significant improvements in memory, focus, and problem-solving after just an hour in natural settings. It's like your brain gets a complete operating system upgrade, but all you have to do is take a walk in the park.

MY JOURNEY TOWARD CONNECTING WITH NATURE

For fifteen years, I lived a mere ten-minute stroll from one of Jersey's most beautiful beaches. I managed to visit it roughly five times annually. It's like owning a portal to paradise and using it primarily as an occasional backdrop for your selfies.

Enter Yeti, with the energy of a toddler doing espresso shots. This 70-pound fur missile pup hasn't just changed our routines. He's completely hijacked them, dragging us (sometimes literally) into a lifestyle we didn't know we were missing.

Before Yeti, my Fitbit recorded an average of about 6,000 steps. Just enough to prevent complete muscle atrophy. Now, thanks to his boundless determination to chase every duck, wave, and suspicious-looking piece of seaweed, I'm clocking 10,000 steps daily like some born-again fitness prophet.

Our beach pilgrimages have become as non-negotiable as coffee. There's something mind-altering about watching a creature experience pure joy without self-consciousness. Nose to the ground, tail wind-milling with delight, occasionally rolling in something that requires immediate bathing.

During these sandy expeditions, I've consumed hundreds of podcasts and other great books. The combination of sunshine, movement, belly laughs at dog antics, and brain food from podcasts has become my personal therapy. Looking back, this book was born on the beach. One pawprint, one podcast, one revelation at a time.

Here's the cosmic joke: I rescued Yeti, but he rescued my step count, my appreciation for the sunrise, and, without knowing it, gave me the headspace to write this book.

REFLECTING ON CONNECTING WITH NATURE

When was the last time you felt truly awestruck by something in nature. A sunset, a thunderstorm, or even just the perfect pattern of a leaf? How did that moment change your perspective, even temporarily? What's one small way you could incorporate more nature into your daily routine, even if it's just for five minutes?

ACTION STEPS TOWARD CONNECTING WITH NATURE

Ready to tap into nature's recharging power? Here are six ways to make it happen, no matter your circumstances:

- **City life? Head to a park or keep houseplants**: Even tiny nature moments lower stress and lift mood when skyscrapers outnumber trees.
- **Too busy for nature? Slip in 5-minute nature breaks**: Watch clouds from your office window or touch the bark of a tree on your lunch break. Brief nature moments still count.

- **Doubt nature helps? Next time you're anxious, walk in greenery**: Notice how your breathing naturally slows and your shoulders drop. Nature's calming effect is automatic.
- **Bugs or bad weather put you off? Start with nature sounds or videos**: Rain sounds during work or nature documentaries can provide similar benefits while you build comfort.
- **Always on screens? Take a short nature walk with your phone off:** The combination of natural surroundings and digital silence creates a powerful reset for your overtaxed attention.
- **Limited mobility? Bring nature to you**: A bird feeder outside your window or fresh flowers indoors can benefit nature when getting outside is challenging.

WRAPPING UP THE CHAPTER

What makes these four tools so powerful is that they work with your brain's natural wiring, not against it. Your brain is constantly adapting to what you repeatedly do.

Every time you choose movement over inertia, quality sleep over one more episode, mindful eating over mindless snacking, or nature over screens, you're literally building new neural pathways.

Your brain is essentially a prediction machine, constantly anticipating what's coming next based on what you've done before. When movement, quality sleep, mindful nutrition, and nature connection become consistent practices, your body begins to expect and even crave these health-promoting activities. That's when the transformation happens. Caring for your physical energy becomes your default setting rather than something you have to force.

This adaptation occurs regardless of your age, background, or past attempts. Your body responds to what you're doing now, not your history of false starts.

TRANSFORMATION STORY

Let's call her Maya. At 42, her life looked successful from the outside:

decent job, two healthy kids, nice house. But inside, she was running on empty.

"I don't have time for self-care," she'd snap whenever friends suggested solutions. Between single parenting and work deadlines, adding anything felt impossible. She'd abandoned her crash diet and exercise program by February.

Her turning point came on a random Tuesday, sitting in her parked car, too exhausted to walk inside. "Something has to change," she whispered. "I can't keep living like this."

That night, she made one small change: setting her alarm 20 minutes earlier and placing walking shoes by her bed. The next morning, she dragged herself through a short neighborhood walk, certain she'd abandon this effort like all the others.

But she didn't. Walking became her gateway habit. The one thing she could manage even when everything else felt overwhelming. "Some days it was literally just walking around the block while still half-asleep. But it was mine."

Three weeks in, she noticed something odd. She was getting sleepy earlier. Without stress hormones keeping her wired, her body actually signaled when it needed rest. She started respecting those signals.

Better sleep naturally led to conscious eating. "I just started noticing how certain foods made me feel afterward. When you're exhausted, everything sugary feels like medicine. When you're rested, you can tell the difference between foods that fuel you and those that drain you."

The nature connection happened accidentally. Cutting through a park on her way to work, ten minutes among trees changed something fundamental. Her shoulders dropped, her breathing deepened. She began spending lunch breaks under a particular oak tree, her "unofficial therapist."

Six months later, Maya's circumstances hadn't changed. Same job, same kids, same house. But she had changed. The constant anxiety had quieted. She had energy reserves previously unknown. Most surprisingly, she'd become more patient with her children, work challenges, and herself.

"I thought changing habits meant forcing myself to do things I hated," she reflected. "Turns out, it's about discovering what you actually need, and then giving yourself permission to receive it."

Looking back at where this chapter started, me calling myself a walking contradiction, I realize something important. I'm still that guy who can knock out push ups while nursing a beer, who tracks every workout but sometimes disappears from the gym for months, who knows exactly what to do but doesn't always do it. The difference now? I've stopped fighting these contradictions and started working with them.

My operating system isn't broken because it's inconsistent. It's human. Some days I'm the health warrior; other days I'm searching for the snacks that I asked Suzy to hide from me. Some mornings Yeti drags me to the beach; other mornings we both agree the couch has gravitational superpowers. Maya's story taught me that your body doesn't need a complete overhaul. It needs small, consistent acts of kindness, the same patience you'd show a good friend who's doing their best. And on those days when your contradictions feel over-whelming? Remember that even a walking contradiction is still walking forward.

YOUR ENERGY CHEAT SHEET

Consider this your go-to reference when life gets hectic and you need a quick reminder of what actually works:

- **Motion creates emotion**: Your body isn't just transportation for your brain; it's a mood-altering machine. Even five minutes of movement can transform your mental state faster than anything else.
- **Sleep is non-negotiable**: If you wouldn't drive a car with no gas, don't try running your brain with no sleep. Everything looks worse through exhausted eyes.

- **Food is information**: Every bite sends messages throughout your body and brain. Choose messengers that support your energy rather than sabotage it.
- **Nature is your reset button**: When overwhelmed, step outside. The natural world has a remarkable way of shrinking problems down to a manageable size.
- **Small habits beat grand gestures**: Consistency trumps intensity every time. A daily five-minute walk outdoors beats a monthly three-hour hike for long-term well-being.
- **Start where you are**: Perfect conditions never arrive. Begin with whatever modest step you can manage today, and build from there.

YOUR ENERGY REVOLUTION STARTS NOW

Take a look at what I've learned after decades of inconsistent exercise, countless sleep-deprived nights, beer-fueled regrets, and missed opportunities to experience the natural beauty right outside my door: perfection isn't the goal. Progress is.

Every single day offers a fresh chance to stop stealing from tomorrow and start investing in today. You don't need to overhaul your entire life at once. You don't need special equipment, expensive memberships, or superhuman willpower. You just need to start making slightly better choices, one small decision at a time.

The tools we've explored aren't just about having more energy, though that's certainly a wonderful benefit. They're about creating a life where you feel fully alive, present, and capable of handling whatever comes your way. They're about building resilience from the inside out.

Here's my challenge: Pick one action from this chapter. Something so small it feels almost silly. Do it today. Then do it again tomorrow. Because small steps don't stay small. They create unstoppable momentum. Let it be imperfect. Let it be messy. Let it be a starting point rather than a finished product. Because that's how real, lasting change happens. Not through dramatic transformations, but through consistent, imperfect efforts that gradually reshape your life.

This isn't just about feeling better tomorrow. It's about rewriting the way you live today. Starting with one small step.

CHAPTER 6:

DESIGNING A LIFE THAT ACTUALLY WORKS

If someone stopped me on the street and asked if I live purposefully and productively, I'd probably break into a nervous sweat. The same kind I get when I see unexpected mail from the tax office. That question feels like a pop quiz I forgot to study for, administered by the universe itself.

See, I'm supposed to have this figured out by now, right? Some profound mission statement tattooed on my forearm, a TED talk rehearsed in my back pocket, maybe a vision board with magazine cutouts spelling out my destiny. Instead, I've got a barn full of half-finished projects and a vague sense that I'm making it up as I go along.

Truth is, I've spent decades chasing this mythical "purpose" like it's some exotic bird that'll land on my shoulder if I just whistle the right tune. Those motivational mission statements people post in their offices? I tried writing one once. Spent a whole afternoon crafting something that sounded impressive but meant nothing. Pretty sure it ended up in the trash with the losing lottery tickets.

Instead, I've focused on doing things that make a positive impact while ensuring I enjoy waking up each day. That's been my makeshift purpose. And you know what? Maybe that's enough.

As I've stumbled through life, I've realized that the things that provide meaning and joy, my purpose, aren't static. It's not a single North Star but a shifting constellation that changes as we grow. There were seasons when Suzy and I were all-in on helping the homeless, literally opening our home as a shelter. Fast forward, and that season of purpose shifted to orchestrating joy at the marina. Hosting cookouts, organizing cornhole tournaments, and taking other people's kids out for unforgettable afternoons of tubing.

Each of these seasons brought wonderful people into our lives who touched our hearts, and through them, I discovered a profound truth: purpose doesn't require a grand revelation or a perfectly crafted mission statement. It grows from small, deliberate choices that align with what matters to you. Let's explore five practical tools that have helped me, and can help you, build a life that actually works.

- Setting meaningful goals that actually matter to YOU
- Taking proactive steps instead of just dreaming
- Making lifelong learning part of your everyday routine.
- Creating financial well-being (without obsessing over money)
- Managing your time so you actually feel time-rich instead of time-starved

These aren't just nice ideas. They're science-backed tools that can transform your daily experience from "just getting by" to "actually thriving." So let's dive in, shall we?

SETTING MEANINGFUL GOALS
WHY SETTING MEANINGFUL GOALS MATTERS

Running on a hamster wheel, busy as all get-out but not actually getting anywhere that matters, describes life without meaningful goals. It's like driving cross-country without a GPS or even a destination in mind. Sure, the scenery might be nice, but eventually, you'll wonder where you're headed.

Setting goals that actually matter to you isn't just some corporate productivity hack. It's about giving your days direction and your efforts purpose. Something magical happens when your goals align with what you truly value, not what your neighbors value or what Instagram suggests you should value. When your goals align with your values, you wake up with more energy. Problems start looking more like interesting puzzles than insurmountable walls.

Evidence suggests that people with meaningful goals tend to be more resilient when life throws curveballs their way. Instead of seeing setbacks as failures, they see them as detours or even learning opportunities. "Well, that didn't work. What's next?" becomes your mindset instead of "I'm a total failure."

Measuring progress taps into something incredibly powerful. Our brains absolutely love this stuff. Each small win triggers a little hit of dopamine that says, "Hey, keep going, this feels good!" Without goals, those natural rewards are harder to come by.

But this is what nobody tells you: *the real power isn't in achieving the goal itself. It's in who you become while pursuing it.* The person who finishes a marathon isn't just someone who can run 26.2 miles; they're someone who built discipline, overcame doubt, and pushed through discomfort. And the research backs up this transformative power of meaningful goals.

THE SCIENCE BEHIND SETTING MEANINGFUL GOALS

Ever notice that some people seem to bounce through life with energy and purpose while others just drift along? It turns out that science has been wondering, too. Researchers Hill and Turiano discovered something pretty mind-blowing in 2014: having a strong sense of purpose isn't just good for your mood. It can literally extend your lifespan.[23]

Think of purpose like the ultimate health supplement, except you can't buy it on Amazon. Their study showed that people with clear goals and a sense of direction had lower rates of heart disease, better immune function, and, believe it or not, lived longer than their purpose-challenged counterparts.

It's like your brain and body are designed to thrive when they're working toward something meaningful. Without that north star, they start running on low power mode. Just enough to get by, but not enough to truly feel alive. Your goals are basically telling your entire system, "Hey, stick around, we've got important stuff to do!"

MY JOURNEY TOWARD SETTING MEANINGFUL GOALS

In college, I scraped by digging clams in New Jersey. My friends and I rose before dawn, piled into a rickety boat, and worked in cold water, earning ten cents at a time. Those were golden days, something about being with fun people on the water spoke to me.

Twenty-five years later, I was broke. Still, I couldn't shake the dream of owning a boat again.

Suzy and I would bike to the river in the evenings, watching boats drift past. One evening, I pointed to a small Boston Whaler and said, "That's my dream." Suzy grabbed my hand and said, "Let's make it happen... someday." We wrote it on a small piece of paper. Not a fantasy, a plan. It lived on our fridge as a daily reminder.

After years of saving, working overtime, and setbacks, we finally got our boat. It's created countless memories with the people we love. That boat once felt impossible. But it happened... because we made a plan.

REFLECTING ON SETTING MEANINGFUL GOALS

Take a minute and think about the last time you felt truly excited about something you were working toward. How did that goal connect to what matters most in your life? And if you're having trouble coming up with an example, what might that tell you about the goals you've been setting (or not setting)?

ACTION STEPS TOWARD SETTING MEANINGFUL GOALS

Alright, let's get down to brass tacks. Here are six ways to set goals that matter:

- **Values first, goals second**: Unsure what goal to set? Identify what truly matters to you first. Evidence suggests that meaningful goals emerge from personal values.
- **Start small but significant**: Think goal-setting is overrated? Commit to one small, meaningful goal. Achieving a small milestone boosts confidence and happiness, proving it's worthwhile.
- **Break it down to build it up**: Big dream overwhelming? Break it into micro-goals. Each small win triggers a dopamine boost that sustains momentum without intimidation.
- **Embrace the experiment**: Afraid to fail? Treat your goal as a learning experiment, not all-or-nothing. This growth mindset reduces fear, backed by resilience research.

- **Quality over quantity**: Too many goals at once? Prioritize one or two. Studies show focusing on fewer goals increases success and prevents burnout.
- **Write your "why"**: Lose motivation? Write down your 'why' and keep it visible. Research shows remembering your goal's purpose boosts persistence through roadblocks.

Ultimately, the shift from a life of 'have-to' goals to one of 'get-to' goals is the core of building your happier life. It reclaims your daily actions as part of a journey you have chosen, not a sentence you are serving. Even chores and obligations can feel different when they serve a 'get-to' purpose.

MOVING ON FROM SETTING MEANINGFUL GOALS

Now that we've discussed setting meaningful goals, let's shift gears and discuss what happens next. Because let's face it. Having a goal is just the beginning. The fun happens when you start taking action, which brings us to our next tool.

TAKING PROACTIVE STEPS TOWARDS GOALS

WHY TAKING PROACTIVE STEPS TOWARDS GOALS MATTERS

We've all been there. Staring at a goal that seems to mock us from a distance while we're stuck in "someday" mode. The truth is, goals without action are just fancy daydreams. Taking proactive steps, even tiny ones, is what transforms wishful thinking into actual results.

Something powerful happens in your brain when you take consistent action toward your goals. Each small step triggers a hit of dopamine, that feel-good neurotransmitter that keeps you coming back for more. This creates a positive feedback loop: action leads to feeling good, motivating more action, and creating more progress.

Being proactive also dramatically reduces stress and anxiety. There's something uniquely uncomfortable about having unfulfilled goals hanging over your head. Each intentional step forward releases some of that pressure, replacing it with a calm sense of control. You stop feeling haunted by what you "should" be doing and start enjoying the satisfaction of simply making progress.

Plus, taking action builds self-efficacy. Your belief in your own ability to achieve things. Each tiny win proves to yourself that you can do hard things, creating a snowball effect of confidence that carries over into every area of your life.

THE SCIENCE BEHIND TAKING PROACTIVE STEPS TOWARDS GOALS

Remember how you'd get all excited as a kid after finishing just one piece of a big puzzle? That wasn't just childish enthusiasm. You were experiencing what scientists call the "progress principle." Researchers Amabile and Kramer found that making progress, even tiny progress, is the single most powerful motivator in our day-to-day lives.[20]

Your brain is actually wired to get a little happiness boost from making headway on meaningful work. It's like having a built-in reward system that says, "Hey, good job taking that step: here's a little shot of feel-good chemicals as your prize!" This internal reward system works whether you're building a business or finally organizing that garage nightmare.

The really cool part? The good feeling you get from making progress doesn't just fade. It actually makes you more creative and productive the next day. **It's a virtuous cycle. The more you do, the better you feel, and the better you feel, the more you can do.**

MY JOURNEY TOWARD TAKING PROACTIVE STEPS TOWARDS GOALS

Sometimes the universe drops a challenge in your lap that forces you to either step up or face-plant spectacularly. For me, that moment arrived disguised as my daughter's wedding. Specifically, when budget and reality collided with reception dreams.

In what can only be described as temporary insanity, I thought we could cater the entire event. Now, let me put this in perspective for you. This was a full-blown celebration for 125 guests. At a beautiful venue in New Jersey, no less. As the father of the bride, the "speech" had me freaking out on its own. Clearly, I needed a psychological evaluation.

Once the words left my mouth and my daughter's eyes lit up with both hope and skepticism, there was no turning back. I still remember her saying. "I believe in your cooking, Daddy!" Thankfully, while I might be the family dreamer, Suzy and our kids are the logistics ninjas who transform chaos into order.

We prepped for months. Things got downright chaotic in those final weeks. With a ragtag crew of helpers, we eventually stormed that venue's kitchen like friendly pirates just hours before all those dressed-up folks started pouring in. When the fire alarms started wailing as we seared sous-vide filet mignon for 125 hungry souls, we didn't panic. Just assigned someone to fan the smoke detector. Then I remembered that I forgot the mashed potatoes were still cold. Meanwhile, Suzy's homemade wedding cake was doing its best impression of the Leaning Tower of Pisa.

It was a blast. Our guests actually shared that these "disasters" played a big part of what made the day beautiful.

That grease-stained, checkmark-covered wedding planning sheet was eventually moved from the refrigerator to a drawer. A testament not to perfection but to breaking down seemingly impossible goals into actionable steps. It gave us confidence to take on even bigger challenges, including our next daughter's wedding for 180 guests, where I not only cooked but officiated. (The "Bishop Billy" nickname unfortunately did not stick.)

REFLECTING ON TAKING PROACTIVE STEPS TOWARDS GOALS

When was the last time you felt stuck on a goal that matters to you? Looking back, what was the real obstacle. Was it truly lack of time or resources, or was it something deeper like fear of failure or uncertainty about where to start? What tiny step could you take right now that would move you forward?

ACTION STEPS TOWARD TAKING PROACTIVE STEPS TOWARDS GOALS

Time to roll up our sleeves and get moving! Here's how to kick procrastination to the curb:

- **Set the timer trick:** Procrastinating on a goal task? Set a 5-minute timer and start. Often that's enough to overcome inertia. A quick-start trick backed by research.
- **Carve out sacred goal time**: No time for goals? Carve out a recurring 15-minute slot in your schedule. Consistent small progress beats rare big efforts, studies show.
- **Eat that frog**: Avoiding a tough task? Do it first when your willpower is strongest. This 'eat the frog' method reduces dread and jump-starts momentum.
- **Reward small wins**: Losing steam mid-way? Give yourself a small reward after each step. Tiny treats trigger dopamine that boosts motivation.
- **Get an accountability buddy:** Struggling to follow through? Recruit an accountability partner or share your goal publicly. Social pressure significantly increases follow-through, studies show.
- **Embrace the 1% rule:** Doubt tiny steps add up? Embrace 1% daily improvements. Consistent small actions compound into big results. An approach validated by habit science.

MOVING ON FROM TAKING PROACTIVE STEPS TOWARDS GOALS

Now that we've got you taking action on your goals, let's explore something that makes the journey productive and genuinely enjoyable. Because taking steps toward your goals is great, but continually expanding your horizons through learning makes the process infinitely more rewarding.

ENGAGING IN LIFELONG LEARNING
WHY ENGAGING IN LIFELONG LEARNING MATTERS

Remember that kid in elementary school who'd get wide-eyed with excitement over the science fair project while everyone else was groaning? Turns out that kid was onto something. That natural curiosity we're born with, the one many of us gradually pack away like childhood toys, is actually a powerful happiness engine.

When we actively learn new things, our brains come alive. New neural connections form, creating what scientists call "cognitive reserve". Brain resilience that helps us stay sharp and adaptable as we age. But the benefits go way beyond brain health.

Learning builds lasting self-esteem, unlike the fleeting ego boost of social media likes. There's something deeply satisfying about looking back and thinking, "I couldn't do that last month, and now I can." That sense of competence and growth fulfills one of our core psychological needs.

Plus, learning naturally pushes us out of our comfort zones, where the magic of personal growth happens. Whether you're learning Spanish, growing tomatoes that actually survive, or mastering woodworking, you're expanding your sense of possibility.

And perhaps most importantly in our increasingly isolated world, learning connects us with others. Whether joining a cooking class, discussing books, or learning alongside YouTube communities, shared learning creates meaningful bonds based on common interests and mutual growth.

THE SCIENCE BEHIND ENGAGING IN LIFELONG LEARNING

Ever wonder why some people seem sharp as a tack well into their 80s? Research suggests that lifelong learning might be their secret weapon. Scientists studying cognitive aging have found that people who continuously challenge their brains with new learning experiences build what they call "cognitive reserve". Essentially a buffer against age-related decline.[25]

But the benefits go beyond just brain health. Studies on learning communities show that when people learn together, they experience significant decreases in loneliness and increases in overall life satisfaction. It's like hitting a happiness trifecta: you get the joy of mastering something new, the fulfillment of connecting with others, and the confidence boost that comes from stepping outside your comfort zone.

The really cool part? Your brain doesn't care what you're learning. Whether it's quantum physics or how to make the perfect sourdough bread, the neural benefits of tackling something new and challenging are surprisingly similar. It's not about becoming an expert; it's about enjoying the growth journey. Each new item you learn forms neural connections that facilitate subsequent learning, building a reinforcing cycle of growth and discovery.

MY JOURNEY TOWARD ENGAGING IN LIFELONG LEARNING

Learning has become one of my top priorities in life, right alongside love. Learning for me has been more about following curiosity wherever it may take me, from learning how to build a van despite having little mechanical aptitude to learning about happiness science for this book.

My home brewing phase proved hobby learning doesn't care about success. My pumpkin ale could knock friends down, but it lit up my unused brain cells. Problem was, I drank the good batches faster than I made them. Gained 20 pounds. Suzy finally intervened and helped sell the kit online. Thanks, Suzy.

Every failed batch was still building those neural connections the scientists talk about. My brain got sharper even as my waistline got wider.

But the craziest learning leap? Learning about happiness and writing this book!

I never dreamt of writing a book. Are you kidding? I still have to Google "effect vs. affect" every single time. But following that curiosity about happiness, listening to hundreds of podcast episodes while walking Yeti on the beach, diving into research I barely understood at first. It all changed me in ways I couldn't have imagined.

Here's what I know now: I'm genuinely happier than that guy frantically Googling at 2 a.m. Not because I've mastered all these tools (I haven't), and definitely not because I wrote a book (still can't believe that happened). I'm happier because I finally learned that learning itself, messy, imperfect, sometimes embarrassing learning, is what keeps us growing.

Every crazy leap, from failed brewing to accidental authorship, taught me something I'd never have discovered by playing it safe. Turns out the willingness to look foolish while learning something new? That's not something to avoid. That's exactly where the growth lives.

REFLECTING ON ENGAGING IN LIFELONG LEARNING

Think back to something you learned recently that brought you genuine joy. Not something you had to learn for work or because someone expected it, but something you chose to learn because it interested you. How did that process affect your mood and energy? And what's something you've been curious about lately but haven't permitted yourself to explore?

ACTION STEPS TOWARD ENGAGING IN LIFELONG LEARNING

Ready to fire up those brain cells? Here's how to make learning a regular part of your happiness routine:

- **Challenge the "too old" myth**: Think you're too old to learn? Adult brains remain adaptable (neuroplasticity). Set a tiny daily learning goal to see if your brain can still improve.
- **Embrace micro-learning**: No time to study? Try micro-learning: podcasts on commutes, quick articles at lunch. Even five minutes daily builds knowledge, studies show.
- **Follow your curiosity**: Not sure what to learn? Pick something that genuinely interests you, no matter how niche. Studies show intrinsic interest fuels persistence and deeper learning.
- **Welcome beginner status**: Afraid to look foolish as a beginner? Embrace a growth mindset and allow yourself mistakes. Studies show accepting errors speeds up learning.
- **Use free resources**: Limited budget? Use free resources: library books, online courses, tutorials. Free content can build your skills. Formal classes aren't the only path to learning.
- **Learn for happiness**: Doubt learning brings happiness? Studies link lifelong learning to better mental health. Learn something fun and notice how pride in progress lifts your mood.

MOVING ON FROM ENGAGING IN LIFELONG LEARNING

Now that we've explored how continual learning enriches our lives, let's discuss a topic enabling many other positive choices: financial well-being. Because when we get our money situation under control, we create the freedom to pursue what truly matters.

PRACTICING FINANCIAL WELL-BEING

WHY PRACTICING FINANCIAL WELL-BEING MATTERS

oney doesn't buy happiness, but financial stress can definitely steal it. When we're constantly worried about making ends meet or drowning in debt, our brains get stuck in survival mode, making it nearly impossible to focus on bigger dreams or even simple daily joys.

Financial well-being isn't about being rich. It's about creating enough stability and breathing room that money worries don't dominate your mental landscape. When you're not constantly stressing about bills, your mind can focus on relationships, creativity, and purpose. The stuff that fills your happiness tank.

The research is pretty clear on this: financial stress is linked to higher rates of anxiety, depression, and even physical health problems like high blood pressure and disrupted sleep. On the flip side, gaining control of your financial situation, even if you're not wealthy, significantly boosts your sense of agency and confidence.

Financial well-being also transforms your relationship with the future. Instead of fearing what might happen if your car breaks down or viewing retirement as an impossible fantasy, you can approach life with a sense of possibility and choice. That psychological freedom is priceless.

And perhaps most importantly for relationships, financial well-being reduces one of the most common sources of conflict between couples and within families. When you're not constantly fighting about money, you have more emotional energy for connection, fun, and tackling life's challenges as a team.

THE SCIENCE BEHIND PRACTICING FINANCIAL WELL-BEING

It's crazy how money worries can hijack your entire brain. Right? There's solid science explaining that feeling. A comprehensive 2020 review by Ridley and colleagues exploring the links between poverty, financial strain, and mental health highlighted that chronic financial stress, like persistent debt or the struggle to pay bills, is strongly linked to higher rates of anxiety and depression, and can even impact physical illness.[26]

This isn't just a vague feeling; it's backed by large-scale data. For instance, nationally representative surveys consistently show that adults grappling with high financial worries report significantly greater psychological distress than those who feel more financially at ease, even when other demographic factors are taken into account. Your brain essentially treats severe financial threats with a high-alert stress response.

But here's the empowering part: the research also points to a way forward. Studies and reviews suggest that individuals who take proactive steps to manage their finances, like creating a budget, tracking spending, or seeking sound financial advice, often experience less psychological distress. It's not always about suddenly having more money; it's often about creating a sense of control, predictability, and direction with what you have.

MY JOURNEY TOWARD PRACTICING FINANCIAL WELL-BEING

You'd think a chapter on financial well-being would start with advice about making more money or building the perfect retirement portfolio. Plot twist: for me, financial well-being has been all about finding creative ways to NOT spend money and keeping life beautifully, intentionally simple.

I was still recovering from the housing market crash in 2008 and a divorce. A financial double whammy that sent me spinning. When I met Suzy I was a single father of four lovely kids treading some very deep water.

When we first got married, we had nothing but each other and credit scores that looked like golf scores. Except in finance, lower isn't better. We couldn't even get approved to rent a decent place.

After countless rejections, we finally found a rent-to-own deal on a house that had seen better days. We were thrilled! Fourteen years later, we're still here. Same house, same creaky floors, but now it's ours. Turns out staying put was the smartest financial move we ever made.

Suzy and I slowly rebuilt, focusing on widening that critical gap between earning and spending. We celebrated paying off debts like birthdays.

The reward wasn't just a healthier bank account. It was sleeping through the night without money anxiety jerking me awake at 4 AM. The freedom that comes from financial breathing room? Absolutely priceless.

REFLECTING ON PRACTICING FINANCIAL WELL-BEING

When's the last time you felt genuinely good about your relationship with money? Not just having enough of it, but feeling like you were in control of what came in and what went out? What's one small financial habit that, if you started today, might help you sleep better at night six months from now?

Action Steps Toward Practicing Financial Well-Being

Enough money talk. Let's get to the doing part. Here are six simple moves to boost your financial well-being:

- **Schedule money dates**: Avoiding money matters? Schedule a 10-minute weekly money check-in. Scientists found that facing finances in small doses builds confidence and reduces anxiety.
- **Recognize the money-grabbing tricks**: Let's face it, just about everywhere we turn, there's some clever marketing whiz trying to hypnotize our wallets into opening for stuff we flat-out don't need. Those commercials aren't accidentally making you hungry at 10 pm! Take a second to spot these mind games when you're being pelted with all that shiny, tempting junk. Trust me, once you see the strings they're pulling, it's like watching a magician after you've figured out where the rabbit was hiding; way less impressive and a whole lot easier to walk away from.
- **Start stupidly small:** Tight budget? Save just a few dollars a week. Automate it if possible. Even tiny savings add up and increase peace of mind, findings demonstrate.
- **Implement the pause:** Impulse spender? Impose a 24-hour rule on non-essential purchases. This pause curbs impulse buys. Studies find waiting reduces regret and overspending.
- **Budget with breathing room**: Hate budgeting? Make a flexible plan that includes some 'fun money'. Studies indicate that a bit of guilt-free spending makes budgets more sustainable.
- **Connect money to mood**: Doubt money habits affect happiness? Financial stress fuels anxiety. Creating a simple budget or debt plan can lower stress and boost happiness, research confirms.

MOVING ON FROM PRACTICING FINANCIAL WELL-BEING

Now that we've discussed creating financial breathing room, let's explore another type of abundance that's just as crucial for happiness. Having enough time. Because no matter how much money you have, if you're constantly racing against the clock, true happiness will remain elusive.

MANAGING YOUR SCHEDULE FOR "TIME AFFLUENCE"

WHY MANAGING YOUR SCHEDULE FOR "TIME AFFLUENCE" MATTERS

Ever feel like you're rich in stuff but completely broke when it comes to time? You're not alone. In our hyper-connected, productivity-obsessed world, time poverty has become the new normal: and it's killing our happiness.

When we're constantly rushing from one commitment to the next, our stress hormones stay elevated, our attention fragments, and we miss the small moments that actually make life worth living. We end up speeding through our days on autopilot, wondering where all the time went and why we feel so empty despite being so "productive."

Evidence suggests that feeling time-affluent, having breathing room in your schedule, moments to savor experiences, and the freedom to be spontaneous, is one of the strongest predictors of happiness. More than money or possessions, having control over your time creates a sense of autonomy and possibility that fuels well-being.

Time affluence also enhances your relationships. When you're not constantly checking your watch or mentally jumping ahead to the next task, you can actually be present with the people you care about. And meaningful connection, as countless studies confirm, is the foundation of lasting happiness.

Perhaps most importantly, having breathing room in your schedule allows for both rest and play. Two crucial ingredients for creativity, resilience, and overall mental health that often get sacrificed in the name of productivity.

THE SCIENCE BEHIND MANAGING YOUR SCHEDULE FOR "TIME AFFLUENCE"

Ever notice how your happiest days often aren't the ones when you are running around like a madman non-stop, but the ones where you have breathing room to actually enjoy what you were doing? There's fascinating research backing up that feeling. Studies by Mogilner and colleagues found that people who feel "time-rich" consistently report greater life satisfaction than those who feel "time-poor". Even when controlling for income and work hours.[27]

This research suggests that your subjective experience of time, whether you feel rushed or spacious, impacts your brain chemistry in measurable ways. When you're constantly racing against the clock, stress hormones like cortisol stay elevated, keeping your nervous system in a low-grade fight-or-flight state that's terrible for both happiness and health.

Here's where it gets really interesting: psychological experiments show that simply shifting your mindset about time can change how stressed you feel. When people are prompted to focus on having "enough time" rather than "not enough time" before doing the same activities, they report less stress and greater enjoyment, even though their actual time constraints haven't changed.

MY JOURNEY TOWARD MANAGING YOUR SCHEDULE FOR "TIME AFFLUENCE"

Earlier in this chapter I shared a joy that had unexpectedly become a burden. Like many good things in life, what started as pure pleasure had morphed into obligation.

Suzy calls it my "optimization obsession". The urge to squeeze maximum value from every opportunity. Whether it was a gym membership, a garden plot, or my boat, I felt guilty whenever I wasn't using it. The mental math was exhausting: every minute had to count, or I'd feel like I was wasting potential.

Then life happened. My daughter wanted to explore a food festival in the city in mid-July. Friends invited us to a gathering thirty miles inland during prime boating season. A kids birthday party landed on the perfect Saturday for cruising.

My gut reaction was almost visceral: *What about the boat?!* The thought was followed instantly by mental calculations of dollars sitting idle at the dock, as if some celestial bookkeeper was tallying our enjoyment-to-dollar ratio.

The irony hit me like a wayward wake. I'd bought something meant to represent freedom, then tied myself to it tighter than my work schedule! That vessel that was supposed to help us escape the tyranny of commitments had become its little captain, barking orders.

Everything changed when I realized my "optimal fun strategy" wasn't all that fun for anyone. I still have that boat today, and I'm learning that true time affluence isn't about squeezing value from every minute. It's about having the freedom to say yes to joy that doesn't come with advance notice.

REFLECTING ON MANAGING YOUR SCHEDULE FOR "TIME AFFLUENCE"

When was the last time you had a day where you weren't rushing or checking the clock constantly: where you felt like you had plenty of time for what mattered? What was different about that day compared to your typical schedule? And what's one thing you could remove from your calendar this week to create more breathing room?

ACTION STEPS TOWARD MANAGING YOUR SCHEDULE FOR "TIME AFFLUENCE"

Time to tackle the clock! Here are six practical strategies to help you feel less rushed and more in control of your hours:

- **Calculate the Cost of "Yes"** When you say "yes" to something, visualize what you're actually saying "no" to. Your time is a limited currency. Choose wisely.
- **Celebrate saying "No"**: Celebrate your "no" by savoring the freedom on days when declined activities would have happened. Notice the space you've created for what truly matters to you.
- **Practice saying "no"**: Overcommitted? Start declining non-essential requests without elaborate excuses. "That doesn't work for me" is a complete sentence: and a sanity-saving skill.
- **Use time blocks**: Always distracted? Dedicate specific chunks of time to single tasks and silence notifications. Focused work is exponentially more efficient than multitasking.
- **Identify time-wealthy activities**: Feel constantly rushed? Some activities actually expand your perception of time. Reading, being in nature, and deep conversations create "time affluence" regardless of actual duration.
- **Prioritize experiences over efficiency**: Think being busy equals success? Studies find prioritizing time over money increases happiness. Skip a low-value task and use that hour for something meaningful instead.

WRAPPING UP THE CHAPTER:

Now that we've explored these five powerful tools for living more purposefully and productively, let's step back and see how they all fit together. Creating individual improvements and a completely transformed approach to daily life.

READER TRANSFORMATION TIMELINE

Real change in how you approach productivity and purpose unfolds in stages, not overnight transformations. When you commit to these five specific tools, meaningful goals, proactive steps, lifelong learning, financial well-being, and time management, take a look at what you might experience:

First Month: The Awakening

You'll catch yourself pausing before automatically saying yes to commitments that don't align with your values. That little voice inside your head starts whispering, "Wait, does this actually matter to me?" Your shoulders drop about half an inch as you realize you don't have to chase everyone else's definition of success.

Three Months In: Finding Your Rhythm

Those small proactive steps are stacking up now, creating momentum that carries you through tough days. You'll notice anxiety doesn't grip you quite as tightly when unexpected bills arrive because that tiny financial cushion you've been building is actually working. Friends might comment that you seem "different somehow". More present, less scattered.

Six Months Later: The Shift

Learning has become as natural as breathing. You're picking up books you never would have touched before, falling down fascinating YouTube rabbit holes about topics you never knew you'd love. Time feels different too. Somehow more expansive, like you've discovered hidden pockets throughout your day. You're saying no without apologizing for it.

One Year: The New Normal

Goals that once seemed like distant fantasies are now checkmarks on your list. Not because you've become some productivity robot, but because you've aligned your daily choices with what actually matters to you. The gap between earning and spending has widened enough that you sleep differently. More deeply, without the 2 a.m. money panics. **Most surprisingly, you've stopped measuring your worth by your output.** Life feels less like a performance review and more like, well, living.

Remember, friend. Transformation isn't a straight line upward. Some weeks you'll slide backward so far you'll wonder if you've made any progress at all. That's not failure; it's just being human. The difference now is you know how to gently guide yourself back to the path.

YOUR BRAIN ON PURPOSE

Each time you use these five purpose tools, you're creating neural pathways that make purposeful living more automatic. Think of your brain like learning to play an instrument. When you first pick it up, every note requires conscious effort, your fingers fumble, and it sounds pretty rough. But with regular practice and the right techniques, muscle memory develops and music begins to flow naturally.

The beauty of this process is that using these tools might feel forced or unnatural at first, like those awkward first guitar chords, but gradually become your new normal. Eventually, you're playing without thinking about where your fingers go. Just like my first attempts at brewing beer were disasters (who puts their wallet in the wort?), your initial efforts at living more purposefully might be messy. But stick with it, and soon you'll naturally gravitate toward choices that align with your deeper values.

Remember, this isn't about perfection. It's about practice. Your brain doesn't expect you to get it right every time. It just needs enough repetition to recognize the pattern and start automating it. So be patient with yourself as you build these new neural highways of purposeful living.

YOUR DAILY PURPOSE CHEAT SHEET

When life gets chaotic (and when doesn't it?), here's your quick reference guide to staying on the purposeful path:

- **Purpose isn't fixed, it evolves**: Your sense of purpose doesn't need to be carved in stone. Let it shift and grow as you do, staying true to your values while embracing new possibilities.
- **Small steps create big momentum**: Remember that taking any action, however tiny, creates forward motion. Perfect conditions never come; doing something small today beats waiting for the perfect moment.
- **Learning is living fully**: Approach each day with curiosity rather than certainty. The quality of your questions often matters more than having all the answers.
- **Mind the gap**: Keep that critical space between what you earn and what you spend. Financial breathing room isn't luxury. It's essential for peace of mind and true freedom.
- **Time is the ultimate currency**: Protect your time as fiercely as your money. It's far more precious and impossible to earn back

once spent. "No" is a complete sentence when something doesn't serve your purposeful life.

- **Joy matters as much as achievement**: Building a purposeful life isn't just about accomplishing goals; it's about enjoying the journey. Schedule play with the same seriousness you schedule work.
- **Purposeful living is a practice, not a destination**: Like any worthwhile skill, living with purpose gets easier and more natural with consistent practice. Be patient with yourself as you build your skill with these tools.

THE PURPOSE PARADOX

Here's the funny thing about living purposefully and productively. The more you chase it as some distant, perfect state, the more it slips through your fingers. But when you simply show up daily with these small tools, purpose has a way of finding you.

I never set out to be "purposeful" or "productive" in any grand, inspirational way. I just tried to find work I didn't hate, create a life with plenty of laughter, and maybe leave things a little better than I found them. Along the way, I've stumbled into moments of meaning so profound they took my breath away: and they almost always came from using these five simple tools we've been discussing.

So here's my closing thought for you, friend: *Purpose isn't something you discover once and hold onto forever. It's something you build daily through small choices that align with what truly matters to you. It's messy and imperfect and constantly evolving.* And that's not a bug in the system. It's the whole beautiful point.

Your purposeful life won't look like mine or anyone else's. But if you lean into these tools, setting meaningful goals, taking proactive steps, embracing lifelong learning, creating financial well-being, and managing your time for richness rather than just efficiency, you'll create something uniquely yours and genuinely fulfilling.

There's an old saying I've always loved: 'The best time to plant a tree was twenty years ago. The second-best time? Right now.

CHAPTER 7:

THE ART OF SUSTAINABLE LIVING

I'm a master of recreation and a disaster at rest. When it comes to play, I'm ALL IN. It's one of the most important things in the world to me. But when it comes to prioritizing actual rest? I absolutely suck at it, despite my body finally sending me the bill for decades of ignoring the fine print.

I'm living proof that work hard, play hard is a terrible life strategy when you forget the rest smart part. And I'm not alone. Most of us have bought into the crazy idea that grinding ourselves into dust somehow equals success. We wear our exhaustion like a badge of honor, competing to see who is the most worn out. "Oh, you think you're tired? Let me tell you about MY week!" Sound familiar?

Who knows why we're like this? Are we "go-getters" or just "can't-stoppers"? Probably a bit of both.

But what if the secret sauce of a truly fulfilling life isn't found in your inbox or to-do list, but in those moments when you're fully engaged in something that lights you up? When you're laughing so hard your face hurts or when you're so absorbed in a hobby that you lose track of time?

Science is crystal clear: Rest isn't laziness. It's essential maintenance. And recreation isn't a frivolous luxury. It's the reset button your brain and body desperately need. This chapter will explore five game-changing tools that can transform your relationship with rest and play.

The following explains what I've learned (the hard way, naturally):

- Regular breaks and vacations make you better at literally everything else
- Our digital world is designed to hijack your attention. Unless you fight back
- Hobbies and flow activities aren't just fun. They're literal brain medicine
- Decluttering your physical space declutters your mental space too
- Experiences create longer-lasting happiness than more stuff ever will

Let's rediscover what it means to truly rest, recharge, and play. Because that's not just the good stuff in life, my friend. That IS life.

TAKING BREAKS & VACATIONS

WHY TAKING BREAKS & VACATIONS MATTERS

've watched people wear their "I haven't taken a vacation in a long time" badge like it's some kind of Nobel Prize. Meanwhile, their eye is twitching, they're on their fourth cup of coffee, and they've snapped at every person who's crossed their path that day.

Here's the truth bomb: Your brain and body aren't designed for constant output. They're designed for rhythms. Exertion and recovery, focus and rest. Fighting against this biological reality is like trying to drive cross-country without stopping for gas. Eventually, you're going to sputter to a stop, probably in the middle of nowhere with no cell service.

Regular breaks aren't a sign of weakness. They're strategic pit stops that keep your engine running smoothly. These range from five-minute breathers between tasks to two-week vacations where you completely unplug. Such pauses are the secret weapon of high performers.

But perhaps the most powerful reason to prioritize breaks is what happens to your relationships when you don't. Ever notice how the people you love most get your leftovers when you're burned out? Taking breaks isn't selfish. It's ensuring you have enough in your tank to show up as your best self for the people who matter most.

THE SCIENCE BEHIND TAKING BREAKS & VACATIONS

Your brain is basically a muscle that gets fatigued, except the exhaustion is invisible until it's too late. Scientists studying mental performance can literally watch your cognitive abilities decline when you push without breaks. Your attention splinters, your error rate climbs. Your creative problem-solving falls off a cliff.

Researchers at UCLA found that even brief breaks can reset your brain's attention system, kind of like rebooting a glitchy computer.[28] And those micro-breaks matter! A 2019 study showed that a simple 10-minute nature walk can immediately lower stress hormones and improve working memory.

When it comes to vacations, the science gets even more interesting. Your brain actually processes and consolidates information during downtime. That brilliant solution that "magically" pops into your head in the shower or on the beach? That's your resting brain connecting dots your busy brain was too overwhelmed to see.

Studies show that a well-rested brain is significantly more productive and efficient than a chronically tired one, with some reports suggesting substantial gains in productivity.

MY JOURNEY TOWARD TAKING BREAKS & VACATIONS

Okay, I'm gonna come right out and say it. This is the part of the book where I'm not just the author; I'm my own target audience. Writing this section was a painful reminder of how much work I still have to do.

On paper, I should be the poster child for work-life balance. I lead a team at a company that offers unlimited PTO. We're fully remote, saving me roughly two hours of daily commute time. This setup is basically the holy grail of flexible work. The kind people quit good jobs to find. Yet I haven't taken two consecutive days fully off in three years. Not once.

I've become a master of the micro-break instead, stealing 20 minutes between Zoom calls to walk, celebrating the commute time I don't waste, occasionally working from the dock with my laptop precariously balanced. I tell myself these stolen moments are enough, that I'm "hacking" the system by integrating mini-breaks throughout my day.

But even as I write this, I hear the hollowness in my excuses. I sound like someone justifying why it's perfectly reasonable to live on nothing but protein bars. Technically survivable but missing the whole point of nourishment.

When I ignore this wisdom, chaos follows. I get short-tempered and protective about guarding my "free moments." It's not fair to anyone who deals with the depleted version of me that emerges.

I keep promising myself, *I'll take a real break after this project...* It's the classic procrastinator's promise, always pushing rest into a theoretical future that never arrives.

Sometimes honesty is the best first step toward transformation.

REFLECTING ON TAKING BREAKS & VACATIONS

What's the story you tell yourself about rest? Is it "I'll rest when I'm dead" or "I don't deserve a break until everything is done"? And what would happen if you challenged that narrative and gave yourself permission to rest not because you've earned it, but because you need it?

ACTION STEPS TOWARD TAKING BREAKS & VACATIONS

Let's get specific. Here are 6 ways to take those breaks you desperately need:

- **Schedule breaks like meetings:** Feel guilty taking breaks? Science says they're vital for performance. Block 15 minutes between Zoom calls for a walk around the block. Your brain will thank you.

- **Eat lunch away from your desk:** Workaholic? Create a physical boundary. Take your sandwich to a park bench or coffee shop. Stepping away prevents burnout and improves focus, as demonstrated by research.
- **Start with a staycation:** Can't afford travel? Plan a local adventure. Even sleeping in your own bed but exploring nearby attractions recharges you; findings demonstrate just anticipating a break boosts happiness.
- **Long weekend rescue:** No time for week-long trips? Take a Friday and Monday off occasionally. Evidence suggests that even a 4-day break reduces stress and prevents burnout better than scattered single days.
- **Try a digital detox weekend:** Afraid to disconnect? Start small. From Friday night to Sunday night, put the phone in a drawer. Studies confirm that it might feel weird at first, but unplugging lowers stress and improves sleep.
- **Remember: rest = productivity:** Think constant work is noble? Think again. Overwork hurts output. Data indicates that vacations boost job satisfaction and performance. Well-rested people get more done in less time.

MOVING ON FROM TAKING BREAKS & VACATIONS

Now that we've challenged our workaholic tendencies (I'm talking to myself here too), let's focus on something that pairs perfectly with breaks. Digital resilience. Because all that downtime we're trying to create won't mean much if we spend it mindlessly scrolling through our phones instead of actually being present.

STRENGTHENING DIGITAL RESILIENCE
WHY STRENGTHENING DIGITAL RESILIENCE MATTERS

Remember when the internet was supposed to make our lives easier? Yeah, that didn't exactly pan out as advertised. Instead, most of us are now tethered to devices that ping, ding, and vibrate with notifications that trigger the same neurological pathways as a slot machine. We've basically turned our pockets into mini casinos.

Digital overwhelm isn't just annoying. It's rewiring our brains in ways we're only beginning to understand. Our attention spans are fragmenting. Our ability to be fully present is eroding. And weirdly enough, despite being more "connected" than ever, rates of loneliness and isolation are skyrocketing.

Building digital resilience isn't about becoming a tech hermit. It's about reclaiming your brain's incredible capacity for deep thought, genuine connection, and being fully present in your own life. It's about using technology as the tool it was meant to be, rather than letting it use you.

The most powerful reason to strengthen your digital boundaries? The quality of your relationships depends on it. Looking someone in the eye without feeling the phantom vibration of your phone is becoming a rare skill. Yet it's in those fully present moments that the deepest human connections are formed.

THE SCIENCE BEHIND STRENGTHENING DIGITAL RESILIENCE

Every time your phone lights up with a notification, your brain gets a tiny squirt of dopamine. The same chemical involved in gambling addiction. It's not your fault you find it hard to resist checking. Your brain is responding exactly as it's designed to.

A groundbreaking study by Ward and colleagues (often called 'brain drain' research) from the University of Texas at Austin found that just having your phone nearby, even when it's off. Reduces your brain's available processing power.[29] Participants who kept their phones in another room significantly outperformed those who kept phones in their pockets or on their desks. Your brain is constantly using resources to not check your phone.

The news cycle is particularly damaging. The constant exposure to negative news creates a chronic stress response, a phenomenon researchers call 'headline stress disorder.' Importantly, research by Michelle Gielan showed that watching just three minutes of negative news in the morning made people 27% more likely to report having a bad day six to eight hours later.[30]

The good news? Your brain's neuroplasticity works both ways. A 2018 study found that people who limited social media use to 30 minutes per day reported significantly reduced loneliness and depression after just three weeks.[31] Your brain can relearn focus and presence. It just needs some help breaking the digital habit loops.

MY JOURNEY TOWARD STRENGTHENING DIGITAL RESILIENCE

My digital resilience journey started with a jarring observation in a poor neighborhood in India. TV antennas sprouting from nearly every tin-roofed shack with dirt floors and unreliable water.

I learned something unsettling: TVs were intentionally made afford-able because watching commercials makes people want things, which makes them work harder to buy those things. The television pays for itself many times over in increased consumer spending.

Flying home, that conversation haunted me. My two daughters were about 5 and 6 years old. Impressionable, curious, and growing up in the world's most advertising-saturated culture. The parallels between Mumbai shacks and American suburbs suddenly seemed painfully obvious. On the flight, I decided that I was going to cut the cable line.

My daughters mostly just looked confused. "Why are we doing this, Daddy?" they asked, while I fumbled through an explanation. Other parents looked at me like I'd announced plans to live in a tree. A mixture of confusion and that special kind of pity reserved for the voluntarily eccentric.

But that cable stayed cut for nearly twenty years. Instead of Disney marathons, they devoured books. They read "Lord of the Rings" cover to cover by age 10. Instead of Saturday cartoons, we had many fun adventures.

Today, my now-adult daughters thank me for what many friends of mine considered child abuse. That single decision fundamentally changed our family's relationship with media designed to trigger wanting rather than appreciation.

I genuinely believe our family has lived a fuller life because instead of watching screens, we went out and actually did things.

REFLECTING ON STRENGTHENING DIGITAL RESILIENCE

How often do you reach for your phone when you're bored, anxious, or uncomfortable? What would happen if you sat with those feelings instead? And what activities or connections might fill the space if you weren't reflexively checking social media or news?

ACTION STEPS TOWARD STRENGTHENING DIGITAL RESILIENCE

Time to turn theory into practice with these 6 digital detox helpers:

- **Create no-phone zones**: Always glued to your phone? Designate tech-free spaces (dining table, bedroom) and times (first hour after waking, last hour before bed). Research shows these boundaries reduce anxiety and improve sleep quality.
- **Schedule news checks**: Addicted to doom scrolling? Limit news consumption to set times once daily. **Kill TV news if possible.** Constant updates keep your stress hormones elevated; a scheduled approach keeps you informed without the emotional rollercoaster.
- **Curate ruthlessly**: Social media making you feel inadequate? Unfollow accounts that trigger comparison or negativity. Follow fewer people who make you feel worse and more who genuinely inspire you. Your feed should lift, not drain you.
- **Practice JOMO:** Fear missing out? Embrace the Joy Of Missing Out sometimes. Skip the group chat for a day or ignore a trending topic. You'll likely discover the world keeps spinning. Studies show we overestimate the importance of staying constantly updated.
- **Try app time limits**: Phone eating your day? Use screen time settings to limit social media apps to 30 minutes. Evidence suggests most people check their phones 96 times daily: that's once every 10 minutes of waking life!
- **Take a digital sabbath**: Choose one day a month to completely unplug. No email, no social media, no news. Just nature, people, books, and presence. Studies show even short digital breaks significantly restore attention and lower stress levels.

MOVING ON FROM STRENGTHENING DIGITAL RESILIENCE

Now that we've established healthier boundaries with our digital devices, let's explore activities that can fill that newly reclaimed time and attention in ways that truly enrich our lives. By moving away from unconscious scrolling and notification-checking, we create the ideal setting for doing what digital existence has a tendency to distract us from: being fully immersed in activities that bring profound enjoyment and satisfaction.

ENGAGING IN HOBBIES & FLOW ACTIVITIES

WHY ENGAGING IN HOBBIES & FLOW ACTIVITIES MATTERS

Let's be honest. Sometimes life can feel like a giant to-do list. Between work deadlines, family responsibilities, and the never-ending stream of emails, it's easy to forget what it feels like to do something just because it lights you up inside. But that's exactly what makes hobbies and flow activities so powerful.

When you're completely absorbed in something you love, whether it's cornhole, painting, cooking, or making stuff with old wood pallets, something magical happens. You enter what psychologists call a "flow state," where time seems to disappear and your brain gets a much-needed vacation from its usual worrying. It's like hitting a reset button on your stress levels.

But the benefits go way beyond just feeling good in the moment. Regular engagement in hobbies builds confidence as you develop new skills, creates opportunities for meaningful social connection, and gives you a sense of identity outside your job title or family role. Plus, there's something deeply satisfying about creating something or mastering a skill that has nothing to do with making money or checking boxes.

In a world obsessed with productivity, choosing to spend time on activities that seemingly "produce nothing" is a radical act of self-care:

and ironically, one that will make you more productive and creative in every other area of your life.

THE SCIENCE BEHIND ENGAGING IN HOBBIES & FLOW ACTIVITIES

Remember how I mentioned that hobbies are like brain medicine? I wasn't just throwing words around. Research tracking people's daily creative activities found something remarkable: folks reported significantly higher happiness, energy, and life satisfaction on days they engaged in creative hobbies.[32]

Think of your brain like an old truck engine that's been running too hot for too long. Engaging in a hobby you love is like pouring in fresh coolant. It doesn't just prevent overheating; it helps everything run smoother. When you're in that flow state, your brain releases a cocktail of feel-good chemicals like dopamine and endorphins, which are the same ones that get triggered when you accomplish something meaningful.

The key detail to remember is that, **unlike the temporary high from scrolling social media or binge-watching shows, the happiness boost from hobbies sticks around.** The difference between chugging an energy drink (quick spike, then crash) and slow-burning fuel keeps your engine purring all day.

MY JOURNEY TOWARD ENGAGING IN HOBBIES & FLOW ACTIVITIES

My cornhole obsession started innocently enough. Just tossing bean bags while nursing a cold beer, the kind of mindless activity you do while chatting about nothing important.

What I didn't expect was how this simple game could transform my social life. The satisfying thunk of a perfect shot, the smell of fresh-cut wood as we built boards in the garage, the sound of genuine laughter replacing small talk. These became the soundtrack of real connection. We became part of this weird little tribe, united by nothing more profound than landing bean bags in holes. And somehow, that was enough.

Then we ramped it up a notch when Suzy and I started making cornhole boards together. What began as a practical project (buying new ones every couple years was not working out!) evolved into our shared creative outlet. We've spent countless hours designing, building, and painting over a hundred sets for friends, family, and eventually, customers through our modest side business.

The shared experience while throwing bags created bonds that transcended the game itself. Those hours spent playing, laughing, and good-naturedly trash-talking have become some of our favorite memories. Not because they were extraordinary, but because we were fully present, just having fun together.

REFLECTING ON ENGAGING IN HOBBIES & FLOW ACTIVITIES

Take a mental stroll back to childhood for a second. What activities made you lose track of time? What were you doing when your mom had to call you three times for dinner because you were so absorbed? What's stopping you from finding that feeling again now?

ACTION STEPS TOWARD ENGAGING IN HOBBIES & FLOW ACTIVITIES

Alright, folks, enough theory. Let's roll up our sleeves and get this hobby train moving:

- **"No time" is no excuse**: Pencil in a 30-min weekly hobby session. It's essential downtime. Hobbies lower stress and boost productivity, as proven by experts.
- **Ditch the guilt:** Realize hobbies spark creativity and resilience. Investigations reveal that guilt-free leisure reduces burnout and can even improve work performance.

- **Revive childhood passions**: No hobby interest? Revisit what delighted you as a kid or try a free hobby class. Evidence suggests that curiosity-driven hobbies stick and boost enjoyment.
- **Embrace being terrible**: Afraid you'll be bad? Of course you will be! Evidence suggests even novices entering 'flow' gain mood and focus boosts, no expertise required.
- **Add structure**: Always quit hobbies? Set small goals or join a weekly group. Research finds that social support and small wins keep you engaged when motivation wanes.
- **Start micro:** Too old or busy? Try a micro-hobby: 10 minutes a day of something fun. Data reveals that even short flow states boost well-being and build toward longer sessions.

MOVING ON FROM ENGAGING IN HOBBIES & FLOW ACTIVITIES

Now that we've explored how hobbies and flow activities can transform your daily experience, let's talk about creating the physical environment that serves this mental liberation. Though engaging in an activity we enjoy replenishes our minds, for many of us it is difficult to be fully present in these activities if we surround ourselves with a cluttered physical environment. After all, it's hard to lose yourself in painting, woodworking, or any creative pursuit when you can't find your supplies under piles of stuff or feel overwhelmed by the chaos around you.

DECLUTTERING
WHY DECLUTTERING MATTERS

There's a reason those decluttering experts skyrocketed to fame and weren't just some passing trend. They tapped into something many of us feel but couldn't quite articulate: our stuff is literally weighing us down.

Every item you own demands something from you. It requires space, maintenance, cleaning, organizing, and mental bandwidth. Each object in your home silently shouts for a slice of your attention. When you multiply that by hundreds or thousands of possessions, it's no wonder we feel mentally scattered and overwhelmed.

But decluttering goes beyond just creating a pretty Instagram-worthy space. It's about clearing both physical and mental roadblocks. When your environment is chaotic, your brain constantly processes that chaos in the background, like a computer running too many programs at once. Everything slows down.

The magic happens when you start creating space. Suddenly you can think more clearly. Decisions come easier. Creativity flows more freely. And perhaps most importantly, you regain a sense of control that spills over into other areas of your life. It's as if clearing your physical space gives you permission to clear out mental and emotional junk too.

THE SCIENCE BEHIND DECLUTTERING

Your brain is basically playing "Where's Waldo?" every time you walk into a cluttered room. Seriously! Neuroscientists using fMRI scans can actually see your visual cortex getting overwhelmed when it's trying to process too many objects at once. The result? Your brain gets tired out faster, just from being in a messy space.

And get this: a fascinating study from Princeton University (from the lab of neuroscientist Sabine Kastner) found that all that physical clutter directly competes for your attention. It makes it way harder for your brain to focus and process information effectively because it's trying to deal with too many things vying for the spotlight.[33] While the exact minutes of focus gained from tidying might vary from person to person, the science is clear: an orderly room allows your brain to concentrate much better. Imagine the productivity boost, and the mental relief, just from clearing your desk!

But wait, there's more. It even messes with your stress hormones! Researchers have delved into how our home environment links to cortisol, that main stress hormone we're always hearing about. Studies, like important work by Darby Saxbe and Rena Repetti, suggest that when people describe their homes as more stressful, less organized, or not very restorative (which, let's be honest, often goes hand-in-hand with clutter), they tend to show less healthy patterns of cortisol throughout the day.[34] These patterns can mean your body isn't managing stress optimally. Those folks living in spaces they perceived as more organized and restful? They generally had healthier cortisol rhythms, which often translates to better moods and even sounder sleep.

MY JOURNEY TOWARD DECLUTTERING

I'm eternally grateful for Facebook Marketplace to sell our stuff. My digital therapist, where each listing is a step toward mental freedom, each pickup a celebration, each cash transaction validating my excellent taste in things I no longer want.

My shame is this: I hoard anything vaguely technical. If it's got wires, connectors, or could be useful on a future project, my reptilian brain shouts 'KEEP IT!' like someone who's just spotted the last lifeboat on a sinking ship. My collection of cables could supply a small nation's infrastructure needs. I have cables from devices that haven't existed since the Clinton administration. I'm pretty sure one of them is for a Betamax player.

But at what mental cost? When my workspace gets messy, I experience a brain meltdown... the visual noise drowning out clear thinking.

Yet my growing-up-poor mentality screams that wasting anything is sinful. The voices of depression-era grandparents echo: 'You might need that someday!'

Thank God for Suzy, who's mastered storage systems that keep our house looking civilized. She's created a clutter containment strategy preserving my sanity while accommodating my bizarre attachments. And she is great at peddling our used goods online.

It's a work in progress, but I'm learning that less stuff equals more mental freedom.

REFLECTING ON DECLUTTERING

What's one space in your home that creates stress every time you see it? And how would your daily mood change if that space brought you calm instead of chaos? What's the smallest step you could take today to begin transforming that area?

ACTION STEPS TOWARD DECLUTTERING

Grab a pencil or just your good intentions. It's action time:

- **Start ridiculously small:** Overwhelmed by clutter? Clear one drawer or tidy for just 5 minutes. Evidence suggests that small wins build momentum and confidence, and even brief decluttering reduces stress.

- **Take memory photos**: Too sentimental to toss items? Photograph cherished but unused things before donating them. The memory stays while the clutter goes. Psychologists confirm this eases the emotional letting-go process.
- **Create a "maybe box"**: Afraid you'll need it someday? Put questionable items in a sealed box with today's date. If in 6 months you haven't opened it, donate it without looking inside. You've proven you can live without it.
- **Follow the one-in-one-out rule**: No time for big cleanouts? For each new item you bring home, remove one similar item. This simple habit prevents clutter buildup without requiring massive time commitments.
- **Clear just one surface**: Skeptical decluttering affects mood? Try this experiment: completely clear your desk or kitchen counter and notice how you feel. Most people report an immediate sense of calm when looking at an orderly space.
- **Make it a game**: Hate tidying? Set a 10-minute timer and see how many items you can properly put away. When it's playful, you're more likely to follow through. Findings demonstrate gamifying chores increases completion rates.

MOVING ON FROM DECLUTTERING

As we release the extra physical baggage holding us back in our homes and minds, we can't help but wonder what really enriches our lives. Decluttering is not about eliminating possessions: but about consciously deciding what warrants space in our homes and lives. This shift in thinking leads to a freeing aha moment: maybe the most meaningful things in life aren't things at all. Allow us to discover how experiences instead of more possessions can lead to lasting joy that no shopping spree can ever equal.

CHOOSING EXPERIENCES OVER POSSESSIONS

WHY CHOOSING EXPERIENCES OVER POSSESSIONS MATTERS

L et me ask you something: When you're on your deathbed (cheery thought, I know), will you be thinking about that fancy watch you bought or the time you laughed until you cried on that road trip with friends?

We live in a world constantly telling us that happiness comes in Amazon packages. Buy this gadget! Upgrade your phone! Get the bigger house! Meanwhile, the happiness boost from new stuff typically fades faster than cheap jeans in a hot wash.

Experiences, though? They're like the gift that keeps on giving. First, there's the delicious anticipation. Planning that trip or concert gives you weeks of happiness before it even happens. Then there's the actual experience itself. And finally, there's the reminiscing afterward, which can bring joy for years or even decades.

But perhaps the most powerful aspect is how shared experiences weave the fabric of our relationships. That inside joke from your camping disaster or the story of that time you all got lost in a foreign city. These shared moments become the glue that binds us together. No 72-inch TV can do that, no matter how crisp the picture.

THE SCIENCE BEHIND CHOOSING EXPERIENCES OVER POSSESSIONS

Your brain constantly compares what you have against what others have. With possessions, this creates what researchers call the "hedonic treadmill". The new purchase thrill quickly fades as items become the new normal.

The fascinating thing? This comparison trap doesn't hit experiences nearly as hard. In landmark studies by Dr. Thomas Gilovich at Cornell, people reported longer-lasting happiness because they become part of your identity rather than just temporary possessions.[35] **Plus, sharing experiences connects you with others, while talking about possessions often creates distance or envy.**

The science is clear: if you want more happiness bang for your buck, invest in doing rather than owning.

MY JOURNEY TOWARD CHOOSING EXPERIENCES OVER POSSESSIONS

Let me address the seven refrigerators in the room. Yes, SEVEN! I'll confess, I have a love-hate relationship with stuff. Although I preach about experiences over things, our house has amassed an impressive collection of cooking equipment.

This confession might seem to contradict my "experiences over possessions" preaching. But here's my defense: these aren't dust-collecting status symbols. They're memory-making machines with plugs and warranties that bring people together.

What I've learned in this paradox is the crucial distinction between possessions that enable experiences and those that simply take up space. For each person, this line is different.

Every refrigerator has been filled for block parties where neighbors became friends. Our grills have transformed over a thousand pounds of ingredients into meals where strangers became family.

I've made possession-related blunders too. See motorcycle story above.

That's the distinction: stuff that sits versus that serves. The value isn't in what you own. **It's in the stories those possessions help you create.**

REFLECTING ON CHOOSING EXPERIENCES OVER POSSESSIONS

Think about your last three major purchases. Now think about your last three memorable experiences. Which set of memories brings a genuine smile to your face? And if you had to give up either all those possessions or all those memories, which would hurt more to lose?

ACTION STEPS TOWARD CHOOSING EXPERIENCES OVER POSSESSIONS

Time to get our hands dirty. Here's how you make this happen:

- **Test the memory formula**: Skeptical about experiences? Try this: Wait a month after your next purchase and experience. See which you're still talking about. Empirical results prove that you'll cherish an experience's memory longer than a new gadget's shine.
- **Enjoy the triple happiness hit**: Experiences give three doses of joy: planning, doing, and remembering. Next time you're eyeing a purchase, ask if it offers the same triple boost. Studies show even anticipating an experience boosts mood more than waiting for a delivery.
- **Start small and free**: Low budget? The best experiences often cost nothing. Try a sunset picnic, explore a new hiking trail, or join a free community event. Studies find even simple adventures spark more joy than another trinket.
- **Redirect shopping energy**: Shopaholic? Channel that excitement into planning experiences. Creating a bucket list or researching your next adventure gives a similar dopamine hit with longer-lasting rewards.

- **Find everyday adventures:** No time for trips? Add novelty to your routine: take a different route home, try a new recipe, or watch the sunrise. Adding even small new experiences to ordinary days boosts happiness more than buying stuff.
- **Run the deathbed test:** When stuck in a buying decision, ask: "Will this matter when I'm 80?" Experiences almost always win this test because they become part of who you are, not just something you own.

WRAPPING UP THE CHAPTER:

THE RIVER JOURNEY OF REST & RECREATION

Think of these five tools as a river journey. Your hobbies are the current carrying you forward. Breaks provide calm waters for recharging. Experiences become memorable landmarks. Decluttering removes obstacles blocking your flow. Digital resilience creates clean boundaries.

Notice how each element supports the others. Declutter your life, and you find space for flow activities. Strengthen digital boundaries, and you discover time for real breaks. This isn't about perfection. It's about progress.

TRAINING YOUR BRAIN FOR REST & JOY

These five tools aren't just good ideas. They're literally rewiring your brain for greater well-being. Each time you engage in a flow activity, take a real break, choose an experience over a possession, declutter a space, or set a digital boundary, you're creating and strengthening neural pathways.

Like we referenced before, our brains physically change based on repeated behaviors. This means every small choice matters. That ten-minute hobby session, that lunch break away from your desk, that decision to plan a road trip instead of buying a new gadget is physically altering your brain's structure in subtle but powerful ways.

The most amazing part? These changes compound over time. What feels difficult or unnatural at first gradually becomes your default setting. The path of least resistance slowly shifts from burnout and accumulation to rest and meaningful engagement.

YOUR REST & RECREATION CHEAT SHEET

When life gets crazy (and when isn't it?), come back to these fundamental truths:

- **Your productivity doesn't measure your worth**: The world will take everything you're willing to give. It's up to you to set the boundaries.
- **"I don't have time" really means "This isn't a priority."**: Be honest about your choices, then adjust if they don't align with what truly matters to you.
- **Rest is a skill that requires practice**: Not something that happens automatically when you finally collapse from exhaustion.
- **The best possessions create experiences**: If it doesn't bring joy or enable meaningful connections, question why it's taking up space in your life.
- **Your attention is your most valuable resource**: Be intentional about where you invest it. What you focus on literally becomes your life.
- **Small, consistent habits beat grand gestures every time**: Five minutes of daily play adds up to more than the "someday" plans you never get around to.
- **When in doubt, ask: "Will doing this create a memory I'll treasure?"**: If the answer is yes, that's your compass pointing true north.

THE ULTIMATE PERMISSION SLIP

At the end of the day, this chapter isn't really about hobbies or decluttering or digital boundaries. It's about giving yourself permission to rest without guilt, play without justification, and enjoy your life while you're living it. Not just in some distant future when everything on your to-do list is magically done.

Somewhere along the way, we bought into a whopper of a lie: that running ourselves ragged is somehow noble, like we deserve a gold medal for the dark circles under our eyes.

That rest is some fancy spa treatment, not the basic maintenance our bodies are hollering for.

That success comes in the form of an empty inbox (ha!), or those shiny toys that "everyone" has.

It's like we're all competing in the Exhaustion Olympics, and nobody's stopping to ask why the heck we signed up in the first place. I've got the participation trophy for that competition gathering dust. Right next to all those "must-have" gadgets I barely remember buying.

But what if the real measure of success isn't what we accomplish, but what we experience?

Not what we own, but the stories we collect?

Not the promotions, but the kitchen dance parties, the belly laughs, the sunset views shared with someone we love?

Here's your permission slip, my friend. Written not by me, but by the universe itself:

You are allowed to rest.

You are meant to play.

Your joy isn't an indulgence. It's the whole damn point.

Now, go do something that makes your face hurt from smiling.

WRAPPING UP YOUR SUCCESS SYSTEMS:

THE BODY-MIND CONNECTION: BUILDING YOUR HAPPINESS FOUNDATION

Well, we've made it through fourteen tools, some embarrassing stories about my life, and what feels like enough science to qualify for college credits. If you've stuck with me this far without throwing this book across the room and muttering, "This guy needs therapy, not a publishing deal," then I consider that a roaring success.

I'm reminded of my backyard setup when I think about all we've covered in this physical and lifestyle section. It's nothing fancy. Just a collection of grills, coolers, cornhole boards, and that questionable-looking bar we built ourselves. But it's important to understand that each piece works in harmony with the others. The smoker needs the right wood, the coolers need ice, and the sound system needs to be playing something that gets people moving. When one element fails, the whole party suffers.

That's exactly what we've been exploring here. Not just random tools tossed together because they sound nice, but a deliberately designed system where each piece supports the others. Your body isn't separate from your mind, and your daily habits aren't separate from your happiness.

The magic happens in the connections. When you move your body regularly, you naturally sleep better. When you sleep better, you have the energy to pursue meaningful goals. When you're working toward what truly matters, you're more motivated to fuel your body properly. When you're eating mindfully, your brain works better for learning new things. When you're learning and growing, you're more likely to prioritize experiences over possessions. It's this beautiful upward spiral where each positive choice makes the next one easier.

I'm not going to pretend I've mastered all of this. I still have days when I choose the extra beer over the early bedtime. My shed organization system would make the "declutter experts" break out in hives. **But I know this for sure: I'm better than I was. And for all of us, "better than before" is a victory worth celebrating.**

The tools in this section aren't about achieving some Instagram-perfect lifestyle where you're running marathons at dawn before whipping up an organic smoothie bowl that looks like abstract art. They're about building a foundation sturdy enough to hold your dreams and disappointments without crumbling under either.

If I could go back and give my younger self one piece of advice about these tools, it would be this: **begin with what feels doable, let go of the pressure to nail it, and find humor in the hiccups. These tools aren't about fixing what's broken in you. They're about nurturing what's already working, one tiny choice at a time.**

My hope for you isn't that you master these tools flawlessly. I hope that a few months from now, you find yourself naturally craving a walk after a stressful day, automatically turning off your phone an hour before bed, or instinctively making time for that hobby that lights you up: and suddenly realizing that something has shifted inside you. Not dramatically, but fundamentally.

Change that sticks rarely comes from sweeping overhauls. It builds in the quiet, consistent moments that eventually carve new paths through the wilderness of your life until the new way becomes the obvious way.

And speaking of paths and connections, all of these physical and lifestyle changes? They're designed to fuel something even more essential to your well-being. Your bonds with others. Because what good is having energy, purpose, and quality rest if you don't have people to share your life with?

So let's keep going. In the next section, we'll explore the tools that help you build meaningful connections with others. From your romantic partner to your friends, family, colleagues, and even your broader community. Because while your body needs movement, your heart needs connection. We'll also discover how sharing and teaching these happiness practices to others creates a powerful ripple effect.

The journey continues, and the best parts are still ahead.

Remember this, if nothing else: Your daily habits aren't just what you do. They're who you become. Choose wisely. And hey, don't try to overhaul your whole lifestyle tomorrow. If all you do this week is get a little more sleep or take a few deep breaths, you're already winning. Pick one habit, make it yours, and let the momentum grow.

CONNECTION THAT MATTERS
SECTION THREE

We humans are hard wired for connection like boats are built for water. It's what we're made for, even when we convince ourselves otherwise. It took me thirty-some years to figure this out.

After spending time chasing just about everything under the sun that promised happiness, careers, achievements, stuff that can make stuff, I eventually figured out what my Aunt Marge and Uncle Bob knew all along: the path to joy isn't paved with accomplishments or acquisitions. It's lined with faces. The people we love. The neighbors we wave to. The strangers who become friends over a shared meal.

I somehow became that guy who learned to love creating spaces where folks can just be together. From turning my backyard into the neighborhood hangout and roasting whole pigs at block parties, to opening that little coffee shop where musicians could jam without judgment and taking hundreds of people out on our boat. I've been accidentally collecting people ever since.

What I've learned from all that gathering is that we're starving for real connection. In an age of digital noise and growing division, the ability to forge genuine bonds isn't just a happiness skill. It's a survival tool. The problem is, modern life keeps serving us a flashy menu of counterfeit connections, digital junk food that looks appealing but leaves us feeling empty and malnourished. It's built on a foundation of myths that I, and maybe you, have spent years believing. Ideas that encourage us to isolate ourselves while pretending we're more connected than ever. Before we go any further, let's expose five of the biggest lies that keep us lonely:

- Social Media Connects Us and Improves Happiness
- Complete Independence Leads to Happiness
- The Perfect Relationship Will Make You Happy
- Happiness Is a Purely Individual Pursuit
- Helping Yourself First Leads to Happiness

Believing these myths is like trying to survive on a diet of digital junk food. It might give you a quick hit, but it offers zero real nourishment. They steer us toward isolation, shallow interactions, and the endless, lonely pursuit of self-sufficiency. The chapters ahead are the antidote. They are the guide to cooking up the rich, meaningful, and sometimes messy feast of true human connection. (As always, you can find the complete recipe book for dismantling all 37 myths in the Appendix.)

My hope is that this book becomes something that sits dog-eared on coffee tables and kitchen counters, sparking conversations in what sociologists call "third places". The coffee shops, book clubs, and community hubs that serve as the heart of our social lives. These are the crucial spaces, not quite work and not quite home, where we can drop our guard and truly find each other.

Think of this book as a shared toolbox meant to be passed around, discussed, and practiced together in these third places. Whether in book clubs, community groups, or informal gatherings at local coffee shops. Like any good conversation starter, it works best when people compare notes, share their own experiences with these tools, and support each other's journey toward happiness in these neutral, welcoming spaces. **The science is universal, but the stories we create while practicing these principles together in our third places. That's where the real transformation happens.**

As we dive into relationships and social connections, remember that everything else we've talked about, from mindfulness to purpose, ultimately leads here: **to the messy, beautiful business of being truly present with other human beings.** Because at the end of the day, that's what makes a life worth living.

In this section, we'll explore the tools that transform surface-level interactions into soul-nourishing connections. We'll dig into deepening personal relationships, enhancing communication with actual empathy (not the fake kind), and building community through simple acts of kindness.

Fair warning: creating meaningful connections isn't always comfortable. It requires vulnerability, authenticity, and occasionally admitting you're wrong (my personal kryptonite). But my years of fumbling through this stuff have taught me one crucial lesson: every awkward conversation that deepens a relationship, every moment of vulnerability that brings you closer to someone, every time you choose connection over comfort, you're not just improving your relationships. You're literally rewiring yourself for a richer, fuller life. The people who master these tools don't just have better relationships. They build better lives. They have more resilience. More joy. More of that deep-down satisfaction that no amount of stuff can buy.

Because at the end of the day, it's not what we accumulate that matters; it's who we share the journey with. **And once you learn how to truly connect? You'll wonder how you ever settled for anything less.**

Now, let's look ahead to three important chapters that will transform how you build your happiness foundation through the power of genuine human connection.

In Chapter 8, we'll learn how to transform surface connections into soul connections by:

- Prioritizing Quality Time with Loved Ones
- Expressing Appreciation and Love
- Setting Boundaries & Being Assertive
- Resolving Conflicts Constructively

- Practicing Forgiveness

In Chapter 9, we'll master communication that actually connects by:

- Practicing Active Listening
- Tuning into Nonverbal Cues
- Practicing Empathy
- Sharing Authentically & Vulnerably

And in Chapter 10, we'll move from isolation to community by:

- Performing Acts of Kindness
- Contributing Through Volunteering
- Building Community Connections
- Finding & Joining Your "Tribe"

So, as we set off into the chapters ahead, I invite you to bring your whole self. Quirks, hesitations, and all. Because real connection isn't about perfection; it's about showing up, being seen, and making room for others to do the same. Let's get started on building a life that's rich with the kind of connections we're all hungry for

CHAPTER 8:

TRANSFORMING SURFACE CONNECTIONS INTO SOUL CONNECTIONS

Ever notice how some people have incredibly rich, supportive relationships while others feel painfully alone. Despite having hundreds of social media "friends"? The difference isn't luck or charisma. I've been on both sides of that fence, and let me tell you, the view's a lot better when you're surrounded by people who see you.

I value spending quality time with friends and family. For years, I struggled with having difficult conversations. I kept things light and breezy, thinking I was keeping the peace. In reality, I was building walls instead of bridges. I avoided sensitive topics like relationship hurts and everyday conflicts. This seemed easier in the moment but ultimately hurt everyone involved. This pattern affected my relationships with my children and especially with Suzy.

What I've learned, the hard way, as usual, is that avoiding important interpersonal issues causes more lasting damage than any practical mistake ever could. I've wiped away too many tears that honest "heart-conversations" could have prevented. Thankfully, I've found these necessary talks are usually less difficult than I fear. I'm gradually becoming more willing to engage on a deeper level.

The science is crystal clear on this one, folks: meaningful relationships are the bedrock of happiness. Not fancy cars, not impressive job titles. Just good old-fashioned human connection. In this chapter, we'll explore five essential relationship tools that are proven to make all the difference between surface-level acquaintances and those soul-nourishing bonds we all crave:

- Prioritizing quality time (even when your schedule's bursting at the seams)
- Expressing appreciation (even when you think it's obvious)
- Setting healthy boundaries (without feeling like a jerk)
- Resolving conflicts constructively (instead of sweeping them under the rug)
- Practicing forgiveness (without becoming a doormat)

These aren't just nice-to-have social skills. They're the difference between relationships that drain you and relationships that sustain you. So let's dig in, shall we?

PRIORITIZING QUALITY TIME WITH LOVED ONES

WHY PRIORITIZING QUALITY TIME WITH LOVED ONES MATTERS

R emember the last time you canceled plans with a friend because work was "crazy busy"? I've been there more times than I care to admit. Yet somehow, when we look back at life from our deathbeds, nobody ever says, "Gosh, I wish I'd spent more time answering emails."

What stands out about this is spending quality time with loved ones isn't just a nice break from your to-do list. It's literally life-extending. Social connections don't just make us happier; they help us live longer. While we're chasing wealth and fame thinking they'll bring happiness, science keeps pointing to the same conclusion: close relationships keep us happier throughout life.

When life gets overwhelming (and when doesn't it these days?), time with loved ones acts like a stress buffer. Having supportive family and friends nearby makes our problems feel more manageable and gives us a sense of meaning and purpose that no solo achievement can match.

The contrast is stark: warm relationships help people live happier, longer lives, while loneliness harms our well-being as much as smoking or obesity. And unlike our genetic makeup, this is something we have real control over through intentional presence and meaningful engagement. Pretty powerful stuff for something as simple as showing up, huh?

THE SCIENCE BEHIND PRIORITIZING QUALITY TIME WITH LOVED ONES

You know how we all secretly hope there's some magic bullet for happiness out there? Well, Harvard researchers spent 80+ years looking for exactly that. The Harvard Adult Development Study tracked hundreds of men throughout their lives, measuring everything from blood work to brain scans to kitchen-table interviews.[36]

Their breakthrough finding: relationships, not money, fame, or achievement, predicted happiness and health at 80.

Think of relationships like emotional savings accounts. Regular deposits of quality time create security that pays dividends when life gets rough. The researchers found that people with strong social connections had sharper memories, lower stress levels, and even delayed physical pain and disease.

What's fascinating is how this shows up physically: your body actually processes stress differently when you feel socially connected. That fight-or-flight response that makes your heart pound and your muscles tense? It calms down faster when you've got solid relationships in your corner.

I love this research because it validates something we intuitively know: we're wired for connection. Our brains literally function better when we regularly engage with people we care about. No wonder isolation feels so darn uncomfortable. It's like trying to run a car without oil!

MY JOURNEY TOWARD PRIORITIZING QUALITY TIME WITH LOVED ONES

Every morning, I meet with my small work team, about six wonderful people scattered around the world, for an hour. Over time, I've grown surprisingly close to them, not just because they're wonderful people, but because we intentionally show up, day after day.

It hit me one morning like a brick: I was sometimes closer to these coworkers than certain family members I'd known my entire life.

Why? Because we had structured, consistent time together. During these times each one of them claimed a chunk of my heart. It reminded me of my childhood when monthly family birthday gatherings ensured we all stayed connected. Something that gradually disappeared as we scattered across the country.

The irony wasn't lost on me. I had let many of my most important relationships drift while maintaining work connections simply because one had a recurring calendar invite and the others didn't. Talk about missing the forest for the trees!

Recently, prompted by our adult children with grandkids (who are apparently wiser than their old man), my family committed to actively scheduling get-togethers. We finally understood that relationships don't magically thrive on good intentions. They need purposeful time allocation. Otherwise, connections naturally fade as life's current pulls us in different directions.

Reflecting On Prioritizing Quality Time with Loved Ones

Think about the people who matter most in your life. When was the last time you gave them your full, undivided attention. Not just being physically present while mentally rehearsing your to-do list, but really being there? What's one small step you could take this week to create more meaningful moments with them, even if you're crazy busy?

ACTION STEPS TOWARD PRIORITIZING QUALITY TIME WITH LOVED ONES

Alright folks, let's get practical. Here are six ways to make quality time happen, even when life gets hectic:

- **Calendar your loved ones:** Add family and friends to your schedule like important meetings; even the busiest doubters find regular connection boosts mood and longevity.
- **Combine tasks with togetherness**: Turn everyday chores into bonding time; cooking dinner together removes the "I don't have time" barrier.

- **Start small but consistent**: Begin with just 15 minutes of device-free conversation daily; consistency naturally deepens closeness over time.
- **Create virtual rituals:** If distance separates you, establish a weekly video dinner date; consistent rituals keep bonds strong despite miles.
- **Choose side-by-side activities**: Not a talker? Try walking or cooking together; parallel activities ease conversation pressure while strengthening connection.
- **Extend that simple invitation**: Think it's too late to reconnect? Send a quick "coffee next week?" text; small consistent efforts can revive long-neglected relationships.

MOVING ON FROM PRIORITIZING QUALITY TIME WITH LOVED ONES

Creating space for meaningful connection is like building a beautiful room: but an empty room, no matter how lovely, needs to be filled with warmth to become a home. You've carved out the time, shown up physically and mentally, but now what? The magic happens when we fill those precious moments with what our loved ones need most: genuine appreciation and expressions of love that leave no doubt about how much they matter.

EXPRESSING APPRECIATION AND LOVE

WHY EXPRESSING APPRECIATION AND LOVE MATTERS

Y ou know that warm glow you feel when someone genuinely thanks you for something? Turns out, that feeling isn't just nice. It's transformative. Appreciation is like emotional fertilizer, strongly linked to greater happiness and positive emotions that help everything else in your life grow.

When we regularly express appreciation, we train our brains to spot the good stuff instead of fixating on problems. Thankful people become more optimistic and resilient, bouncing back faster from life's inevitable challenges. It's like developing an emotional immune system.

But here's where it gets really interesting: expressing appreciation isn't just about making others feel good (though it definitely does that). When you vocalize your gratitude or show affection, whether through words, notes, or even physical touch like hugging, you're actually triggering changes in your own body. Those affectionate actions reduce stress hormones and lower blood pressure, lifting your mood from the inside out.

The truth is: showing love benefits your own well-being just as much as the receiver's. Let's face it, **love is an action verb**. By practicing regular compliments and sincere expressions of love, you create a positive feedback loop that strengthens relationships while making you both feel closer, more secure, and, bottom line, happier..

THE SCIENCE BEHIND EXPRESSING APPRECIATION AND LOVE

Ever wonder if a simple 'thank you' actually creates measurable change? Research by Algoe and others found something remarkable: appreciation doesn't just feel good. It transforms relationships at work and home.[37]

When appreciation becomes a regular practice, something magical happens. For instance, picture this: in workplaces where teams started doing things like "gratitude days", making a point to thank a colleague, they actually saw real jumps in trust and people working better together. No kidding! And it's not just at the office. In families, studies indicate that when teens feel genuinely appreciated by their parents, it gives a solid boost to their mental health. Turns out, everyone, and I mean everyone, is wired to crave that feeling of acknowledgment and to know they matter.

So, what's the big secret? It's that making it a habit to voice your appreciation. You know, actually saying "I love how you did that!" or "Seriously, thanks for being you". It creates this amazing atmosphere of support. And that supportive vibe? It cranks up the well-being for both the person giving the props and the person getting them! People who make a point to frequently dish out appreciation often report feeling more positive and more tuned into others' feelings (that's empathy, folks!), mainly because it shifts their whole focus to the good stuff in people.

And don't forget the cool brain chemistry! When you express or receive that heartfelt appreciation, your brain often gets a nice hit of oxytocin: that famous 'bonding hormone.' It's like nature's own recipe for trust and connection. This all feeds into an upward spiral: you appreciate someone, they feel great and appreciated, they're more likely to be awesome and appreciative back, and the whole positive cycle just strengthens your bond.

Think of appreciation like relationship sunshine; it might seem subtle, but it provides the warmth and energy that makes all your connections, from your family to your work buddies, grow stronger and healthier!

MY JOURNEY TOWARD EXPRESSING APPRECIATION AND LOVE

For me, expressing love and appreciation has always felt natural. Maybe too natural. Growing up in chaos taught me early that you never know when someone might disappear from your life. That's why I've never been shy about telling people how I feel about them. But what I didn't fully understand for years was just how transformative those simple words could be for the people hearing them.

This lesson hits closest to home with my siblings. Having been torn apart as kids, we now sit face to face perhaps once or twice a year. During those cherished visits, they bring both love and lingering pain from our decades apart. We all carry scars we're still healing from, yet to be given their vulnerability and words of affection is a gift each time.

I've witnessed how saying "I love you" amidst brokenness can bring profound healing. There is something about speaking the good that we see in each other, especially when life has given us every reason to be gazing at what is broken, that can heal wounds time alone never could.

REFLECTING ON EXPRESSING APPRECIATION AND LOVE

When was the last time you told someone exactly what you appreciate about them. Not just a generic "thanks" but a specific quality or action that made a difference to you? And what holds you back from expressing appreciation more often? Is it discomfort, forgetfulness, or perhaps the assumption that people already know how you feel?

ACTION STEPS TOWARD EXPRESSING APPRECIATION AND LOVE

Ready to boost your appreciation game? Here are some simple ways to start expressing more love and gratitude today:

- **Voice one daily thank-you:** Feel awkward? Start small; expressing gratitude releases bonding oxytocin and improves your relationship quality.
- **Write it down**: Worried it won't sound genuine? Put appreciation in writing; seeing appreciation and love on paper often feels more meaningful and lasting.
- **Show don't tell**: Not the sentimental type? Show appreciation through actions like doing a chore or offering a treat; gestures count when words are hard.
- **Make it explicit**: Afraid they "already know" you care? Even so, verbalizing appreciation enhances intimacy and trust in measurable ways.
- **Trust the impact:** Think compliments go unnoticed or to their head? Research proves otherwise. Heartfelt thanks spark positivity for both giver and receiver.
- **Be detailed with praise:** Rather than general compliments, comment on specific qualities or behaviors: "I like the way you always ask about my mother" is more meaningful than "You're really nice."
- **Receive different languages of appreciation:** Some people like words, others prefer acts of service, quality time, thoughtful gifts, or physical touch. Learn how your loved ones receive appreciation best and modify your expression accordingly.

MOVING ON FROM EXPRESSING APPRECIATION AND LOVE

Freely showing love is a superpower. But here's the catch: the same people who freely express appreciation often struggle with its flip side. Clearly expressing their needs and limits. When we pour out love but forget to maintain the vessel that holds it, we risk depleting ourselves. Yet healthy relationships require both generosity and self-respect, both giving and protecting what we have to give. It's the difference between being a generous spring and a dried-up well. That's why setting boundaries isn't the opposite of love. It's what makes sustainable love possible.

SETTING BOUNDARIES & BEING ASSERTIVE

WHY SETTING BOUNDARIES & BEING ASSERTIVE MATTERS

Ever notice how some people seem to get walked all over while others somehow command respect without being jerks about it? The difference often comes down to one skill: healthy boundary-setting.

Setting clear boundaries isn't selfish. It's essential self-care that lowers stress and dramatically increases life satisfaction. Think of boundaries as the guardrails that keep your relationships on safe, healthy roads instead of careening off cliffs.

When you communicate your needs and limits clearly, something remarkable happens: your anxiety and depression levels drop, and your self-esteem and confidence rise. There's something powerfully affirming about knowing your own limits and having the courage to express them.

The payoff extends beyond your internal state. Assertive people tend to have fewer conflicts and frustrations in their daily interactions. Instead of letting resentment build up until they explode (or implode), they address issues early and directly, preventing small irritations from becoming relationship-ending blowups.

Perhaps most surprisingly, healthy boundaries don't push people away. They build stronger relationships while filtering out the unhealthy, draining ones. Through clear communication and establishing healthy limits, you're essentially teaching others how to treat you, creating the foundation for authentic connection based on mutual respect.

THE SCIENCE BEHIND SETTING BOUNDARIES & BEING ASSERTIVE

Remember back in school when some teachers let chaos reign while others maintained order without being dictators? Turns out, there's fascinating science behind why boundaries make everyone feel safer and happier.

Wonder why boundaries help everyone feel safer and happier? Research offers answers. For instance, a 2016 study with adolescent girls tested an 8-week assertiveness training program where they learned to respectfully communicate their needs and set personal boundaries (Eslami et al.)[38]. The results were compelling: the trained girls showed a significant increase in assertiveness and a significant decrease in their levels of anxiety and stress compared to a control group.

What's happening in your brain when you set healthy boundaries is pretty cool. Your amygdala, that ancient alarm system that triggers fight-or-flight responses, calms down when you feel in control of your personal space and time. It's like telling your brain, "We're safe here. We've got this covered."

The really interesting part? Setting boundaries doesn't just help you. It clarifies expectations for everyone. It's like painting those bright lane markers on a busy highway. Without them, drivers swerve unpredictably into each other creating complete chaos and dangerous accidents. With them, everyone clearly knows their designated driving space, creating much smoother traffic flow for all.

So when you clearly communicate your limits. Whether it's saying "I need to leave by 8," or "Please don't borrow my tools without asking". You're not being difficult. You're actually creating the conditions for less anxiety and more genuine connection for everyone involved.

My Journey Toward Setting Boundaries & Being Assertive

I'm the guy who says yes before you finish asking the question. Want to borrow my truck? Keys are on the counter. For reasons I'm still untangling, I'm wired to be the "yes" guy. Giving pieces of myself away like Halloween candy.

Let me tell you about our Van Life experiment. Suzy and I offer our driveway as a free overnight spot for folks traveling America in vans. We've met software engineers turned nomads, retired teachers exploring all 50 states, young couples living their dreams. About 90% have been absolute gems. Sharing stories, fixing things on our vans together, teaching us to make sourdough bread. These connections? Pure gold.

But then there was that other 10%.

First, the guy whose devil dog went after my gentle Yeti like he was made of bacon. The owner just shrugged: "Yeah, he does that sometimes." Next came the woman who wanted to rent out her shore house for profit while living in our driveway for free. And don't get me started on the guy who thought it might be ok to park his oversized RV in my front yard.

I was ready to shut everything down. Told Suzy we were done, no more van-lifers. I was building this righteous anger story about ungrateful people ruining a good thing.

Then Suzy asked one simple question: "Why don't you just say no to the ones that feel off?"

I stared at her like she'd explained quantum physics. It hadn't occurred to me that I could be selective. That saying yes to some didn't mean saying yes to all. She was right. We even had a hunch about most of the challenging guests.

Now we have the "Van Life Vibe Check." Dogs? Tell me about their temperament. Planning to profit off our hospitality? There's a Holiday

Inn down the road. Simple questions help us filter out takers while welcoming genuine travelers.

Setting boundaries isn't selfish. It's actually kind. Without them, I'd have killed the entire program. With them? We're still meeting amazing people, just without the drama. Those 90% of beautiful souls? They're worth protecting the space for. That's what boundaries really do. They protect the good stuff.

REFLECTING ON SETTING BOUNDARIES & BEING ASSERTIVE

Think about a recent situation where you said "yes" but deep down, you wanted to say "no." What made it difficult to honor your limits at that moment? And what might have happened if you had respectfully declined instead. Both for the relationship and for your well-being?

ACTION STEPS TOWARD SETTING BOUNDARIES & BEING ASSERTIVE

Let's get those boundary muscles working! Here are six practical ways to become more assertive without turning into a jerk:

- **Remember the relationship benefit:** Feel guilty saying no? Remember real friends respect limits. Saying no prevents burnout and resentment.
- **Reframe assertiveness as honesty**: Too nice to speak up? Assertiveness is simply honest communication with respect; studies show it strengthens relationships.
- **Start small to build confidence:** Afraid of backlash? Begin with a low-stakes boundary (like picking the movie); it builds courage for bigger conversations.
- **Prevent relationship poison**: Think boundaries hurt connections? In fact, clear limits prevent the silent resentment that truly damages relationships.
- **Practice in safe settings**: Not assertive by nature? Start with a

barista (ask them to fix your order); skill builds gradually in low-pressure situations.

- **Focus on the health benefits**: If you fear conflict, remember that assertiveness significantly reduces anxiety and boosts self-worth over time.

MOVING ON FROM SETTING BOUNDARIES & BEING ASSERTIVE

Setting boundaries is like drawing a map of your emotional territory: but what happens when someone accidentally (or intentionally) crosses those lines? Even with the clearest boundaries, friction is inevitable when two whole human beings try to share life together. The good news? Those moments of conflict, handled well, can actually strengthen your connection rather than damage it. Think of conflict resolution as boundary-setting in action, where you practice honoring both your needs and theirs in real time.

RESOLVING CONFLICTS CONSTRUCTIVELY
WHY RESOLVING CONFLICTS CONSTRUCTIVELY MATTERS

We've all been there: that stomach-dropping moment when tension rises and you realize you're heading into conflict territory. While your instinct might be to run for the hills (or maybe that's just me), learning to face conflicts head-on is surprisingly one of the best things you can do for your relationships and your happiness.

Resolving conflicts reduces stress by preventing the silent buildup of resentment and hurt. It's like regularly cleaning out a pipe instead of waiting for the toxic backup that requires emergency intervention. Each time you respectfully work through a disagreement, you tell your nervous system, "We can handle hard things together."

When you tackle a problem as a team, something beautiful happens. You create a shared sense of accomplishment that actually bonds you closer. It's like climbing a mountain together; the challenge itself strengthens your connection.

Constructive conflict resolution helps both sides feel heard, understood, and valued. Even when you disagree. Studies indicate that happier couples aren't those who never fight; they're those who take a solution-oriented approach to conflict, leading to higher relationship satisfaction.

You create emotional safety and closeness by addressing issues openly through respectful disagreement, non-violent communication, and active listening. Counter-intuitive as it seems, healthy conflict doesn't pull people apart. It's often the very thing that brings them closer together.

THE SCIENCE BEHIND RESOLVING CONFLICTS CONSTRUCTIVELY

Some couples can disagree about major life decisions without breaking a sweat, while others implode over dinner plans. To better understand why this is, relationship researchers Gottman and Levenson spent years figuring out this exact mystery.

Their landmark 1999 study discovered something fascinating: it's not whether couples argue that predicts relationship success. It's how they argue.[39] Couples who stayed happily married for decades weren't conflict-free; they just had specific patterns for resolving disagreements respectfully.

The researchers could actually predict with over 90% accuracy which couples would divorce based on just a few minutes of watching them argue. The magic formula wasn't about avoiding arguments, but about the relationship's overall climate. **For every one negative interaction during a conflict, successful couples had at least five positive interactions outside of it**. A shared laugh, a quick hug, a word of appreciation. This created a 'love bank' so full that a single conflict couldn't bankrupt the relationship.

Think of conflict like weather in your relationship. Storms will come. That's just nature. But how you weather those storms makes all the difference. Couples who use contempt, criticism, defensiveness, or stonewalling (what Gottman calls the "Four Horsemen of the Apocalypse") create relationship-eroding patterns.

In contrast, those who stay curious instead of furious, asking questions, validating feelings, and taking responsibility, strengthen their bond through conflict. It's like their disagreements become opportunities for deeper understanding rather than wedges driving them apart.

Learning to fight fair doesn't just save relationships. It makes them stronger and more satisfying for everyone involved.

MY JOURNEY TOWARD RESOLVING CONFLICTS CONSTRUCTIVELY

I used to pride myself on winning arguments, mistakenly equating verbal sparring with intelligence. For decades, I'd leave debates feeling victorious, oblivious to how the other person felt, all for the hollow satisfaction of being "right."

The wake-up call came from the person I love most. Suzy and I are kinda newlyweds. 14 years as of today. For both of us, it's a second chance at getting love right. But early on, I brought my debate champion routine into our marriage like it was some kind of asset.

One evening, we were discussing something trivial. I can't even remember what we were talking about. But I was in full prosecutor mode, building my case point by point. Finally, Suzy just stopped. "I don't want to debate," she said quietly. "I don't like it. You're good at debating, but I don't want to do this."

Here's where I showed my true genius: I argued with her about arguing. I actually said, and I cringe writing this, "It's not that I'm good at debating. I'm just right." I kept going, blah blah blah, completely missing the irony of debating someone about not wanting to debate.

Eventually, Suzy got increasingly tired, and then she cried. Actually cried. Over my need to be right about something so stupid I can't even remember what it was.

Seeing her tears stopped me cold. This wasn't some courtroom victory. This was me hurting the person I'd promised to love and cherish, all for the cheap thrill of winning a pointless argument.

We eventually sat down and really talked about it. Not debated, talked. That conversation shifted our entire relationship. Just having the awareness that I have this tendency has made all the difference. Now when I feel that familiar urge to launch into closing arguments, I picture Suzy's tears and ask myself: Do I want to be right, or do I want to have a great marriage?

I'm slowly learning that **being kind is far more important than being right**. And it's a whole lot easier. It turns out that "I hear you" leads to more happiness than "Well, actually…" ever could.

These days, I measure success not by whether I've changed someone's mind, but by whether we both feel heard and respected. Suzy doesn't cry during our discussions anymore. In fact, she actually seeks me out to talk about things. That's when I knew I'd finally learned something worth knowing.

Who knew that the secret to a happier marriage wasn't being right all the time? It was shutting up and listening. They should really put that in the wedding vows.

I still don't love hard conversations, and I haven't 'mastered' them. But I am a happier husband and a happier father today because I have the tools to show up for them more often and more skillfully. The quality of my life improved not when the conversations became easy, but when I became more willing to try.

REFLECTING ON RESOLVING CONFLICTS CONSTRUCTIVELY

Think about your default response when conflict arises. Do you tend to charge in, retreat completely, or something in between? How might your approach to disagreements be affecting the depth and quality of your most important relationships? What's one small shift you could make to create more constructive conversations, even when topics get heated?

ACTION STEPS TOWARD RESOLVING CONFLICTS CONSTRUCTIVELY

Ready to transform how you handle conflicts? Here are six practical ways to make disagreements more productive and less painful:

- **Take a cooling timeout**: Hot temper? Allow a 20-minute pause before discussing; even skeptics find conflicts go smoother when emotions settle first.
- **Aim to understand, not win**: Feel like conflict is a pointless battle? Shift your goal from victory to understanding. The win isn't proving you're right; it's leaving the conversation with the relationship intact. Happier couples focus on solving the problem together, not on scoring points.
- **Ask open-ended questions**: Partner shuts down in conflict? Try "What do you think about this?" instead of accusations; a collaborative tone eases defensiveness.
- **Start small and early**: Hate confrontation? Address minor issues promptly with calm "I feel" statements to prevent emotional buildup and practice respectful dialogue.
- **Own your part first**: Think apologizing means losing? In reality, acknowledging your contribution disarms tension and often prompts reciprocity from others.
- **Mind the 5:1 Ratio:** Take time to build trust outside of conflict. The healthiest relationships maintain what Dr. Gottman calls a 5:1 ratio. Five positive interactions for every one negative interaction. Make daily deposits of appreciation, affection, and shared laughter so that when conflict arises, your emotional bank account can easily cover the withdrawal.

MOVING ON FROM RESOLVING CONFLICTS CONSTRUCTIVELY

Sometimes, despite our best efforts at healthy conflict resolution, wounds happen. Words cut deeper than intended. Trust gets dented. Someone crosses a line that can't be uncrossed. This is where we face a choice that determines whether a relationship recovers and grows stronger, or slowly bleeds out from old injuries. Forgiveness isn't just the final tool in our relationship toolbox. It's often the one that makes all the others possible again. Because when we're carrying yesterday's hurt, we can't fully show up for today's connection.

PRACTICING FORGIVENESS

WHY FORGIVENESS MATTERS

We've all been there. Nursing that emotional wound from what someone said or did, replaying it in our minds like a sad movie on repeat. While it's completely natural to feel hurt when someone wrongs us, hanging onto that hurt comes with a surprisingly steep price tag.

Forgiveness isn't about excusing bad behavior or pretending everything's fine when it's not. **It's a gift you give yourself, releasing the emotional burden of anger and resentment.** Research consistently links forgiveness with greater life satisfaction and significantly less depression and anxiety.

The physical benefits are equally striking. Letting go of grudges lowers stress levels, reduces blood pressure, and improves overall health. It's as if your body physically relaxes when you unclench that emotional fist.

When you practice forgiveness, you essentially trade toxic emotions like anger and resentment for healthier ones like empathy and compassion. This emotional alchemy calms your body's stress response, making you feel more at peace in your daily life.

Perhaps most powerfully, being forgiving improves your relationships and rebuilds trust, contributing to long-term happiness. By releasing resentment and developing forgiveness techniques, you're not just healing past wounds but creating the foundation for healthier connections moving forward.

THE SCIENCE BEHIND PRACTICING FORGIVENESS

Ever wonder if forgiveness is just a nice spiritual concept, or if it actually does something measurable in your life? Researchers led by Dr. Robert Enright asked the same question in their groundbreaking research beginning in the 1990s, and what they found might surprise you.[40]

Their research showed that forgiveness therapy significantly reduced depression and anxiety while boosting self-esteem in participants. We're not talking minor improvements either. The effects were comparable to other established therapeutic approaches.

The following explains what's happening in your body when you forgive. Your stress hormones, like cortisol, actually decrease, your immune system functions better, and your heart rate and blood pressure normalize. It's as if your body has been running a constant low-grade fever of resentment, and forgiveness breaks the cycle.

Think of grudges like carrying a heavy backpack everywhere you go. You might get used to the weight, but it's still draining your energy with every step. When you forgive, you put that pack down: and suddenly you have more strength available for everything else in your life.

What's particularly fascinating is how forgiveness creates a neurological shift. Brain scans show that when people practice forgiveness, activity decreases in regions associated with negative emotions and increases in areas linked to empathy and problem-solving. You're literally rewiring your brain to process hurt differently.

The science is clear: **forgiveness isn't just about being nice. It's a powerful practice that transforms your mental and physical health from the inside out.**

MY JOURNEY TOWARD PRACTICING FORGIVENESS

My life began amidst chaos. It was a difficult upbringing with insta-bility and loss being constant companions.

Yet, looking back, it strikes me as odd that even as a child, I never truly harbored hatred towards my parents. I see now that I could have easily chosen a path of deep resentment, carrying that anger through life like a heavy piece of luggage.

The real test came when I became a parent myself. Suddenly, I under-stood both how easy it is to love a child, and how spectacularly my own parents had failed at basic care. That realization could have deep-ened my anger. Instead, it opened a door to deeper understanding.

I saw them clearly for the first time. They weren't the all-powerful figures who'd let me down. They were confused, overwhelmed young people wrestling with demons I'd never fully understand. They hadn't failed me out of lack of love. They'd failed because they were drowning in their own unhealed pain.

The forgiveness didn't happen overnight. It came in waves. Some days forward, some days back. I'd think I'd forgiven them, then another memory would surface and I'd have to forgive all over again. But each time got easier, like loosening a knot strand by strand.

The transformation wasn't just about them. It was about me. When I stopped defining myself by their failures, I could finally see my own journey more honestly. Sure, I showed up for my children in ways my parents couldn't, but I also stumbled plenty, losing my patience, making promises I couldn't keep, sometimes being the parent I needed rather than the one they needed. Yet even my imperfect presence was better than absence. Every day I tried again. I showed up as my flawed but committed self. These were my answers to the past. Not perfection, but presence. Not flawlessness, but the willingness to keep trying.

Forgiveness freed me. It felt like cutting chains I'd been dragging so long I'd forgotten they weren't part of me. This doesn't mean I emerged unscathed. I still grapple with the complexities. But I chose to transform pain into purpose, resentment into resilience. Against the odds, that choice has led to a genuinely happier life.

REFLECTING ON PRACTICING FORGIVENESS

Consider someone in your life you've struggled to forgive. Not necessarily a major betrayal, but perhaps a lingering hurt you still carry. What would it feel like to set down that burden, not for their sake but for your own peace of mind? How might your life be different if you weren't carrying that particular weight anymore?

ACTION STEPS TOWARD PRACTICING FORGIVENESS

Time to lighten your emotional load! Here are six practical ways to cultivate forgiveness in your daily life:

- **Forgive for your sake:** Reluctant to forgive? Remember, forgiveness is for your peace, not their pardon; it's linked to less anxiety and more life satisfaction.
- **Separate forgiving from excusing**: Worried forgiving means condoning behavior? Not so. You can release anger while still maintaining appropriate boundaries.
- **Write an unsent letter**: Can't move on? Pour your hurt onto paper without sending it; this private catharsis can ease resentment and start healing.
- **Try an empathic perspective**: No apology forthcoming? Consider their possible struggles without excusing harm; understanding often naturally softens anger.
- **Practice on minor annoyances**: Still fuming? Start by immediately forgiving small frustrations like rude drivers; it builds the forgiveness muscle for bigger hurts.
- **Extend self-forgiveness**: Can't forgive yourself? Imagine how you'd treat a friend who made the same mistake and offer yourself that same compassion.

WRAPPING UP THE CHAPTER

A s we wrap up our journey through these five relationship-strengthening tools, let's take a moment to see how they all work together. Because these aren't isolated skills. They form an interconnected system that transforms how we connect with others and, ultimately, how we experience life itself.

SYNTHESIZE THE SCIENCE

These tools aren't just good habits. Just like a carpenter develops muscle memory through daily use, the more consistently you practice connection-building behaviors, the more natural they become. Once again, neural pathways change, making empathy, communication, and boundaries easier over time.

The science of relationships shows us something fascinating: your brain processes social pain in the same regions it processes physical pain. That's why rejection or conflict can hurt in such a tangible way. But here's the flip side. Positive social connections trigger the same reward centers in your brain as food or other physical pleasures.

Think of your relationship skills like your truck's electrical system. At first, you might need jumper cables to get things moving, deliberate effort to use new tools. But once the engine's running, it generates its own power. The more you practice quality time, appreciation, boundaries, conflict resolution, and forgiveness, the more natural they become.

What's remarkable is how these small actions compound. A five-minute conversation, a sincere compliment, a respectful 'no': these tiny moments literally rewire your brain for better relationships.

Applying The Five Relationship Tools: Your Transformation Journey

Changing how you connect with people isn't like flipping a light switch. It's more like growing tomatoes. You plant the seeds, water them consistently, and then one day you look up and think, "Well, would you look at that! We've got ourselves some actual tomatoes here!" The transformation happens so gradually you barely notice it... until suddenly, you do.

Wondering what this transformation actually looks like in real life?

First Two Weeks: The Awkward Beginning

Those first couple of weeks feel about as natural as wearing someone else's shoes. You'll schedule "quality time" in your calendar and then stare at each other thinking, "Now what?" You'll try expressing appreciation and sound like you're reading from a script. That's normal! Your brain is literally building new pathways.

You'll notice your thoughts starting to shift, though. Instead of automatically thinking "I'm too busy" when someone wants to connect, you'll catch yourself considering how to make it work. That little pause before automatic rejection? That's the first sign things are changing.

One Month In: Finding Your Footing

By the one-month mark, using these tools will start feeling less like homework and more like, well, just how you do things. The awkwardness begins to fade. You might notice yourself taking three deep breaths before diving into a conflict conversation, or actually saying "no" to something without apologizing seventeen times afterward.

Emotionally, this is when you'll likely experience the first real payoff. That moment when expressing appreciation makes someone's entire face light up, and you think, "Huh, that felt really good." Or when you set a boundary and the world doesn't end. The relief that comes with that is like taking off your shoes that were pinching your feet all day.

In your daily life, you'll start seeing small wins. Maybe your partner mentions how nice it is that you've been really listening lately. Or you'll resolve a minor disagreement without anyone sleeping on the couch. These aren't coincidences, my friend.

Three Months: The Practice Honeymoon

Around the three-month mark, these tools stop feeling like something you're trying and start feeling like something you're living. This is when the real magic starts happening.

Your thinking patterns shift from "I should make time for this person" to "I want to make time for this person." The mental energy you once spent ruminating over past hurts gets redirected to planning your next meaningful conversation.

Emotionally, you'll likely notice a level of ease in your relationships that wasn't there before. Anxiety about whether you're connecting "right" takes a backseat to actually enjoying the connection itself. It's like when you finally learn to drive a stick shift. Suddenly you're enjoying the ride instead of worrying about stalling out.

Your relationships will start showing tangible improvements. Conversations go deeper naturally. You'll find yourself laughing more with the people you love. Little irritations that once seemed like relationship deal-breakers now just seem like... well, little irritations.

Six Months: The New Normal

Six months in, you won't remember how you did relationships any other way. These five tools have become your relationship operating system. Running quietly in the background, supporting everything else.

Your default thinking now includes other people's perspectives almost automatically. Before reacting to something, you naturally wonder, "What might be going on with them right now?" This empathetic thought pattern becomes as automatic as checking both ways before crossing the street.

The improvements in your daily life are undeniable by this point. People actively seek you out. They tell you things they don't tell others. Your relationships feel less like work and more like refuge. You've created spaces where people can truly be themselves, including you.

The Full Transformation: Your Relationship North Star

When these five tools are fully integrated into your life, your relationships become a source of energy rather than something that depletes you. You've built what psychologists call "secure attachments". Relationships where both people feel safe, seen, and supported.

This doesn't mean everything's perfect. I still mess up these tools regularly, usually when I'm angry or hungry (or both. Watch out world when Billy's hangry!). The difference is that now I have a compass to find my way back. I know what works and how to repair things when I inevitably go off course.

Remember, transformation isn't about reaching some final, perfect state. It's about changing your relationship trajectory, degree by degree, until you're heading somewhere beautiful instead of somewhere painful. I learned early on that even a one-degree change in direction will take you to a completely different place if you give it enough time.

Give these tools enough time, my friend. I promise, the view is worth it.

YOUR RELATIONSHIP TRANSFORMATION CHEAT SHEET

Let's boil all this down to a quick-reference guide you can keep handy when relationship challenges arise:

- **Schedule connection like you schedule everything else**: Relationships don't thrive on leftover time; they require intentional slots in your calendar.
- **Turn appreciation into a daily practice**: The most powerful words in any relationship are simple: "I noticed what you did, and it matters to me."
- **Draw your lines with love**: Setting boundaries isn't selfish; it's the foundation for sustainable, resentment-free connections.
- **Seek understanding before agreement**: The goal of conflict isn't to win but to create solutions where both people feel valued.
- **Release resentment to reclaim your energy**: Forgiveness isn't about excusing behavior; it's about freeing yourself from carrying unnecessary emotional weight.
- **Remember that relationships are skills, not traits**: Nobody is "just bad at relationships"; we're all learning, one interaction at a time.
- **Trust the small moments**: Life-changing connections aren't built in grand gestures but in consistent, tiny acts of showing up for each other.

This isn't just feel-good advice. It's your practical roadmap to stronger, more fulfilling connections that sustain you through life's ups and downs.

THE HEART OF CONNECTION

At the end of the day, relationship skills aren't extremely complicated: but they are transformative. We're not talking about grand gestures or perfect words. We're talking about showing up, day after day, with good intentions and heart.

I've spent too many years thinking relationships should just "happen naturally" if they're meant to be. What a load of hogwash! The truth is, meaningful connection requires the same dedication you'd give to any worthwhile endeavor. Restoring a classic car or mastering a craft.

The quality of your relationships determines the quality of your life more than any other single factor. Not your job title. Not your bank account. Not your achievements. Your connections.

And the beautiful part? These five tools are completely within your control. You don't need special talents or perfect circumstances. Just the willingness to put down your phone, look someone in the eye, and say, "You matter to me, and I'm showing up for this."

So tonight, make that call. Tomorrow, express that appreciation. Next week, have that difficult conversation. The tools are in your hands now. It's time to build something beautiful.

Remember: Relationships aren't something you have; they're something you create. One intentional moment at a time.

While deepening our closest relationships forms the foundation of connection, how we communicate within those relationships determines their quality and longevity. It's time to master the art of communication that actually connects.

CHAPTER 9:
COMMUNICATION THAT ACTUALLY CONNECTS

We've just explored five ways to transform our relationships. But here's the thing, even the strongest connections need a special glue to hold them together, meaningful communication. And believe me, this is a lesson I've had to learn the hard way.

My attempts at empathetic communication have always been like my DIY home repairs. Enthusiastic but usually requiring professional intervention. Thankfully, I live with a master. Suzy has this uncanny ability to make everyone feel understood and valued.

When one of our kids vents about troubles with their job or a friend, I instinctively gear up for full-on dad advice mode. But Suzy. She's got this gift. She'll notice our kid starting to shut down, and she'll just say something like, "Man, that really sounds awful. Doesn't it?" And you should see their face. Instant relief washing over them. Finally, someone who isn't rushing to solve their problem, but is actually trying to get what they're feeling.

I've started a mental checklist I call "What Would Suzy Do?". Wait until someone's finished speaking, ask at least one follow-up question, and resist the urge to immediately solve problems. Some days, I channel her beautifully. Others, my solutions-focused brain hijacks conversations. I'm learning that real connection isn't about having the right answers. It's about asking the right questions and genuinely absorbing the responses.

Here's the thing: most of us think we're good communicators. We've been talking since we were toddlers, after all. But there's a world of difference between exchanging words and truly connecting. The tools in this chapter aren't rocket science but relationship science, backed by research and capable of transforming even the most strained connections into sources of genuine joy.

Whether you're struggling with a teenager who communicates exclusively in grunts, a partner who feels distant, or coworkers who make you question your sanity, these four tools will help you break through the static and create real understanding. Not the superficial "I hear words coming out of your mouth" kind, but the deep "I see you, I get you, and I'm with you" kind that makes life worth living.

PRACTICING ACTIVE LISTENING

WHY PRACTICING ACTIVE LISTENING MATTERS

L et me be straight with you. Most of us are terrible listeners. We're usually just waiting for our turn to talk, mentally rehearsing our brilliant response while someone else is mid-sentence. Sound familiar? I thought so.

This matters because when your partner feels truly heard, they're not just happier. They're better equipped to handle life's inevitable dumpster fires with you. Scientists have discovered that couples who practice attentive listening navigate stress better and report higher satisfaction. It's like relationship superglue.

Good listening isn't just about making others feel warm and fuzzy (though that's a nice bonus). It actually prevents those frustrating "that's not what I meant!" arguments that can spiral into days of cold-shoulder treatment. When you listen mindfully, seeking to understand rather than just waiting to respond, you're building an emotional safety net that transforms relationships from transactional to transcendent.

The payoff is enormous: deeper trust, genuine closeness, and the kind of intimacy that can't be faked. This changes everything because it costs you nothing but a little patience and attention.

THE SCIENCE BEHIND PRACTICING ACTIVE LISTENING

Ever wonder why some conversations leave you feeling connected while others make you want to fake a medical emergency to escape? Science has some answers.

A fascinating study by Weger and colleagues in 2014 concluded that active listening not only feels good, it also measurably alters interactions.[41] They discovered that when someone uses active listening skills (like paraphrasing before responding), their conversation partner feels significantly more heard and supported. The incredible part is how quickly this happens: this difference is often perceived very quickly by your conversation partner, partly due to the nonverbal cues inherent in active listening, which signal engagement even before you verbally respond. The impact can feel like switching from dial-up to fiber optic in your relationship connectivity, a near-superpower in fostering connection.

Think of your brain during conversation like a TV with picture-in-picture. When you're half-listening, the main screen shows your own thoughts while the tiny box in the corner shows what they're saying. Active listening flips that arrangement. Their words get the big screen, your thoughts get the small one. This simple switch lights up different neural pathways, creating what researchers call "high-quality connections" that boost well-being for both people.

MY JOURNEY TOWARD PRACTICING ACTIVE LISTENING

Twenty years ago, at a business dinner, I desperately tried to make my point, cutting off others mid-sentence like it was an Olympic sport and I was going for gold.

The lawyer at the table set down his fork, looked me dead in the eye, and said, "Billy, do you understand you're interrupting me? You're moving so fast you're even interrupting yourself."

We laughed, but his words stopped me cold. I was so busy thinking about my brilliant next point that I wasn't present for anyone, not even letting myself finish a thought before jumping to the next one.

That moment changed how I view conversations. I began noticing the urge to interrupt bubbling up like a sneeze. Almost uncontrollable but definitely noticeable before it happens. Today, active listening remains a daily practice. I still catch myself jumping in prematurely, but now I recognize the pattern and pull myself back.

The truth: people remember how you listened far more than what you said. My relationships transformed not when I found better words, but when I learned to be quiet long enough to hear the ones offered to me.

REFLECTING ON PRACTICING ACTIVE LISTENING

Think about the last time someone truly listened to you, not just waited for their turn to talk, but heard you. How did it feel in your body? What changed in that conversation because you felt understood? Now flip it around: when was the last time you gave someone else that same gift of your complete attention?

ACTION STEPS TOWARD PRACTICING ACTIVE LISTENING

Alright, let's roll up our sleeves and get practical about this listening business:

- **Catch the interruption itch:** When you're itching to interrupt, pause and take a breath instead; letting them finish shows respect and often reveals details you'd have missed.
- **Question your impact**: Do you doubt that listening matters? Remember that active listeners are consistently rated as more understanding and likable.
- **Hunt for something new**: Find it hard to focus? Challenge

yourself to pick out something new in what they're saying; this keeps your mind engaged and shows you're paying attention.

- **Fight the phone urge**: Resist checking your phone and give full attention for 5 minutes; partial attention reads as disinterest, while focus builds trust.
- **Embrace silence**: Not great with words? Remember, listening isn't about a perfect reply; it's about presence. A sincere "I understand" or even a head nod shows you're actually hearing them.
- **Holster your solutions**: Impatient problem-solver? Hold back advice unless they ask. People value suggestions more when they feel heard first; try summarizing their concerns to show understanding before responding.

MOVING ON FROM PRACTICING ACTIVE LISTENING

Moving On: From Hearing Words to Reading the Room. Now that we've learned to truly hear the words, let's tune into the music behind them. Because if what someone says is the lyric, how they say it is the melody: and the real story is in the song. Let's dive into the fascinating world of nonverbal communication, where the truth often lives in the silence between the words.

TUNING INTO NONVERBAL CUES

WHY TUNING INTO NONVERBAL CUES MATTERS

Have you ever had someone tell you, "I'm fine," while their face screams, "I'm plotting your demise"? Welcome to the fascinating gap between words and reality, my friend.

Here's the deal: what people say is just the tip of the iceberg. The vast majority of emotional communication happens through facial expressions, tone, and posture. The language your body speaks even when your mouth is trying to be polite. Evidence suggests that being "in sync" with your partner's nonverbal cues dramatically impacts intimacy. It's like you've discovered the relationship cheat codes.

Noticing these unspoken signals is like having an early warning system for relationship issues. When you can spot the slight furrow in your partner's brow or the subtle shift in their voice before things escalate, you can address concerns while they're still molehills, not mountains.

The most successful relationships aren't built by mind-readers, but by people who've simply developed the habit of paying attention to the full message. Words, tone, and body language together. It's not magic; it's just noticing what's already there. Your accuracy in reading these signals with the people you love might be the difference between a relationship that thrives and one that just survives.

THE SCIENCE BEHIND TUNING INTO NONVERBAL CUES

Think you're getting the full story from just listening to words? Science says you're missing a huge part of the message. While specific percentages vary and are often debated, landmark research in nonverbal communication (with key contributions from researchers like Albert Mehrabian and Judith A. Hall) has highlighted that nonverbal cues, like tone of voice, facial expressions, and body language, carry a vast majority of the emotional and attitudinal content in our interactions, especially when feelings are involved.[42, 43]

The following explains what happens in your brain when you tune into nonverbal cues: specialized cells called mirror neurons fire both when you perform an action AND when you see someone else perform it. It's basically a biological empathy machine. When someone smiles genuinely, your brain prepares your facial muscles to smile back before you're even conscious of it. This unconscious mimicry creates emotional contagion. We literally "catch" feelings from each other through body language.

The research gets even cooler: couples who accurately read each other's nonverbal signals show significantly higher relationship satisfaction and lower stress levels. It's like having an emotional GPS that helps you navigate around potential relationship potholes before you hit them.

And the best part? Unlike learning a foreign language, you're already fluent in nonverbal communication. You just need to start paying conscious attention to what your instincts are already picking up.

MY JOURNEY TOWARD TUNING INTO NONVERBAL CUES

I stumbled upon a superpower hiding in plain sight. The ability to read what's never spoken. Though "stumbled" is generous. More like "crashed into it headfirst out of sheer desperation."

Reading nonverbal cues doesn't come easy to me. Never has. But twenty years ago, life threw me into the deep end of the body language pool when I adopted my two sons from Russia. They were 4 and 5 years old, straight from the streets of Russia, and they spoke exactly zero English. I spoke exactly zero Russian. You can see the problem.

Picture this: two little guys who'd survived God-knows-what, suddenly living with me and my family. They had no idea what to do with this mixed-up American guy trying to give them my best version of a normal life. We couldn't exchange a single word beyond our pitiful set of phrases like "Do you want chicken?" But I had to figure them out fast, because these kids could go from zero to nuclear meltdown in seconds.

So I became a student of the tiniest movements. The way their shoulders would tense before a fight. How their eyes would dart toward the door when they felt trapped. The little fists clenched when they got overwhelmed. I watched them like my life depended on it: because honestly, in church on Sundays, it kind of did.

My secret weapon? "Do you want chicken?" Somehow, this magical phrase could stop an uprising mid-launch. Kid's face turning red, fists balling up, looking ready to flip a pew? "Do you want chicken?" Instant de-escalation. To this day, I have no idea why it worked. Maybe it was the familiarity, maybe the promise of food, or maybe they just thought I was so weird they forgot to be angry.

One evening, I noticed them huddled together, whispering and pointing. Full-on strategy mode. Their body language screamed "conspiracy," and I got nervous. These two could've been planning anything from a midnight food raid to burning down the house. So I did what any rational parent would do: I called my Russian-speaking friend and left my phone hidden in the room like some kind of suburban spy.

He listened for twenty minutes, then called me back laughing. "Billy, they're planning to steal some cookies and hide under the bed." All that suspicious body language? Just two hungry kids being kids.

But here's where the magic happened. Over months, their rigid shoulders relaxed. The darting eyes started making actual eye contact. The defensive postures melted into something softer. And then one day, instead of watching for danger signals, I realized I was seeing trust. Love, even.

We couldn't say it in words, but our bodies spoke volumes. Wrestling matches that started cautious became full-on giggle fests. Hugs that once felt like capturing wild animals turned into little boys melting into safety. We built an entire language out of gestures, expressions, and the occasional "Do you want chicken?"

This completely upended my understanding of communication. I realized words were just the subtitle track. The real story? It's written in shoulders, eyes, hands, and hearts. Those boys taught me that when you can't speak the same language, you better learn to read the silence. And sometimes, that's where the most important conversations happen anyway.

REFLECTING ON TUNING INTO NONVERBAL CUES

When was the last time you noticed a disconnect between what someone said and what their body was telling you? How might your relationships change if you started giving as much weight to how something is said as to what is being said? Consider one person in your life. What nonverbal patterns have you never consciously noticed before?

ACTION STEPS TOWARD TUNING INTO NONVERBAL CUES

Let's get practical about reading the signals that speak louder than words:

- **Start small and specific**: Think you're bad at reading people? Focus on noticing just one nonverbal cue (fidget, tone change) in your next conversation. With practice, you'll train yourself to catch emotional signals you used to miss.

- **Recognize the numbers**: Believe body language is overrated? Actually, most emotional communication happens nonverbally, making it the majority shareholder in meaning.

- **Build eye contact gradually**: Uncomfortable with eye contact? Try looking at someone's face just briefly to read their expression; even a quick glance can reveal emotion, and you'll build comfort over time.

- **Check rather than assume**: Afraid of misreading signals? It's okay to double-check: "You seem quiet today. Are you okay?" Clarifying prevents false assumptions and shows you care enough to notice.

- **Turn observation into a game**: Not naturally observant? Make it fun: during each interaction, spot one nonverbal detail (clenched hands, smiling eyes). This keeps you engaged and, over time, sharpens your ability to read emotional cues.

- **Practice with muted media**: Tech-savvy but unsure emotionally? Use a video with no sound (mute a TV show or TED talk) to practice reading nonverbals. This fun exercise builds your decoding skills in a low-pressure way.

MOVING ON FROM TUNING INTO NONVERBAL CUES

Moving On: From Noticing Cues to Understanding Feelings. We've learned to read the room, but reading the room isn't the same as reading a heart. Noticing a furrowed brow is a skill; understanding the worry behind it is a superpower. Let's move beyond observation and develop that critical superpower: empathy.

PRACTICING EMPATHY
WHY PRACTICING EMPATHY MATTERS

Remember the last time someone really got what you were going through? Not just nodding along, but understanding your experience? That feeling of being seen is like emotional oxygen. We all need it to thrive.

Empathy isn't just nice to have; it's essential for our happiness. Research consistently shows that people who regularly practice empathetic engagement report significantly higher life satisfaction and overall well-being. It turns out that understanding others actually helps us feel less alone ourselves. Weird how that works, right?

But the benefits go beyond just feeling good. Empathetic people are more likely to engage in acts of kindness and volunteering, which creates a positive feedback loop. Helping others boosts your mood, which makes you more likely to help again. It's like a perpetual happiness motion machine.

Empathy is the secret sauce in your closest relationships that makes forgiveness possible and conflicts manageable. It's hard to stay angry at someone when you genuinely understand where they're coming from. And let's be honest. In a world where we're all just trying our best, a little understanding goes a long way toward making daily life not just bearable, but beautiful.

THE SCIENCE BEHIND PRACTICING EMPATHY

Some people glide through relationships like they've got the secret playbook, while others stumble through one emotional minefield after another. Science offers some potent clues: and empathy is sitting right at the heart of it.

Empathy isn't a fixed superpower; it's a skill honed with practice, leading to better cooperation. Consider research by Adam Galinsky and Gordon Moskowitz: in their 2000 study published in the Journal of Personality and Social Psychology.[44] Participants wrote an essay imagining a day in an elderly person's life. The results were significant: this exercise reduced their stereotyping and increased the perceived overlap between themselves and the elderly. By imaginatively stepping into another's shoes, participants saw the 'other' as more like themselves, effectively breaking down 'us vs. them' biases.

This kind of perspective-taking is a powerful way to kickstart empathy. The following explains what happens in your brain, and it's pretty amazing: when you practice empathy, your prefrontal cortex (the sophisticated "thinking" part of your brain) and your limbic system (the ancient "feeling" part) light up and work in concert. This dynamic duo creates what neuroscientists call "cognitive empathy" (I get what you're thinking) and "emotional empathy" (I get what you're feeling), operating together. It's like having both the detailed architectural blueprint and all the quality building materials you need for a solid connection.

The most fascinating part? This dual activation, really getting someone else's world both logically and emotionally, actually helps to calm down your amygdala. That's your brain's built-in alarm system, the part that can make you reactive and defensive during difficult conversations. So, when you're truly practicing empathy, it's like you're engaging emotional shock absorbers, allowing you to cruise more smoothly over life's bumpiest relational roads. Instead of bracing for impact, you're equipped to understand and connect.

MY JOURNEY TOWARD PRACTICING EMPATHY

I used to think empathy was just a fancy word for being nice. Turns out I couldn't have been more wrong. The hardest lesson came from being on the receiving end of well-meaning "help" when all I needed was someone to hear my hurt.

As I mentioned earlier, my siblings and I were separated at an early age. Fifty-plus years later, that hurt still stings. When I was 13, my mom decided to leave New Jersey for Florida. I decided to stay. That decision separated us 1,000 miles apart for the rest of our lives.

During one visit to Florida, I needed to share something that had been eating at me for decades. We were sitting at a bar on the boardwalk. The same kids who used to share bunk beds, now with gray in our hair and a lifetime of separate stories between us, trying to bridge fifty years of distance over beers and ocean breeze.

"I need to tell you both something," I started, throat already tightening. "I'm sorry. I should have come with you. I was the oldest. Maybe if I'd been there..." The words tumbled out, five decades of regret spilling onto that weathered bar top.

Before I could finish, they both jumped in. "Billy, no! You were just a kid!" "It wasn't your fault!" Their words overlapped, desperate to absolve me.

I know they meant well. But with each interruption, I felt more frustrated. I didn't need them to fix my guilt. I needed them to understand the weight of it.

Finally, I pulled the big brother trump card: "Both of you, stop. Please. Just let me finish. Don't fix it. Don't make it better. Just hear me."

The silence was thick as Florida humidity. But they listened. Really listened. As I laid out five decades of wondering if they'd had someone to protect them from bullies or help with homework, they just sat there. My sister crying. My brother reaching for my hand.

The freedom I felt after they truly heard me? Like setting down a back-pack full of rocks I didn't know I was carrying. That release could never have come from them telling me it wasn't my fault. It came from them witnessing my pain without trying to edit it.

That moment taught me how often I'd been rushing to fix instead of sitting in discomfort. Now when someone shares their pain, I remember that boardwalk bar. The greatest gift we can offer isn't wisdom. It's presence.

Though I'll admit, keeping my mouth shut when I have a perfectly good solution is still harder than watching someone eating soup with a fork. But I think that experience accidentally taught my brother and sister how to listen with empathy. As their big brother, I'm totally taking credit for that. It just took me fifty years and a complete emotional breakdown to deliver the lesson.

REFLECTING ON PRACTICING EMPATHY

Think about a recent disagreement where you felt misunderstood. How much energy did you spend trying to make your point versus trying to understand theirs? What might have changed if you'd approached the conversation with curiosity instead of conviction? How might your closest relationships transform if you made under-standing, not agreement, your primary goal?

ACTION STEPS TOWARD PRACTICING EMPATHY

Time to turn understanding into action with these empathy-building moves:

- **Build your empathy muscle**: Not naturally empathetic? Each day, imagine yourself in someone else's situation for one minute. Regular perspective-taking practice increases empathy over time, just like reps at the gym build strength.
- **Seek understanding, not agreement**: Think empathy is too touchy-feely? Remember, it's about understanding, not

agreeing. If you're a logical type, ask "What might they be feeling?" and you'll gain insight without getting sappy.

- **Get curious with opponents:** Hard to empathize with someone you disagree with? **Swap judgment for curiosity** by asking about their story. You don't have to agree, but understanding their perspective humanizes them and can reveal common ground.
- **Create emotional boundaries:** Overwhelmed by others' emotions? Remind yourself, "their feelings are theirs, not mine." Empathy means acknowledging their pain, not absorbing it. This mental boundary lets you care without burning out.
- **Recognize the peace dividend**: Think empathy won't change anything? Actually, showing understanding can de-escalate conflicts and strengthen relationships faster than proving you're right ever will.
- **Take a fictional empathy workout:** Want a fun empathy workout? Read a novel or watch a character-driven film and put yourself in the protagonist's shoes. Research suggests engaging with stories boosts empathy by exposing you to diverse perspectives.

MOVING ON FROM PRACTICING EMPATHY

Moving On: From Understanding Others to Being Understood. Empathy builds a bridge to someone else's world, but connection is a two-way street. A bridge that only carries traffic in one direction isn't a bridge. It's an observation deck. The final, bravest step is to allow others to cross over to our side. Let's explore the transformative power of lowering our own shields through vulnerability.

SHARING AUTHENTICALLY & VULNERABLY

WHY SHARING AUTHENTICALLY & VULNERABLY MATTERS

R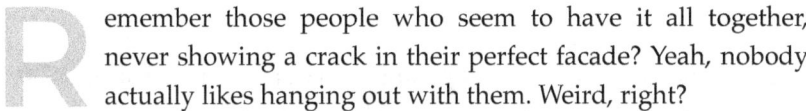emember those people who seem to have it all together, never showing a crack in their perfect facade? Yeah, nobody actually likes hanging out with them. Weird, right?

Here's the truth: authenticity isn't just some buzzword from your company's mission statement. It's the foundation of genuine human connection. Research consistently shows that people who express their true thoughts and feelings report significantly higher life satisfaction and lower psychological distress. Turns out, maintaining a perfect image is exhausting, while being real is rejuvenating.

When you open up about your struggles and fears, you're building bridges of trust with others. Even sharing quirky opinions matters. These vulnerability bridges are the only way to reach the island of genuine intimacy. There are no shortcuts.

Most importantly, sharing your authentic self relieves that heavy burden of shame or fear many of us carry. There's something incredibly freeing about being known, really known, and discovering you're still accepted. It's like finally taking off shoes that are two sizes too small after wearing them all day. The relief is immediate, and you wonder why you put up with the discomfort for so long.

THE SCIENCE BEHIND SHARING AUTHENTICALLY & VULNERABLY

Think vulnerability makes you look weak? Science suggests exactly the opposite, thanks to something called the 'beautiful mess effect.' Research, such as a key 2018 study by Anna Bruk and her colleagues, found there's a fascinating mismatch: we tend to view our own vulnerability much more negatively than we view it in other people.[45] While we might fear being judged harshly for sharing our imperfections or struggles, observers often see these displays of openness more positively, perhaps as courageous, authentic, or relatable. So, when college students, for example, are more open about their emotions and challenges with peers rather than trying to appear perfect, it stands to reason they'd be seen as more likable and approachable. Peers can connect with that realness.

Let's break down what's happening in your brain: when you share something vulnerable, your body releases oxytocin, often called the "bonding hormone." It's the same chemical that floods your system when you hug someone you love or pet a dog. This oxytocin release creates a neurological foundation for trust and connection that simply can't be established through surface-level interactions.

The research gets even more interesting: brain scans show that when someone shares vulnerability with you, your neural patterns actually begin to synchronize with theirs. Scientists call this "neural coupling," and it's a physical representation of that feeling when you're completely in sync with someone. It's like your brains are doing a dance together, and vulnerability is what gets the party started.

Most compelling of all, longitudinal studies show that people who regularly practice authentic self-disclosure report significantly lower levels of stress hormones like cortisol. Being real doesn't just feel better emotionally. It's measurably better for your physical health.

MY JOURNEY TOWARD SHARING AUTHENTICALLY & VULNERABLY

One of the upsides of having to navigate chaos in life is that sharing the struggle almost becomes a requirement. I never set out to be vulnerable. It was simply the language of survival in my unpredictable world.

In those rough high school years following Dad's death, while other kids seemed to float through life on steady ground, I caught the attention of unexpected mentors. Teachers, family friends, and relatives who stepped up. After one particularly raw conversation where I'd laid everything bare, my English teacher looked me straight in the eye: "You have a resilience most adults never develop." But it wasn't just his recognition that changed me: these talks cracked something open inside me, teaching me to speak from the heart instead of hiding behind the armor I'd been wearing.

That unexpected validation created safe spaces where honesty felt possible rather than dangerous. The impact of those early connections rippled through my adult relationships, making openness my default rather than something I had to learn.

Looking back, I recognize that what others view as courage was actually just survival. I simply couldn't maintain both chaos and facades simultaneously. I didn't have the bandwidth to craft a perfect image while my world was falling apart, so I just showed up as I was.

Today, vulnerability remains my most natural language, not because I'm particularly enlightened, but because necessity taught me early that authentic connection requires revealing our unvarnished truths. The lesson was simple: relationships built on carefully constructed images crumble, while those rooted in shared humanity endure.

REFLECTING ON SHARING AUTHENTICALLY & VULNERABLY

Think about your closest relationships. The ones where you feel most comfortable and accepted. How much of your true self do you share in these relationships versus others? What's one thing you've been hesitant to share with someone important to you, and what do you fear might happen if you did? What might become possible in that relationship if you took that risk?

ACTION STEPS TOWARD SHARING AUTHENTICALLY & VULNERABLY

Let's break down the walls and build some bridges with these practical vulnerability steps:

- **Start small but genuine:** Scared to open up? Begin with one trusted person. Share a mild worry or funny insecurity. Even if it's uncomfortable, vulnerability often prompts others to open up too, deepening the connection like nothing else can.
- **Recognize courage, not weakness:** Think vulnerability equals weakness? In reality, it takes guts. People often respect and trust someone more who shares authentically, because it signals confidence in the relationship.
- **Try structured sharing**: Not sure how to be vulnerable? Use structure: try the "The 36 Questions That Lead to Love" exercise of trading increasingly personal questions (proven to increase closeness between even complete strangers).
- **Gauge reactions as you go**: Afraid of oversharing? Share just one personal tidbit at first, then pause. Most people appreciate the honesty more than you expect, and you can gauge their comfort before revealing more.
- **Choose your confidants wisely**: Very private? You don't have to bare your soul to everyone. Pick one or two close friends to practice being open with. Even reserved personalities find confiding in a trusted ally lightens their emotional load.

- **Trust the reciprocity effect**: Doubt anyone wants to hear your problems? True friends do, and are often relieved when you confide in them. Share a small challenge, and you'll likely find they appreciate your trust and feel permission to open up in return.

WRAPPING UP THE CHAPTER:

As we wrap up our exploration of these four essential communication tools, take a moment to notice how they build upon each other. From listening actively to reading nonverbal cues, from empathizing deeply to sharing authentically. Together, they create something much more powerful than anyone could alone: genuine human connection.

LIFE-CHANGING CONTRASTS

The Family Dinner

BEFORE: AFTER

You're physically at the table but mentally writing tomorrow's presentation. Your teenager mentions trouble with a teacher, and you immediately launch into advice mode: "Well, you should just talk to her after class." They roll their eyes, mutter "never mind," and retreat back into their phone. You feel a familiar pang of disconnection, but blame their age. "Teenagers," you sigh to yourself, scrolling through your own notifications.

Same dinner, different presence. When your teen mentions the teacher issue, you put down your fork, make eye contact, and get curious: "That sounds frustrating. What's that been like for you?" You notice their shoulders relax as they elaborate. Instead of jumping to solutions, you reflect: "Sounds like you feel misunderstood there." The conversation flows into their deeper concerns, revealing worries you'd have completely missed before. As they talk, you fight the urge to "fix it" and instead ask what support they need. Later, they actually seek you out to share how things went, something that hasn't happened in months.

The Workplace Disagreement

BEFORE: AFTER

Your colleague proposes an idea that seems obviously flawed. You immediately point out three problems with it, feeling helpful but noticing their face harden. They defend their position, voices rise, and you both leave the meeting frustrated. "Some people just can't take feedback," you think, oblivious to how your "help" landed like criticism.

When your colleague shares their flawed idea, you get curious instead of critical: "Walk me through how you see that working." As they explain, you notice they're twisting their pen. A sign of uncertainty you'd have missed before. Instead of attacking their idea, you validate their intention: "I appreciate how innovative that approach is." Then you authentically share your concern: "I'm a bit worried about how it might affect our timeline. Have you thought about that aspect?" The conversation becomes collaborative rather than combative. You both leave with a better solution and actually look forward to working together again.

The Relationship Rough Patch

BEFORE: AFTER

Your partner sighs heavily while doing the dishes. You ask, "What's wrong?" They respond "Nothing," but their slammed cupboard doors say otherwise. Irritated by the mixed message, you retreat to another room, thinking, "If they won't tell me what's wrong, I can't help." The tension hangs in the air all evening, with neither of you addressing the real issue.

Same sigh, different response. You notice their tense shoulders and distracted gaze. Body language that speaks volumes. Instead of a perfunctory "What's wrong?" you move closer, touch their arm gently, and say, "Hey, you seem upset. I'm here if you want to talk." When they initially say "I'm fine," you take a risk with vulnerability: "I've been feeling disconnected from you lately, and it's making me sad. I miss us." Your honesty creates space for theirs. They finally express feeling unappreciated, a simple truth that would have festered into resentment in your old pattern. That evening, rather than tiptoeing around tension, you reconnect through honest conversation that leaves you both feeling understood.

These communication tools haven't just changed how you talk. They've transformed how you experience your entire life. What once felt like an exhausting game of emotional pinball now feels like flowing downstream in a canoe. There's still effort involved, but you're working with the current of connection rather than against it.

REWIRING YOUR CONNECTION CIRCUITS

The amazing thing about these communication tools is that they don't just change your relationships. They literally change your brain.

Each time you pause before interrupting, each time you notice a nonverbal cue, each time you choose empathy over judgment or vulnerability over facade, you're literally rewiring your neural circuitry.

The coolest part? This rewiring happens fast. Scientists have discovered measurable changes in brain activity after just two weeks of practicing these communication skills for a few minutes daily. Your relationship brain is like a flexible muscle, not a rigid concrete, and it responds quickly to new patterns of use.

COMMUNICATION CHEAT SHEET

When relationships get rocky, come back to these communication fundamentals:

- **Listen first, solve second**: The most powerful response often isn't advice but the simple acknowledgment: "That sounds really hard. Tell me more."
- **Notice the full message**: Words lie, bodies don't. When someone says "I'm fine" through clenched teeth, believe the teeth.
- **Replace judgment with curiosity**: Behind every annoying behavior lies a need or fear you might recognize in yourself if you look closely enough.
- **Create safety, not perfection**: People don't connect with your achievements; they connect with your humanity. Your fears, failures, and funny stories.
- **Recognize that emotions are messages, not problems**: Feelings provide valuable information; trying to fix or dismiss them is like throwing away an important letter unopened.
- **Remember that connection precedes correction**: People rarely change their minds until they feel their current perspective has been understood and respected.
- **Choose presence over performance**: True connection happens in unrehearsed moments when you're fully there instead of thinking about what to say next.

THE ULTIMATE CONNECTION

Here's the truth about communication that most books won't tell you: it's not about becoming perfect. It's about becoming real.

The most powerful connections in your life won't come from saying all the right things or never making mistakes. They'll come from those moments when you messed up but apologized sincerely, when you admitted you were scared, when you laughed until you snorted, when you asked for help instead of pretending to have it all together.

I've spent decades studying communication, and here's my not-so-scientific conclusion: **technical skills matter less than showing up with your whole heart**. The people who make us feel most connected aren't flawless communicators. They're authentic ones who make us feel safe enough to be authentic too.

These four tools, listening actively, reading nonverbal cues, practicing empathy, and sharing vulnerably, aren't separate skills but facets of the same gem: genuine human connection. When practiced together, they create something greater than the sum of their parts. Relationships where people can be fully seen, deeply understood, and truly valued.

So here's my challenge to you: **Don't aim for communication perfection. Aim for communication authenticity. Because at the end of the day, we don't remember the people who spoke eloquently. We remember the ones who made us feel understood. And that's a superpower available to every single one of us.**

As we master the art of authentic communication in our closest circles, we can expand our focus to building meaningful connections throughout our communities. Because true happiness comes not just from deep individual relationships, but from feeling connected to the world around us.

CHAPTER 10:
FROM ISOLATION TO COMMUNITY

We're lonelier than ever in a world of eight billion people. I learned the antidote to this modern plague not in any self-help book or therapy session, but while making chicken salad sandwiches in my kitchen after a hurricane.

After Hurricane Sandy devastated our Point Pleasant community in 2012, our family started making sandwiches for recovery crews. We delivered them to workers in damaged neighborhoods. This modest gesture unexpectedly led us to an 80-year-old man in medical distress and his special needs son. The father couldn't walk, and when the ambulance arrived, the team explained that overwhelmed hospitals couldn't admit him.

Without much deliberation, we offered our unused RV as temporary housing. What began as practical resource sharing unexpectedly transformed both our families, teaching us that community emerges through small decisions to notice and respond to others' needs. The father's primary concern wasn't for himself but for his son's future after he was gone, a worry that resonated deeply with our own parental instincts.

In the months that followed, as we helped secure permanent housing for the son and sat with the father during his final days, I realized community isn't something you discover. It's something you create through countless small decisions to notice others' needs. The irony wasn't lost on me: in our simple attempt to offer help, we had inadvertently formed the very connections that give life its deepest meaning.

PERFORMING ACTS OF KINDNESS
WHY PERFORMING ACTS OF KINDNESS MATTERS

There's something magical that happens when you hold the door for a stranger or send a surprise text to an old friend. It's not just your imagination. When you perform an act of kindness, your brain releases feel-good chemicals like dopamine and oxytocin, creating what scientists call a "helper's high". It's like getting a natural mood booster without the side effects or the price tag.

What amazes me is how little it takes. We're not talking about grand gestures that require planning committees and fundraising campaigns. Even the smallest kindness, a genuine compliment, a thoughtful text, grabbing coffee for a coworker, can significantly boost your mood and well-being. These tiny moments of connection act as happiness micro-doses throughout your day.

The benefits go beyond just feeling good. Kindness literally changes your body's chemistry, lowering those pesky stress hormones like cortisol and reducing your blood pressure. Your body relaxes, your mind clears, and suddenly that presentation you've been worrying about doesn't seem so overwhelming after all.

Researchers have found that people consistently report feeling happier and less lonely during weeks when they perform more kind acts. Think about that. The antidote to loneliness isn't necessarily having more friends; sometimes it's just being kinder to the people already around you. Generosity creates a sense of purpose and connection that turns everyday interactions into meaningful moments. Those brief exchanges remind us we're all in this messy human experience together, and that awareness alone can dramatically increase your happiness.

THE SCIENCE BEHIND PERFORMING ACTS OF KINDNESS

When Sonja Lyubomirsky and her team studied kindness in 2005, they discovered something that might sound obvious but is actually profound: regular acts of kindness significantly enhance happiness and life purpose.[46] But here's the interesting part. They found that how you perform these kind acts matters almost as much as doing them at all.

Think of kindness like exercise for your happiness muscles. Their research revealed something surprising: concentrating several kind acts into one day per week boosted happiness more than spreading them thinly throughout the week. The key insight? Intentional engagement in kindness, however you structure it, contributes to sustained well-being.

But here's the interesting part. How you perform these kind acts matters. Their research revealed something surprising. Think of it like exercise for your happiness muscles: a single, focused 'kindness blitz' once a week, like a dedicated weekly workout, boosted happiness significantly more than spreading the same kind acts thinly throughout the week. This suggests that intentional, concentrated effort creates a more powerful and lasting mood boost.

MY JOURNEY TOWARD PERFORMING ACTS OF KINDNESS

I just hit one of those big birthdays. The kind with a zero after it. Even though I'm no spring chicken, I still found myself deeply moved by the simplest gestures. A text saying "Happy birthday, Billy," with perhaps two sentences recalling a moment we'd shared, could make my entire day brighter. Just a minute of someone's time had that power.

As birthday wishes rolled in, I confronted an uncomfortable truth: I rarely extend the same kindness to others. Partly because I'm admittedly lazy sometimes, but more honestly, I overcomplicate these small gestures, believing they must be perfectly crafted to matter. This paralysis of perfection has kept countless kind messages unwritten, unsent.

This realization struck me while reading a heartfelt message from an older friend. He referenced an old wrestling story from when he coached me as a kid. A memory we'd probably retold dozens of times. That simple acknowledgment of our shared history made my entire day.

I came to realize that kindness doesn't require eloquence. Just sincerity and the courage to press "send." The most meaningful gestures aren't polished performances but authentic moments of connection. For all who take time for those simple hellos, thank you. You've not only brightened my life but also taught me the profound impact of imperfect but timely kindness.

REFLECTING ON PERFORMING ACTS OF KINDNESS

When was the last time a small gesture from someone else completely changed your day? What was it about that moment that made it so meaningful? Now flip that around. What small gesture could you offer today that might create that same feeling for someone else?

ACTION STEPS TOWARD PERFORMING ACTS OF KINDNESS

Alright, folks, enough chit-chat. Let's roll up our sleeves and get kind:

- **Challenge your skepticism**: Doubting that small acts matter? Even brief kindnesses trigger a helper's high (oxytocin release reduces stress).

- **Attach kindness to routines**: Too busy for grand gestures? When buying your coffee, grab one for a coworker, too. No extra time needed, and you'll still get a mood boost and a stronger community feeling.
- **Try anonymous kindness:** Shy about talking to strangers? Leave a kind note or pay for someone's coffee without making it a big interaction. Watching the impact from afar builds confidence for more direct acts later.
- **Keep it targeted**: Worried your gesture might be awkward or unwanted? Offer help with a task you know someone dislikes or give a sincere, specific compliment. Targeted kindness feels natural and is rarely misinterpreted.
- **Embrace simplicity**: Feel silly being nice? It's not about grand heroics; quiet, simple acts count. Studies show even small kindnesses boost happiness for the giver and receiver.
- **Use kindness as medicine:** Having a bad day? Doing something kind can lift you, too. It might feel counterintuitive, but helping others boosts your own mood.

MOVING ON FROM PERFORMING ACTS OF KINDNESS

Now that we've explored how small acts of kindness can transform both your day and someone else's, let's expand our view a bit. What happens when we take that generous impulse and channel it into something more structured? That's where our next practice comes in. Contributing through volunteering, where those momentary sparks of connection can grow into sustained flames of purpose and community.

CONTRIBUTING THROUGH VOLUNTEERING

WHY CONTRIBUTING THROUGH VOLUNTEERING MATTERS

Whenever someone brings up volunteering, I see that flicker of guilt cross people's faces. The "I know I should, but who has the time?" look. I get it. Between work deadlines, family obligations, and trying to maintain some semblance of a social life, adding one more commitment feels impossible. But research has consistently shown that volunteering isn't just another obligation draining your energy. It's actually a powerful source of psychological well-being, life satisfaction, and yes, genuine happiness.

The benefits go far beyond just feeling good about helping others. Studies have found that regular volunteers experience notably lower rates of depression, anxiety, and stress-related problems. It's like your brain rewards you for showing up for others by dialing down the volume on your own worries. When you volunteer, your brain releases dopamine: that feel-good neurotransmitter, while simultaneously reducing stress hormones. The result? You walk away feeling both more relaxed and more energized, a combination that's pretty hard to beat.

What's particularly fascinating is how volunteering provides something many of us secretly crave: purpose. In a world where we're often reduced to our productivity or paycheck, giving your time freely reminds you of your value beyond economic measures. This sense of meaning and contribution boosts self-esteem and creates a deep satisfaction, especially as we age and may question our continued relevance.

Perhaps most surprisingly, volunteering expands your social network in ways that feel natural and meaningful. Unlike the awkwardness of trying to make friends as an adult in other contexts, volunteering connects you with people who share your values across age, background, and experience. These connections create a support system that extends far beyond the volunteer site, and strong social connections are consistently linked to greater happiness and resilience. When life inevitably throws challenges your way, these relationships become the safety net you didn't know you were building.

THE SCIENCE BEHIND CONTRIBUTING THROUGH VOLUNTEERING

When researchers like Jenkinson and his team dug into the relationship between volunteering and mental health in 2013, they found something that might make you rethink your packed schedule.[47] Their comprehensive review showed that volunteering doesn't just make you feel good momentarily. It significantly reduces depression and increases life satisfaction over time.

Think of volunteering like a mental health multivitamin. Just as you might take supplements to address specific physical needs, regular volunteering supplements your psychological well-being in ways that are both preventative and therapeutic. Research demonstrates how volunteering actually generates a "helper's high". Whereas random acts of kindness provide you with fleeting bursts of joy, regular volunteering produces a more long-term positive impact, similar to the distinction between sprint and marathon running for mental well-being

What's particularly interesting is the bidirectional relationship they discovered. Not only does volunteering improve your mental health, but better mental health makes you more likely to volunteer, creating a positive upward spiral. It's like installing solar panels on your happiness house. Once they're in place, you're generating positive energy that powers everything else.

The most compelling finding might be what neuroscientists call "the compassion pathway." When you consistently engage in helping behaviors, you're actually strengthening neural connections that make compassion your brain's default response rather than judgment or indifference. Just as practicing piano rewires your brain for music, practicing kindness through volunteering rewires your brain for connection: and that's a skill that pays dividends in every area of your life.

MY JOURNEY TOWARD CONTRIBUTING THROUGH VOLUNTEERING

My relationship with volunteering resembles my approach to exercise. Enthusiastic bursts followed by mysterious disappearances. We've opened our home to guests from the local 'Tent City' homeless shelter, helping with everything from building tents to drivers test prep. What started as a 'good example for the kids' quickly became more complicated when real humans with real struggles entered our lives, some staying for weeks at a time.

But the commitment waxes and wanes. There have been times when, despite our best intentions, we've been 'too busy' to even show up for sandwich-making duty. I remember one of those times vividly. We were getting ready to go to Costco for lunch meat, and I was mentally calculating if we could even afford it, especially since our own children qualified for reduced lunch at the time. I hesitated, suggesting maybe we should skip it this month.

Then my daughter said with startling clarity, 'Dad, we have hope for a better future. Some of these people don't.'

That sentence hit me harder than any lecture ever could. We went to Costco. I'm still learning the delicate balance between generosity and boundaries. How to give meaningfully without burning out. But her words taught me that volunteering isn't about what you have in your wallet; it's about the hope you have in your heart. It's about showing up with whatever you have to offer, even when it's not perfect.

REFLECTING ON CONTRIBUTING THROUGH VOLUNTEERING

What skill or gift do you have that others might benefit from. Something that feels so natural to you that you might not even recognize its value? And what's one small way you could share that gift, even if just for an hour this month?

ACTION STEPS TOWARD CONTRIBUTING THROUGH VOLUNTEERING

Let's cut to the chase. Here are 6 easy ways to jump in:

- **Start small but consistent**: No time to volunteer? Even a small commitment helps. Volunteering just 1–2 hours a week is linked to better mood and less depression.
- **Focus on what you enjoy**: Feel you have no skills to offer? Most causes just need willing hands for basic tasks. Better yet, volunteer in an area you enjoy so you feel useful and confident.
- **Make it social:** Intimidated to go alone? Bring a friend or join a group event. People stick with volunteering longer when it's social and fun.
- **Reframe the benefits**: Think volunteering is only for do-gooders or retirees? It benefits you too. Even busy young adults gain purpose, skills, and networks. Try a one-off event to test the waters.
- **Set boundaries upfront:** Worried about burnout? Set clear limits: volunteer one Saturday a month or for a 3-month project. Defining boundaries prevents fatigue, so you can contribute consistently.
- **Use matchmaking services**: Unsure where to start? Use volunteer-matching sites to find opportunities by interest and

schedule. Choosing a cause you care about keeps you motivated as the initial excitement fades.

MOVING ON FROM CONTRIBUTING THROUGH VOLUNTEERING

While volunteering connects us to a cause we care about, our happiness is also deeply tied to the ground beneath our feet. The next tool helps us transform our street from a collection of houses into a genuine community, where belonging is built one neighbor at a time.

BUILDING COMMUNITY CONNECTIONS
WHY BUILDING COMMUNITY CONNECTIONS MATTERS

I n our hyper-connected digital world, it's ironic how many of us feel profoundly disconnected from the actual humans living around us. We can video chat with someone across the globe, but barely nod to the neighbor whose driveway meets ours. Yet research consistently shows that a strong sense of community belonging is directly linked to better mental health and happiness. The faces you see regularly at the dog park, corner café, or neighborhood block party aren't just familiar backgrounds in your life. They form a crucial social fabric that supports your well-being.

This sense of community provides something social media can't replace. Genuine support during tough times. When life inevitably throws challenges your way, a health scare, job loss, or family emergency, these local connections become your first line of support, reducing stress and combating isolation when you need it most. The neighbor who brings over a casserole or grabs your mail when you're sick might not be your closest friend, but those small acts create a safety net that catches you before you fall too far.

There's something uniquely satisfying about communal activities that solo pursuits can't match. Whether it's joining a neighborhood cleanup, attending a local festival, or participating in a cookout, these shared experiences bring more joy than doing things alone. It's the difference between watching a sunset by yourself versus sharing that moment with others. The experience itself is enhanced by the connection.

Research has consistently found that active participation in community groups, whether they're centered around hobbies, faith, service, or just social connection, is strongly associated with higher happiness levels. These groups provide regular doses of belonging that satisfy our deeply human need for connection. And ultimately, that feeling of being "at home" in your community, of having your place in the local ecosystem, leads to a more satisfying, grounded, and happier life. No matter how busy or successful you are in other domains, community connections provide a unique form of nourishment you can't find anywhere else.

THE SCIENCE BEHIND BUILDING COMMUNITY CONNECTIONS

In their groundbreaking book, The New Psychology of Health, researchers C. Alexander Haslam, Jolanda Jetten, and their colleagues demonstrated something fascinating: joining community groups doesn't just give you something fun to do on weeknights. It fundamentally boosts your self-esteem and sense of meaning in life.[48] Their research showed that the more groups people identified with, the more robust their psychological health became.

Think of community connections as emotional insurance against life's inevitable storms. When Jetten's team followed people through major life transitions, like moving, changing jobs, or experiencing health challenges, those with strong community ties showed remarkable resilience. It wasn't just that these people had more support; their very sense of identity was more stable because it was anchored in multiple groups rather than a single role.

What's particularly interesting is how community connection affects your brain. Belonging activates your brain's reward centers. The same areas that light up when you eat chocolate or fall in love. But unlike those temporary pleasures, community connection provides a steady, sustainable source of well-being. It's the difference between a sugar rush and a slow-release vitamin.

When we have strong social connections with our communities, our bodies utilize beneficial neurochemical reactions we've previously discussed. Raising the bonding hormone oxytocin and lowering cortisol, the stress hormone. My doctor friends might prescribe medications for anxiety or depression. Yet, many privately share that they've observed community involvement yield significant improvements for some patients, at times comparable to benefits seen with medication.

MY JOURNEY TOWARD BUILDING COMMUNITY CONNECTIONS

Building community connections is at the core of my being, not sure why. It just is. What surprised me most was discovering how these connections would fundamentally reshape my identity and relationship.

This drive led me to open a coffee shop bookstore in places where church folks could gather and make music. What began as a simple idea unexpectedly evolved into a centerpiece of our community life.

The bar in my backyard wasn't planned as a neighborhood gathering spot, but that's precisely what it became when neighbors started dropping by regularly.

I never realized how those community events that I told you about earlier would turn strangers into relatives. What started out as ordinary social interactions ended up demonstrating the profound truth regarding human bonds.

There's a vulnerability to making these invitations that I wasn't prepared for. I've faced rejection countless times, discovering that some people simply don't connect with my approach. In other words, not everyone likes Billy. I know I may be a lot sometimes.

In the end, these unexpected community connections have been worth every difficult moment. We've met wonderful people who've grown as close as family. All while sharing something as simple as a pulled pork sandwich. These experiences haven't just changed our neighborhood; they've defined who Suzy and I are as a couple in ways we never could have predicted.

REFLECTING ON BUILDING COMMUNITY CONNECTIONS

What's one small, low-pressure way you could create more connections in your immediate environment? Is there a neighbor you've been meaning to properly meet, a local shop where you could become a regular, or a community event you've been curious about but haven't made time to attend?

ACTION STEPS TOWARD BUILDING COMMUNITY CONNECTIONS

Time to get our hands dirty. Here's how you make this happen:

- **Be consistently visible:** New in town or introverted? Commit to one local event a month. Showing up regularly signals you're open to connecting, and soon, familiar faces will start to acknowledge you.
- **Start small conversations**: Feel like neighbors keep to themselves? Break the ice with small gestures: a wave, a weather comment, or offering extra garden tomatoes. Consistency builds trust. Over time, those tiny contacts often lead to real conversations.
- **Create what you seek**: No community group that fits you? Host a casual gathering around an interest and invite others. Even if only a few people come at first, you're giving folks a chance to connect. That small start can grow.
- **Remember the health benefits**: Doubt community matters? Strong social ties are linked to better health and longer life.
- **Build micro-connections**: Too busy for community meetings? Chat with your barista or a coworker you usually just nod to.

Community isn't only big events. It's also these small daily interactions that boost belonging.

- **Embrace being new**: Shy about being the outsider? Remember, every member was new once. Pick a cause or hobby you love and attend a meeting; mention you're new to the organizer. Showing genuine interest plus repeated attendance gradually turns you from an outsider to an insider.

MOVING ON FROM BUILDING COMMUNITY CONNECTIONS

Feeling at home in our neighborhood is crucial. But there's another level of connection we all seek. Not just belonging to a place, but belonging with our people. Let's explore how to find the 'tribe' that truly gets us.

FINDING & JOINING YOUR "TRIBE"

WHY FINDING & JOINING YOUR "TRIBE" MATTERS

We all know that moment, when you're with people and suddenly realize you don't have to explain yourself, tone yourself down, or justify your excitement about that obscure hobby or passion. That feeling of "these are my people" is more than just comforting. Scholarly work confirms that finding your tribe (a group you deeply belong to) significantly boosts your overall life satisfaction. In a world where superficial connections abound, finding people who share your values, interests, or outlook provides a rare sense of being truly seen and understood.

The power of belonging to a like-minded group fulfills something fundamental in our human wiring. We evolved as tribal creatures, and that ancient need for connection with people who share our perspectives hasn't disappeared just because we have smartphones and Door-Dash. When you find your tribe, whether it's fellow marathon runners, amateur astronomers, devoted dog rescuers, or passionate home bakers, you experience a unique form of happiness that comes from being in your element with others who value what you value.

Your tribe provides something social media followers can't replace. A genuine support system of people who truly understand the specific joys and challenges of your interests or life situation. Whether you're celebrating a success or navigating a setback, having people who "get it" without lengthy explanations provides validation and comfort that even well-meaning friends or family members sometimes can't offer.

Psychologists have found that identifying with a group of peers significantly boosts your self-esteem and sense of identity. When you find your tribe, you're not just gaining friends. You're gaining mirrors who reflect back aspects of yourself you value, and who affirm your choices and priorities. In a culture that often makes us question ourselves, this validation is powerfully stabilizing.

Perhaps most importantly, sharing experiences with your tribe creates a unique joy and meaning that enriches your life immeasurably. Whether it's the shared satisfaction of completing a challenging project together, the inside jokes that evolve from common experiences, or the specialized knowledge you collectively develop, these connections create a sense of belonging that makes life feel fuller, richer, and more purposeful.

THE SCIENCE BEHIND FINDING & JOINING YOUR "TRIBE"

When Haslam and his colleagues studied interest-based groups in 2018, they discovered something that contradicts our hyper-individualistic culture: joining groups based on shared passions significantly boosts happiness and belonging in ways that individual pursuits alone simply can't match.[49] Their research showed that what psychologists call "social identity", the part of your self-concept based on group membership, is a fundamental component of well-being.

Think of your tribal connections like investing in a specialized happiness portfolio. While general friendships provide broad emotional support, groups centered around shared interests or values deliver unique dividends of understanding and belonging. The science indicates that when you interact frequently with individuals who share your interests, your brain chemistry reacts accordingly, secreting that same bonding hormone we've talked about before, establishing a neurochemical sense of safety that's hard to achieve through incidental interaction.

What's particularly fascinating is how tribal belonging affects resilience. A key reason for this is empowerment; a 2015 study by Greenaway and colleagues found that identifying with a group significantly enhances our sense of personal control.[50] Research reveals that when people face challenges or setbacks, those with strong tribal connections demonstrated remarkable emotional stability. It wasn't just that these connections provided practical support; they offered something even more valuable. A sense of continuity and meaning that transcended individual circumstances.

The research revealed another surprising benefit: belonging to interest-based groups actually increases your capacity for authentic self-expression. Unlike workplace or family settings where you might feel pressure to conform to external expectations, your tribe creates a space where your enthusiasm isn't just accepted. It's actually celebrated. This psychological safety allows you to explore dimensions of yourself that might otherwise remain dormant. As scientists would say, your tribe doesn't just appreciate who you are. It creates the optimal conditions for becoming more fully yourself.

MY JOURNEY TOWARD FINDING & JOINING MY "TRIBE"

The journey of finding one's tribe has led me down numerous paths throughout my lifetime. What surprised me most was discovering how this search intensified after having children. Suddenly, I wanted them to belong to something meaningful.

Religion initially seemed the obvious answer, and I committed completely. This eventually faded away. But the revelation came when I realized belonging doesn't require grand institutions. We've discovered a world of miniature tribes that fulfill our need for connection: our fellow partiers/fisherman at the marina, the cornhole crew, football tailgate gatherings where we prepare meals for the local high school team. Our vanlife friends are cool as hell.

I never anticipated that these smaller, organic communities would provide exactly the belonging we'd been seeking. As humans, we long for connection and unity, similar to the joy of cheering for favorite teams together.

Each person plays a unique role in these tribes. Mine centers around cooking and occasionally fixing things, while Suzy naturally provides nurturing as someone everyone trusts for conversation.

These seemingly accidental tribal connections have brought blessings I never expected when I first began searching for community.

REFLECTING ON FINDING & JOINING YOUR "TRIBE"

When have you felt that unmistakable sense of "these are my people"? What was happening in that moment, and what values or interests were being shared? How might you create more opportunities to experience that feeling of belonging in your weekly life?

ACTION STEPS TOWARD FINDING & JOINING YOUR "TRIBE"

Grab a pencil or just your good intentions. It's action time:

- **Pursue your passions publicly**: Feel like the odd one out? Seek out spaces for your passions, no matter how niche. It might feel vulnerable, but those are exactly where your fellow "weirdos" gather: finding even one person who shares your passion can be a huge relief.
- **Give friendship time to grow**: Think you're too old to make new friends? Not true. Adults form bonds, it just takes time. It takes ~50 hours together to turn an acquaintance into a friend.
- **Try multiple groups**: Tried and didn't click? Finding your tribe is like dating. It may take a few tries to find the right chemistry. Don't quit after one awkward meetup; try again or try different groups. Friendships often spark with familiarity.
- **Recognize the health benefits**: Think you don't need a tribe? Even independent people benefit. Close friendships make you

happier and healthier. A supportive group gives belonging and backup when life gets tough.

- **Expand beyond geography**: No close friends nearby? Your tribe doesn't need to be local. Join an online community or professional network to find kindred spirits. Connecting beyond geography widens your chances of meeting people who truly resonate with you.

WRAPPING UP THE CHAPTER:

Now that we've explored all four community-building tools, let's step back and see how they work together to create a life rich with connection, purpose, and joy. These aren't just nice-to-have additions to your life. They're essential ingredients in the recipe for sustainable happiness.

LET'S PLAY TO WIN

Think of building community and practicing kindness as joining a championship sports team that's built for lasting success. Like any winning team, different elements must work together seamlessly, each playing a crucial role in achieving the ultimate goal. Creating a life rich with meaningful connections that support you through every season.

Small acts of kindness function as your daily practice sessions. The fundamental drills that every great athlete commits to regardless of skill level. These simple, repeated actions might seem basic, but they develop the muscle memory essential for peak performance when it matters most. Just as no championship team was built without countless hours of practice, no meaningful community exists without the foundation of everyday kindness that strengthens your connection reflexes.

Volunteering serves as your coordinated team plays. The strategic, designed movements that accomplish what individual effort cannot. When you commit regular time to causes larger than yourself, you're executing plays that create impact far beyond what you could achieve alone. These experiences build deeper bonds through shared purpose while expanding your roster beyond your starting lineup, much like how well-executed plays transform individual athletes into a cohesive, winning unit.

Building local community connections works like your home field advantage. The familiar territory and supportive crowd that energizes everything you do. These relationships with neighbors and local establishments create the everyday infrastructure of belonging that transforms a mere location into true home territory. Without this advantage, even the most talented teams eventually struggle on unfamiliar ground where they lack the crowd's energy and local knowledge.

Finding your tribe functions as your team chemistry and locker room culture. The deep bonds and shared identity that transform talented individuals into championship material. These connections with people who share your values create a sense of belonging where you're not just playing the same game but truly wearing the same jersey. Great teams aren't just collections of skilled players; they're unified by shared purpose and mutual understanding that elevates everyone's performance.

Remember my Hurricane Sandy experience? What began with the simple "practice drill" of sandwich-making (kindness) evolved into executing a larger "team play" as we provided ongoing support (volunteering). This created an unexpected "home field advantage" as we became part of these strangers' community (community connections), which ultimately led to the "team chemistry" that enriched all our lives (finding our tribe). Each community-building element built upon the others to create an impact that none could have accomplished alone.

In sports and in life, we're not meant to play solo. The most meaningful victories and the most sustainable joy come when we connect with others in purpose and presence. Every time you choose to pass instead of shoot, to celebrate a teammate's success, or to help someone up after a fall, you're not just winning the game. You're building a legacy that extends far beyond the final score.

SYNTHESIZE THE SCIENCE

All these community-building tools share something powerful beneath the surface. Each time you practice kindness, volunteer, connect with neighbors, or engage with your tribe, you're actually strengthening those darn neural pathways again that make connection your default setting rather than isolation.

For years, it's been easier to just follow those familiar paths. The habit patterns of disconnection, busyness, and isolation that modern life encourages.

What's happening biologically is fascinating. Connection-focused activities trigger the release of bonding hormones like oxytocin while simultaneously reducing stress hormones like cortisol. This chemical cocktail creates feelings of trust, safety, and belonging that reinforce the very behaviors that produced them. It's like your brain has its own reward system specifically designed to encourage connection, almost as if we evolved to function best in community (spoiler alert: we did).

The science shows that small, consistent actions create more lasting change than occasional grand gestures. A five-minute daily check-in with a neighbor does more to rewire your connection pathways than a once-a-year neighborhood blowout. It's not the intensity that changes your brain's default settings. It's the consistency and repetition.

YOUR COMMUNITY BUILDING CHEAT SHEET

When life gets hectic and you need a quick reminder of how to stay connected, keep this handy:

- **Start with sandwich-level kindness**: The smallest gestures create ripple effects far beyond their apparent impact. Don't wait until you can do something impressive; do something small today.

- **Show up consistently but imperfectly**: Volunteering isn't about heroic sacrifice; it's about regular presence with whatever you can authentically offer. Perfect attendance isn't the goal. Meaningful connection is.
- **Build your "recognition radius"**: Make it a game to recognize one more face or learn one more name each week in your regular spots. Community belongs to those who notice others.
- **Join before you feel ready**: The perfect moment to connect never arrives. Jump into communities and tribes while still feeling like an outsider; belonging comes through participation, not preparation.
- **Remove the earbuds occasionally**: Digital connection is valuable, but insufficient. Create daily pockets of availability for real-world interactions that ground you in your physical community.
- **Remember the return on investment**: Every minute invested in connection pays dividends in health, happiness, and resilience that far exceed the initial time cost. Connection is never wasted time.

Relationships are built one conversation, one act of kindness, one shared laugh at a time. You don't need to join a parade tomorrow. Just start small, stay real, and keep showing up with intention. The rest will follow.

CREATING COMMUNITY THROUGH SMALL CHOICES

Here's the beautiful truth I've discovered through all my stumbling attempts at connection: community isn't something you find like a hidden treasure or a perfect parking spot. It's something you create through a thousand tiny choices to notice, to care, to show up imperfectly but consistently. Those choices might look like making one more sandwich than you need, inviting neighbors over when your house isn't perfectly clean, or simply removing your earbuds while waiting in line for coffee.

The magic happens in the in-between moments. Not in grand gestures or carefully orchestrated events, but in the impromptu conversations, the small kindnesses, and the gradual accumulation of shared experiences that transform strangers into neighbors, neighbors into friends, and friends into family. Every time you choose connection over convenience or community over comfort, you're not just enhancing your own happiness. You're creating ripples that extend far beyond what you can see.

Remember, the sandwich you extend today might lead to connections that transform your life in ways you cannot possibly predict. In the end, we don't just build community. Community builds us, reshaping our lives into something richer, more resilient, and infinitely more meaningful than we could ever create alone.

As we've experienced the joy of learning to find our tribes and build lasting communities, the next logical step presents itself, giving back what we've learned to others. Once we get to experience the transformational power of connection, kindness, and community, we're usually moved to share these gifts with others. And that takes us to where we go next: from receiving to giving, from learning to teaching, from personal development to creating ripples that continue long after we're gone.

CHAPTER 11:

SHARING WHAT YOU'VE LEARNED

I have a confession to make about this book: I didn't start this journey for you. I did it for me. It turns out that was the best way to help us both.

I've learned these happiness tools from dozens of unexpected teachers over the years. From bestselling authors to homeless guests we sheltered, from business mentors to my insightful children. But I kept forgetting to use them. Until I started teaching them to others.

That's when everything changed. Sharing these tools didn't just help other people; it literally rewired my own brain to practice them automatically. My selfish desire to remember became something much bigger: a chance to help you help others, until maybe, just maybe, we've made this whole world a little happier. Every person who learns these tools and shares them typically teaches 3-5 others, who each teach a few more. Do the math: that's hundreds of people from your single decision to share.

I've been incredibly lucky. Dozens of people have shaped who I am today by simply saying "yes" to sharing their wisdom. Teachers and friends who saw potential I didn't know I had. Authors like Stephen Covey, whose Seven Habits opened my eyes to intentional growth.

Often the lessons came from simply watching how other people lived. How their happiness was contagious and made my heart happier. Even strangers whose names I never caught, but whose lessons stuck.

When you share these tools with others, something magical happens. Not only do you help them discover what works, but the act of teaching deepens your own practice in ways you never expected. Every time you explain a concept or share your experience, you understand it more clearly yourself. And that's exactly what this chapter is about. How sharing what you've learned becomes the most powerful practice of all.

This chapter is deliberately focused on one crucial practice, sharing what you've learned, because it's the bridge between personal transformation and community impact. **Master this one tool, and everything else we've discussed multiplies exponentially.**

I remember the first time someone asked me how I'd gotten through a particularly rough patch. I fumbled around, embarrassed, thinking I had nothing worth sharing. Then I mentioned how practicing self-compassion had kept me afloat. Their eyes lit up. Two weeks later, they told me that our talk had made a profound difference in how they were handling things. That's when I realized: we don't need to be happiness experts to help others. We just need to share what's worked for us, messy journeys and all. And that simple act of sharing? It changes everything: for them and for you.

SHARING & TEACHING THESE HABITS

WHY SHARING & TEACHING MATTERS

You know that feeling when your mood gets a serious boost after helping someone out? That's not just in your head. It's literally baked into our human operating system. When we share what we've learned about joy, we're not just being nice. We're activating one of the most reliable bliss switches in our brains.

You won't hear this often, but every time you show someone else how to practice gratitude or how to reframe a negative thought, you're not just helping them. You're strengthening your own happiness muscles. It's like trying to teach your kid to throw a baseball. You end up practicing your own throw a hundred times in the process. I can't tell you how many times I've explained gratitude to someone and suddenly understood it better myself. Teaching isn't one-way. It's a conversation where both people learn.

Plus, there's nothing that connects people faster than sharing something that matters. When you open up about your own journey toward well-being, including all the times you stumbled face-first into a puddle of self-doubt, you're giving someone practical tools they can use tomorrow morning. Those connections? They're what we call meaningful relationships, and they're absolutely essential for lasting fulfillment.

Teaching what you've learned also reminds you that we're all in this together, figuring it out as we go. Let's be real. We all want to matter to other people. When someone says "Oh, I tried that thing you mentioned and it actually helped," you realize we're all just sharing notes on this exam called life.

THE SCIENCE BEHIND SHARING & TEACHING THESE HABITS

You know that warm glow you feel after helping someone understand something new? Science has uncovered why it's so profoundly rewarding: and it goes way deeper than just feeling nice.

When you mentor someone or share your hard-earned wisdom, you're activating what psychologists call "generativity". Our deep human drive to guide others and leave the world a little better than we found it. This isn't just feel-good philosophy. Researchers have found that people who regularly engage in generative activities report significantly higher life satisfaction and sense of purpose.

The evidence is particularly compelling from intergenerational volunteering programs. When older adults help younger students: like in the well-studied AARP Experience Corps program, the benefits flow both ways.[51] The volunteers consistently report a renewed sense of purpose, increased engagement with life, and what researchers call "zest for life." They're not just passing time; they're actively shaping futures and witnessing their impact firsthand.

But here's where it gets really interesting for your own happiness practice: teaching these habits actually strengthens them in your own life. The scholarly work confirms two key mechanisms at work. First, helping others releases oxytocin: that bonding hormone that creates feelings of connection and trust. Second, explaining concepts to others reinforces your own neural pathways, making the habits more automatic for you.

Researchers call this the "protégé effect". We learn more effectively when we teach. Think of it like physical training: you get stronger not just by lifting weights yourself, but by spotting someone else. Your brain treats teaching as both a social reward and a learning reinforcement, creating what scientists term "durable well-being". The kind that lasts long after the teaching moment ends.

THE MULTIPLIER EFFECT

I'm sorry to get all number-crunchy on you, but I can't help it. I'm a numbers guy. My high school math teacher would be so proud... or possibly confused that I'm using exponential growth to track joy. But stick with me, because this math matters.

When you share these happiness tools, you're not just creating a one-to-one impact. The effect multiplies quickly: If you share a tool with three people, and they each share it with three more, twelve other lives are immediately touched.

But the impact doesn't stop there. Think about those twelve people moving through their day a bit happier. Their smiles and kinder interactions ripple outward, blessing countless others at the grocery store, at their kids' schools, and in their workplaces. The true reach isn't just in who learns the tool, but in who feels the warmth of its effect.

This isn't about theoretical people. It's about actual humans sleeping better, stressing less, and connecting more, all because of one practice you chose to share.

My Journey Toward Sharing & Teaching These Habits

I used to think I needed a fancy degree or had to be perfectly healed before I could share anything about self-care. Who was I to suggest self-compassion when I'd spent that very morning beating myself up for forgetting a friend's birthday text?

Eventually, I began talking about the beauty of self-compassion. I didn't share profound wisdom. Just how speaking to myself like I would to a loved one helped me climb out of my own funk. I felt almost silly offering such a simple tip.

But then something remarkable happened. People told me they were practicing self-compassion daily, and it was the only thing keeping them from spiraling. They were catching themselves when the inner critic got too loud. That hit me in the best way. I'd thought my little habit was too small to matter, but it created a real impact I never expected.

Half the time when I share these tools, people improve on them or tell me about better ways they've found. I started out thinking I was teaching, but really I was starting conversations where we all learned something.

That's when it clicked: we don't need to be perfect to help others. Sometimes the most powerful thing we can share is what worked for us. Messy journey and all. Now, whenever something makes my life even a little better, I look for chances to pass it on. Not as a self-compassion guru, but as a fellow traveler saying, "Hey, this path was a little easier over here."

Not everyone shares the same way, and that's perfectly fine. Some people are natural teachers who can explain concepts clearly. Others lead by example, letting their actions do the talking. Some share through stories, others through asking great questions that help people discover tools themselves. I've learned that the most effective sharing happens when you stop trying to be someone else's version of a teacher and start being your authentic self.

Early on, I tried to sound like the experts I'd learned from. Using their words, their examples, their energy. It fell flat every time. But when I started sharing my actual struggles, my failed attempts at meditation, my gratitude practice that sometimes consisted of "I'm grateful this day is over": that's when people started listening. Your imperfect practice might be exactly what someone needs to hear.

REFLECTING ON SHARING & TEACHING THESE HABITS

Before we dive into some specific ways to share your happiness habits, take a minute to reflect: Who are the people who've shared important life wisdom with you? What made their approach so effective that their lessons still stick with you today?

Now here's the challenging question: if their imperfect journey could help you, what's stopping you from believing your own messy path might be exactly what someone else needs to hear?

THE COURAGE TO START BEFORE YOU'RE READY

People rarely mention this, but sharing happiness tools: you'll never feel ready. You'll always think you need to master them first, to have your life perfectly together, to somehow become the zen master on the mountain. But that's exactly backward. The people who help us most aren't the ones who've arrived. They're the ones walking alongside us, sharing their own stumbles and victories as they happen. Sometimes they're teaching us something they just figured out yesterday. Other times we're the ones with the insight they need to hear.

Here's what sharing actually looks like: It's mentioning during lunch break that you've been sleeping better since you started that gratitude thing. It's texting a friend "Hey, remember when I was super stressed? This breathing exercise helped." It's telling your kids what you do when you're anxious. Nothing fancy, nothing preachy. Just honest sharing of what's working.

So don't wait for perfection. Don't wait until you've meditated for 10,000 hours or achieved unshakeable inner peace. Start sharing what's working today, even if it only worked once. Start with one person, one tool, one honest conversation about what's helped you get through. Because someone out there needs exactly what you've learned, delivered exactly how only you can deliver it.

ACTION STEPS TOWARD SHARING & TEACHING THESE HABITS

Ready to start passing on what you've learned? Here are seven simple ways to begin:

- **Start Small**: This week, tell one person about a specific tool that helped you. Example: "I've been doing this 3-breath thing before responding to angry emails and it's kept me from sending some real doozies."
- **Try the Buddy System**: Instead of lecturing, invite someone to join a gratitude practice or mindfulness session. Positivity is contagious when shared, and you'll both learn from the experience.
- **Schedule Mini-Shares**: Put a 10-minute weekly share on your calendar. Scientists have discovered that small, regular commitments stick better than occasional big efforts. Maybe it's coffee with a coworker where you swap what's working.
- **Experiment with Sharing**: Track your mood before and after helping others. You'll likely find that teaching lifts your own spirits. Keep it real though. Sometimes the person you're sharing with will teach you something better.
- **Live the Life you Love**: Through your courage to live your life to the max, you will encourage others as you teach by example. Actions speak volumes.
- **Find Your Tribe**: Connect with like-minded people online or in person. Social support fuels consistency and confidence in sharing practices. Plus, you'll pick up new tools from them.
- **Celebrate Small Wins**: Notice tiny victories like a friend saying "That actually helped" or "I tried it and felt better." Acknowledging these moments fuels your motivation to keep sharing.

YOUR TEACHING & SHARING CHEAT SHEET

Here's your quick reference guide for sharing and teaching happiness habits:

- **Start with vulnerability**: Share your struggles first; people connect with real experiences, not perfect success stories.
- **Ask before you offer**: "Would you like to hear something that helped me?" respects boundaries and increases receptivity.
- **Make it a two-way street**: Exchange tips rather than lecture; you'll often learn as much as you teach.
- **Right tool, right time**: Match the habit to the person's specific challenge; generic advice rarely helps anyone.
- **Celebrate their wins**: When they tell you something worked, that's gold. Their success reinforces your own practice too.
- **Show, don't just tell**: Demonstrate habits in your own life; people believe what they see more than what they hear.
- **Give without expectation**: Share because it helps, not because you need credit. The best gifts come with no strings attached.

MOVING ON FROM SHARING & TEACHING THESE HABITS

As we close this chapter, the beautiful paradox of this work comes into focus: you become most helpful precisely when you stop trying to be an expert and simply share your honest experience. The goal was never to achieve a state of flawless zen. The goal is connection.

Remember, you don't need to be perfect to be someone's perfect teacher. Sometimes the most powerful gift you can offer is the simple, honest truth: "I struggle with this too, and here's what helped me."

You've now traveled from learning to living to teaching. From receiving wisdom to sharing it forward. And that, my friend, is how we begin to change the world.

EPILOGUE

Remember that desperate 2 a.m. Google search for "how to be happy"? Look how far we've both traveled. Through 42 science-backed tools and past 37 happiness myths, you've transformed from someone searching for happiness into someone equipped to create and share it.

I started this book by being honest. I'm not a traditional happiness guru but someone who's spent six decades gathering wisdom from my own spectacular face-plants. As I sit here in my duct-taped office chair, I'm still figuring things out, still messing up, and still occasionally forgetting there's a boat trailer attached to my truck.

What has transformed is my understanding of what happens when we take this happiness stuff seriously. This journey isn't just about you anymore. In a world that feels more chaotic than ever, every person who uses even one of these tools becomes part of the solution. This is where your true legacy begins: not in what you accumulate, but in the lives you touch through the ripple effect of your own hard-won happiness.

Watch what happens:

That stressed-out parent who learns self-compassion? Picture them at 6 a.m., taking three deep breaths instead of yelling about spilled cereal.

Their kid absorbs that calm, and twenty years later, models the same patience with their own children.

The coworker who finally felt heard by you? She goes home and listens to her teenager's story without once glancing at her phone. The neighbor you invite over for dinner? He's inspired to reconnect with his estranged brother. The lonely retiree who builds community connections? They create gathering spaces that begin to heal neighborhood divisions.

Your smile becomes contagious. Your patience calms someone's terrible day. Your vulnerability creates spaces where real connection can happen. This is how we change the world. Not through a single grand gesture, but through the quiet revolution of ordinary people choosing joy.

So I hope you'll take this seriously. Because in a world that profits from your misery and feeds on outrage, choosing genuine well-being is nothing short of revolutionary. Every time you practice gratitude instead of complaint, build connection instead of isolation, or choose presence over distraction, you are healing more than just yourself.

The toolbox is yours now. Build something beautiful.

Years from now, you might not remember all 42 tools. But you will remember this: the moment you stopped waiting for happiness to find you and started cultivating it yourself. That journey changes everything.

With gratitude and hope for all our tomorrows,
Billy Marshall

P.S. Your journey doesn't have to end here. For more tools, guided practices, and to join a community of fellow builders, visit us at **www. yourhappier.life**.

And if this book helped you, do me a personal favor: pass it on. Loan it to a friend, leave it in a coffee shop, or share your favorite tool with someone who needs it. Because happiness, like love, is one of the only things that multiplies when you give it away. Couldn't we all use a little more of both?

CONNECT WITH OUR HAPPIER LIFE COMMUNITY

The journey to a happier life is better together. Join the conversation, get daily inspiration, and share your own toolbox tips with us online.

Website Hub for All Resources:

www.yourhappier.life

For Daily Inspiration & Visual Tools:

Instagram: @yourhappier.life

Join our Private Facebook Readers' Group:

facebook.com/groups/yourhappier.life

For Quick Insights & Conversation:

X: @yourhappierlife

Share your journey using

#YourHappierLifeToolbox and #YourHappierLife

APPENDIX
SCIENCE-BACKED MYTHS ABOUT HAPPINESS

Well, here we are at the myth-busting portion of our journey together. The part where we take a wrecking ball to some of the most expensive lies you've ever bought. You know what I've discovered after all these years of stumbling toward happiness? Most of us have been working with some pretty outdated information. It's like trying to navigate with a map from 1952. Sure, some of the big landmarks are still there, but you're going to miss a lot of the new roads and probably end up in a cornfield somewhere.

These happiness myths aren't just harmless misconceptions, though. They're more like those "shortcuts" your GPS suggests that end up adding an hour to your trip. They actively lead us away from what actually works. But here's what gives me hope: the research folks have done an amazing job mapping out exactly where we've been taking wrong turns. Consider this appendix your updated GPS for happiness. One that actually knows where the construction zones are.

I. THE FUNDAMENTAL NATURE OF HAPPINESS

For something we all want, we sure have gotten mixed up about what happiness actually is, haven't we?

These fundamental myths about happiness are like building your house on sandy soil. It doesn't matter how nice your house is if the foundation's not solid. The real truth about happiness is both simpler and more hopeful than what most of us learned growing up. It's not locked in stone at birth. It's not about feeling amazing every second. And it definitely doesn't just show up on its own like a pizza delivery you didn't order. Once you understand what happiness really is, and maybe more importantly, what it isn't, you've got solid ground to build something beautiful on. So let's clear up some confusion, shall we?

Happiness Is Fixed by Genetics

Why This Matters: If you believe happiness is all in your DNA, you might as well hang up your happiness hat before the game even starts. "Well, I guess this is just how I'm wired." But once you realize you can actually influence your happiness level through deliberate choices and practices, everything changes. You stop being a passenger and grab the wheel.

Scientific Counter-Evidence: Now, genetics do play a role. What the researchers call your happiness "set point." Those twin studies from

Lykken and Tellegen back in '96 had everyone thinking genes controlled about half the happiness equation.[52] But here's where it gets interesting. Lyubomirsky and her team came along in 2005 and filled in the rest of the story.[46] Yes, maybe 50% is genetic. But, and this is huge, 40% comes from what you actually DO. Your choices, your practices, your intentional activities. Only about 10% comes from your circumstances. So you've got way more control than your DNA would have you believe. Kind of exciting, isn't it?

Happiness Means Constant Pleasure (Hedonism)

Why This Matters: Living for the next thrill is exhausting, and each one delivers less punch than the last. I've been down that road. It's a dead end. Real happiness includes meaning, purpose, connection. The stuff that sticks around long after the party's over.

Scientific Counter-Evidence: The research on what they call "eudaimonic well-being" (fancy term for meaning-based happiness) tells a different story than the pleasure-seekers might expect. Ryff and Singer showed us that purpose and engagement create more lasting satisfaction than chasing thrills.[53] Huta and Ryan ran a head-to-head comparison in 2010.[54] The result? Pursuing meaning, growth, and excellence delivered way more lasting benefits than chasing the next dopamine hit. The pleasure route? Fun for a minute, gone the next. Like that expensive dinner that was great in the moment but leaves you hungry an hour later.

Happiness Means Feeling Good All the Time

Why This Matters: Thinking you need to be sunshine and rainbows every second is like expecting your boat to never rock on the water. It's just not how things work. Real well-being includes the whole emotional spectrum. Yes, even the tough parts. Once you understand that, you can stop beating yourself up for having normal human feelings.

Scientific Counter-Evidence: Davidson's brain scholarly work confirms emotions naturally rise and fall: that's not a bug in the system, it's a feature.[55] Kashdan and Biswas-Diener went even further, proving negative emotions aren't just normal, they're useful.[56] Anger helps you set boundaries. Fear keeps you from doing genuinely dangerous things. Sadness signals you need support. Meanwhile, Bryant and Veroff's work on savoring shows that appreciating good moments as they come, not trying to live in some permanent state of bliss, is what actually builds well-being.[57] It's like trying to keep the sun from setting. Exhausting and impossible.

Happiness Requires No Effort; It Just Happens

Why This Matters: Waiting for happiness to show up is like sitting on your couch expecting to get in shape. Our moods naturally roller-coaster, so without some active maintenance, you're just along for the ride. Think of well-being like tending a garden. Ignore it and watch the weeds take over.

Scientific Counter-Evidence: The evidence is pretty clear on this one: happiness takes some effort. Lyubomirsky and Layous showed in 2013 that practices like gratitude and mindfulness need constant attention, kind of like going to the gym for your mind.[58] Seligman's team found the same thing in 2005.[1] The happiness activities that actually stuck? The ones people kept doing on purpose, not the one-and-done attempts. It's like learning to play cornhole. You don't get good by playing once a year at the family reunion.

You Must Pursue Happiness Directly

Why This Matters: Isn't it weird how obsessing over whether you're happy tends to make you... less happy? It's like watching water boil or constantly checking if your bread dough has risen. The more you monitor your happiness temperature, the more it seems to drop. Focus on doing meaningful stuff instead, and happiness tends to sneak in the back door when you're not looking.

Scientific Counter-Evidence: Mauss and colleagues discovered something fascinating in 2011: people who desperately wanted to be happy ended up more disappointed, especially when good things happened.[59] Talk about irony, right? Schooler's research on what they call the "paradox of happiness" backs this up. Joy shows up when you're absorbed in something that matters, not when you're hunting for it with a net. It's like trying to catch a butterfly. Chase it and it flies away, sit still and it might just land on your shoulder.

Happiness Inevitably Declines with Age

Why This Matters: Believing aging equals misery sets you up to dread every birthday after thirty. But what if I told you many people actually get happier as they get older? Kind of changes how you think about those candles on the cake, doesn't it?

Scientific Counter-Evidence: Blanchflower and Oswald analyzed data from over 500,000 people and found something surprising. Happiness follows a U-shape.[60] It dips around 45-50 (hello, midlife questioning), then climbs back up. The massive MIDUS study confirms it. Older adults often report better emotional well-being than young folks. Turns out wisdom and life experience count for something. So those extra birthdays? They might just be taking you somewhere good.

The bottom line about happiness: It's not some fixed genetic lottery ticket, and it's definitely not about perpetual grinning. Real happiness is more like tending a garden. It takes daily work, includes some rainy days, and grows best when you're focused on the planting, not constantly digging up the seeds to check if they're happy yet. The good news? You've got way more control over this garden than you ever imagined. Now let's talk about all those shiny things we think will make it bloom...

Can't remember all these myth-busters? Here's your cheat sheet:

⬤ HAPPINESS BASICS - REALITY CHECK

✖ Your genes determine your happiness level → You control 40% through your actions

✖ Happiness = constant pleasure → Real happiness includes meaning & purpose

✖ You should feel good all the time → Emotions naturally rise and fall

✖ Happiness just happens naturally → It takes consistent, intentional practice

✖ Chase happiness directly → Focus on meaningful activities instead

✖ It's all downhill after 30 → Many people get happier as they age

II. EXTERNAL CIRCUMSTANCES AND MATERIAL PURSUITS

I can't tell you how many times I've fallen for the old "When I get [insert shiny object here], then I'll be happy" trap. Each purchase gave me a buzz, sure, but it faded faster than my enthusiasm for January gym memberships.

Our culture's got us convinced happiness comes with a price tag. More money, better stuff, perfect location. I've been down that road enough times to know where it leads (spoiler: not to lasting happiness). But the following science has figured out about money, possessions, and circumstances: and friends, it might save you from some of my more expensive mistakes. Those external things we're chasing? They matter way less than we think. And that happiness high from a new purchase? It's got about the same shelf life as gas station sushi. Let's dig into what research really says about all this stuff we think we need.

More Money Will Make You Happier

Why This Matters: Chasing money beyond meeting your basic needs often costs you the real treasures. Time with family, your health, and actually enjoying the life you're working so hard to build. Once you understand money's limited magic, you can stop sacrificing what truly matters for what merely glitters.

Scientific Counter-Evidence: Kahneman and Deaton's landmark 2010 study found something that might surprise you: day-to-day happiness pretty much levels off around $75,000 [61] (in 2010 dollars. Adjust for inflation to $110,000 in 2025). After that? Your daily mood doesn't budge much, no matter how much your bank account grows. Sure, you might feel more "satisfied" looking at your life on paper, but your actual moment-to-moment experience? Pretty much the same. This fits perfectly with something called the Easterlin Paradox. Countries get richer, but citizens don't get happier. Plus, and this one stings a bit, being obsessed with money actually makes you less happy.

Material Possessions Bring Lasting Happiness

Why This Matters: Every advertisement you see is trying to sell you the same story: buy this, be happy. But understanding how little stuff actually delivers helps you invest in what does work. Experiences and connections with people you care about.

Scientific Counter-Evidence: Van Boven and Gilovich figured this out in 2003: experiences beat possessions every single time.[35] That concert with friends, that camping trip where everything went wrong but you laughed until you cried, that cooking class where you made a complete mess. They all deliver more lasting joy than another gadget collecting dust. Why? We don't adapt to experiences as quickly. They connect us to other people. They become part of our story in ways a new TV never will. The research keeps showing that folks focused on accumulating stuff report lower life satisfaction over time. It's like trying to fill a bucket with a hole in the bottom.

Moving to a Better Location Will Make You Happy

Why This Matters: The "geographic cure", thinking paradise is just a moving van away, sets you up for real disappointment. Your problems have this annoying habit of forwarding themselves to your new address, no matter how nice the weather is.

Scientific Counter-Evidence: Schkade and Kahneman's 1998 study is a classic eye-opener. Californians weren't any happier than folks in the

Midwest, despite everyone assuming sunshine equals joy.[62] The happiness bump from moving somewhere "better"? Usually gone within 6 months to 2 years. We adapt. Always do. It's just how we're built. Migration psychology findings demonstrate the truth: your relationships, personality, and sense of purpose, the stuff that actually determines happiness, all fit in the moving truck right next to your coffee maker.

External Circumstances Determine Happiness Levels

Why This Matters: If you think happiness comes from your situation, you'll waste your life rearranging deck chairs instead of learning to swim. The real happiness skills are internal, not external: and that's actually great news because you can work on those anywhere.

Scientific Counter-Evidence: Remember that Lyubomirsky study from 2005? Only 10% of happiness variation comes from circumstances.[46] Ten percent! That's it. The "hedonic treadmill" scholarly work confirms that we adapt to almost everything, good or bad. Lottery winners, accident victims. After the dust settles, most people return pretty close to their baseline happiness.[63] It's both humbling and liberating when you think about it. Your circumstances matter less than you think, which means your happiness is more in your control than you might have believed.

More Free Time = More Happiness

Why This Matters: The dream of endless leisure time? The truth is, it can be more of a nightmare than paradise. Empty hours without purpose or connection can drain your well-being faster than a demanding job.

Scientific Counter-Evidence: Sharif, Mogilner, and Hershfield discovered something fascinating in 2021. There's actually a free time sweet spot.[64] Too little time crushes you (no surprise there). But too much? Also problematic. Beyond about 5 hours of free time daily, well-being actually drops, especially if you're just killing time instead of doing something meaningful. The magic is in the middle. Enough time to breathe and pursue what matters, not so much that you're drowning in aimlessness.

Look, I'm not saying money and stuff don't matter at all. Try paying your mortgage with gratitude journals. But once you've got the basics covered, chasing more toys is like trying to fill a leaky bucket with a fire hose. The happiness you're looking for was never in the Amazon cart or the real estate listing. It's in what you do with what you've already got. Speaking of doing. Let's tackle all those achievements we're convinced will finally make us feel like we've 'made it'...

💰 MONEY & STUFF MYTHS - BUSTED

❌ More money = more happiness → Happiness plateaus around $110k/year

❌ New possessions bring lasting joy → Experiences beat stuff every time

❌ Paradise is a moving van away → Your problems forward to your new address

❌ Circumstances determine happiness → Only 10% comes from situation

❌ Endless free time = bliss → Too much leisure time reduces well-being

III. ACHIEVEMENT, GOALS, AND SUCCESS

Let me tell you about my old way of keeping score. For years, I treated achievements like they were stamps in some cosmic passport to happiness. Got the degree? Stamp. Landed the promotion? Another stamp. Finally organized that disaster of a garage? Well... I'm still working on that one.

What kills me is that every single big win felt amazing for about as long as it takes to reheat leftover pizza. Then poof. Right back to baseline, already eyeing the next mountain to climb. That whole "I'll be happy when..." mindset? Friends, it's a sucker's game. Like trying to catch the horizon. No matter how fast you run, it keeps moving away.

The really twisted part is how these achievement myths keep us living in tomorrow while missing what's happening today. We're so busy chasing future happiness that we step right over the joy puddles at our feet. Time to expose some sacred cows about success, goals, and that particularly exhausting advice about "finding your passion." Grab a comfortable seat: this might sting a little, but in that good way, like antiseptic on a cut.

Achieving Goals Creates Lasting Happiness

Why This Matters: Banking your happiness on future achievements is like putting all your money on one number at the roulette table. You might get a quick thrill, but the house always wins in the end. Once you realize happiness actually helps create success (not just the other way around), you can stop treating achievements like oxygen and start seeing them as nice bonuses in an already good life.

Scientific Counter-Evidence: The research here might surprise you. Goals give you a temporary high, then our brains do this thing called "hedonic adaptation". Basically, we get used to anything, good or bad. Brickman and his team showed this back in '78 with lottery winners.[63] You'd think they'd be dancing in the streets forever, right? Nope. Back to their normal happiness levels within months. Then Lyubomirsky's crew analyzed over 200 studies in 2005 and found something that flipped the script: happy people tend to become successful, not the other way around.[65] Yes, positive emotions boost your performance and creativity. On the other hand those achievement highs expire faster than milk left out on the counter.

You Must Find Your Passion to Be Happy

Why This Matters: That "find your passion" advice has created more anxiety than a thousand final exams. People wander around waiting for lightning to strike, getting more stressed when nothing immediately sets off fireworks. Truth is, passion usually grows slowly, like a friendship or a taste for good coffee. Not like some Hollywood love-at-first-sight moment.

Scientific Counter-Evidence: Back in 2018, O'Keefe, Dweck, and Walton ran a study that basically turned the passion myth inside out.[66] They found that people who believe interests develop over time actually explore more and stick with things longer than those hunting for their "one true passion." The passion-hunters? They bail the second things get challenging. Career researchers back this up as well. Getting good at something and having some control over your work breeds passion way more reliably than sitting around waiting for the universe to send you a sign. It's like waiting for the perfect wave when you don't even know how to swim yet.

You'll Be Happy When You Achieve the Perfect Body

Why This Matters: The perfect body chase is like running on a treadmill in a hall of mirrors. Exhausting, disorienting, and you never actually get anywhere. Body acceptance delivers way more happiness bang for your buck than any diet or workout plan ever could.

Scientific Counter-Evidence: The following study blew my mind: Tylka and Wood-Barcalow proved in 2015 that how you feel about your body matters way more than how it actually looks. People who accept their bodies are happier,[67] period. Regardless of what the scale says or how their jeans fit. Even when folks hit their body goals (lost the weight, got the surgery, achieved those six-pack abs), the joy fades fast. Why? We adapt, then find new "flaws" to obsess over. It's endless, like painting the Golden Gate Bridge. The body acceptance crowd? They're the ones actually winning the happiness game, enjoying their lives instead of postponing joy until they hit some impossible standard.

Extrinsic Goals (Fame, Image, Wealth) Lead to a Good Life

Why This Matters: Our culture's got us chasing all the wrong rabbits. Money, fame, looking good for the 'gram. Problem is, research says these external goals are about as fulfilling as cotton candy for dinner. Understanding this helps you aim for stuff that actually fills you up.

Scientific Counter-Evidence: Kasser and Ryan started documenting this back in '96, and it's held up like a well-built fence.[68] People gunning for cash, fame, and image? More depressed, less energetic than folks pursuing personal growth, relationships, and community contribution. It's not even close. Their follow-up studies showed this isn't just a phase. The longer you chase external validation, the worse it gets. Meanwhile, the people focused on internal stuff like self-acceptance and genuine connection? They're thriving.

Perfectionism Leads to Excellence

Why This Matters: Perfectionism sounds noble, like you just have really high standards, until you realize it's basically self-sabotage wearing a three-piece suit. It breeds anxiety, kills creativity, and ironically makes you perform worse. There's a huge difference between having standards and being a perfectionist. One helps, the other hurts like stepping on a LEGO in the dark.

Scientific Counter-Evidence: Stoeber and Otto drew this important line in 2006: wanting to do well (what they call "perfectionistic strivings") can be okay.[69] But the dark side, beating yourself up, being terrified of mistakes (they call it "perfectionistic concerns"), that's what tanks both performance and happiness. Hewitt and Flett found the worst kind is "socially-prescribed perfectionism". Thinking everyone expects you to be flawless.[70] That particular flavor leads straight to paralysis and procrastination. I've seen it in my own life. The projects I never started because they couldn't be "perfect" versus the imperfect ones (like this book) that actually saw the light of day.

The truth about achievements? They're like Chinese food for your happiness. Satisfying for about an hour, then you're hungry again. Not because there's something wrong with you, but because that's literally how our brains work. So maybe it's time to stop treating life like a resume-building exercise and start asking better questions. Like: What would I do if I knew the high would wear off anyway? And who would I want to share it with when it does? Speaking of which...

🏆 SUCCESS MYTHS - THE TRUTH

❌ Achieving goals = lasting happiness → The high fades fast (hedonic adaptation)

❌ Find your passion or else → Passion develops over time through practice

❌ Perfect body = perfect happiness → Body acceptance beats body perfection

❌ Fame/wealth/image = good life → Internal goals trump external ones

❌ Perfectionism = excellence → It actually paralyzes performance

IV. RELATIONSHIPS AND SOCIAL CONNECTION

Now we're getting to the heart of things. Literally. I've spent years bouncing between two extremes like a ping-pong ball. Sometimes thinking the right relationship would fix everything ("If I could just find my people..."), other times going full hermit mode ("I don't need anybody"). Neither approach worked worth a darn.

I've watched friends hunt for relationship perfection like they're shopping for the perfect avocado. Squeezing and inspecting and never quite satisfied. Others wear their independence like armor, proud they "don't need people," while secretly feeling lonely as a lighthouse keeper. Meanwhile, the scientists have been over here jumping up and down, trying to tell us we've got it all backwards.

These relationship myths are different because they sound so reasonable until you scratch the surface. Whether you're thinking about starting a family, trying to keep friendships alive in our busy world, or wondering what "community" even means when we're all staring at screens, getting these truths straight could change every relationship you've got: including the one with that person in the mirror. So let's dig in and see what's really what.

Children Make People Happier

Why This Matters: Knowing the real deal about kids and happiness helps you make better choices about having them: or helps you feel better about the choices you've already made. Also helps you ditch the fantasy and deal with actual parenthood, which makes everyone happier in the long run.

Scientific Counter-Evidence: Okay, deep breath on this one: parents typically report less day-to-day happiness than non-parents. Glass, Simon, and Andersson proved this in 2016 across multiple countries. It's especially tough in places without good family support policies.[71] Now don't get me wrong, kids bring meaning and those heart-melting moments that make everything else fade away. But the research is honest about this: happiness often takes a hit during the diaper-and-homework years, then rebounds when they finally move out. It's not anti-kid to acknowledge this. It's just being real about the trade-offs. Kind of like boats. Amazing experiences, but nobody talks about the maintenance.

The Perfect Relationship Will Make Me Happy Forever

Why This Matters: Fairy tale thinking kills real relationships faster than leaving the toilet seat up. Expecting another person to be your permanent happiness dispenser sets everyone up for disappointment. Real love takes work, maintenance, and accepting that a good chunk of your happiness still has to come from inside your own heart.

Scientific Counter-Evidence: Helliwell and Grover showed in 2014 that relationship quality beats relationship status every single time.[72] Being married doesn't automatically equal happiness. Being in a good marriage does. There is a big difference there. Gottman's famous research proves it's not about finding your "soulmate" who never annoys you. It's about how you handle the inevitable conflicts.[77] The couples who last? They're not the ones who never fight; they're the ones who fight fair. Studies keep confirming: healthy relationships boost well-being, sure, but the boost is modest and depends entirely on the ongoing quality. It's like having a guitar. Just owning one doesn't make you happy, but playing music with people you love? That's the magic.

Social Media Connects Us and Improves Happiness

Why This Matters: Understanding how social media actually affects your brain helps you use it smarter instead of letting it use you. More real connection, less mindless scrolling: that's where happiness actually lives.

Scientific Counter-Evidence: The data here is not pretty. Heavy social media use links to depression, anxiety, and loneliness. The whole unhappy package. Kross proved in 2013 that Facebook use actually predicts declining well-being over time.[74] Why? Social comparison is a killer. You're seeing everyone's highlight reel while living your own behind-the-scenes blooper footage. Meta-analyses keep finding the same thing: more social media, less happiness. It's especially rough on young people. Like sugar. A little might be fine, but we're all overdosing.

Complete Independence Leads to Happiness

Why This Matters: Our culture worships self-sufficiency like it's the holy grail. But chasing total independence is like trying to move a couch up a flight of stairs alone. Technically possible, but why make life that hard when you could have help?

Scientific Counter-Evidence: We're literally wired for connection. It's not optional equipment. Holt-Lunstad's massive 2010 analysis found that solid relationships boost your survival odds by 50%.[75] That's as powerful as quitting smoking! Every angle of research, attachment theory, social neuroscience, you name it, shows the same thing: humans need humans. Feeling connected doesn't just make you happier, it buffers stress and keeps you alive longer. Independence might sound good in country songs, but interdependence is where the real music happens.

Happiness Is a Purely Individual Pursuit

Why This Matters: Treating happiness like a solo project is like trying to have a party by yourself. Technically possible, but missing the whole point. Once you get that connection is central, not optional, you start investing in relationships and community like your life depends on it. Because honestly? It kind of does.

Scientific Counter-Evidence: Diener and Seligman compared super-happy people to everyone else in 2002.[76] The difference wasn't money, success, or perfect circumstances. It was relationships. The happiest people had better social connections, period. That Holt-Lunstad study I mentioned earlier drives it home. Relationships are as vital to your health as not smoking. This isn't touchy-feely stuff; it's survival. We're pack animals who somehow convinced ourselves we're supposed to be lone wolves. No wonder so many of us feel off.

Social Comparison Helps Gauge Happiness

Why This Matters: Using other people as your happiness measuring stick is like using a rubber ruler. The measurements keep changing, and you'll never measure up. You need your own internal compass, not a constant comparison game that nobody wins.

Scientific Counter-Evidence: Festinger started this research way back, and it's only gotten more relevant in our Instagram world. Vogel's 2014 study linked social media comparison directly to depression.[77] Lyubomirsky and Ross showed that comparing yourself to "better off" people tanks both happiness and motivation.[78] The more you compare, the worse you feel. It's like being in a race where the finish line keeps moving and everyone else seems to have a faster boat (okay, I'll stop with the boat analogies... maybe).

Being Attractive = Being Happy

Why This Matters: We dump ridiculous amounts of time, money, and mental energy into looking good, expecting a happiness payoff that never comes. Knowing looks don't equal joy frees you up to invest in stuff that actually works.

Scientific Counter-Evidence: Diener's 1995 research found almost no connection between how attractive others rated you and how happy you were.[79] What mattered a tiny bit? How attractive you felt. But even that effect was smaller than a minnow. Frederick and Loewenstein's work on adaptation shows why, even dramatic appearance improvements stop making you happy once you get used to them. You could look like a movie star and still be miserable. Happens all the time. Just flip through any celebrity magazine at the grocery checkout. All those beautiful people sure seem to have a lot of problems.

My years have taught me that you could have the perfect Instagram life, beautiful spouse, adorable kids, thousands of 'friends', and still feel lonely as hell. Or you could have a few real connections, people who've seen your messiest moments and stuck around anyway, and feel rich beyond measure. We're not meant to do this life solo, no matter what the self-help gurus preach. We're pack animals pretending to be lone wolves, and it's killing us. But you know what? Even pack animals have to deal with emotions. Let's figure out what to do with those...

👥 RELATIONSHIP MYTHS - GET REAL

✖ Kids automatically make you happier → Day-to-day happiness often drops

✖ Perfect partner = permanent bliss → Relationship quality requires ongoing work

✖ Social media builds connection → Heavy use predicts loneliness & depression

✖ Total independence = freedom → We're wired to need each other

✖ Happiness is a solo journey → Social connections are happiness essential

✖ Compare yourself to others → Social comparison breeds misery

✖ Good looks = happiness → Almost zero correlation exists

V. MANAGING EMOTIONS AND CHALLENGES

For years, I treated negative emotions like warning lights on my car dashboard. Something's broken, fix it NOW. Well, that's about as smart as my legendary attempt to patch a burst pipe with duct tape. These myths about handling life's curveballs? They've got us all twisted up, from dodging sadness like it's contagious to thinking that punching pillows when you're pissed actually helps. (Spoiler: it usually just makes you want to punch more things.)

I've tried every wrong approach in the book. Ignored problems, hoping they'd vanish. Dodged hard conversations like a matador. I even tried to eliminate stress completely from my life. Might as well have tried to eliminate breathing. None of it worked, obviously. The good news? Science has figured out what actually does work, and it's nothing like what most of us were taught. Understanding how emotions really operate doesn't just help you survive the rough patches. Sometimes, those rough patches become the very thing that makes you stronger. Wild, right?

Negative Emotions Signal Something Is Wrong

Why This Matters: Treating every bad feeling like a five-alarm fire means you'll spend your life trying to stuff down perfectly normal emotions. That never ends well. Once you get that even crappy feelings have a job to do, you can work with them instead of against them.

Scientific Counter-Evidence: Kashdan and Biswas-Diener laid it out in "The Upside of Your Dark Side". Our so-called negative emotions are actually pretty darn useful.[80] Anger helps you set boundaries when someone crosses the line. Fear keeps you from doing genuinely stupid things. Sadness? It's basically a bat signal for support. Lisa Feldman Barrett's work on how we construct emotions shows that all feelings, the good, bad, and ugly, are just information.[81] The trick is learning to read the manual.

Venting Anger Relieves It

Why This Matters: That whole "let it all out" advice? Usually makes things worse. You end up escalating conflicts and feeling angrier than when you started. There are way better ways to handle anger that don't involve destroying innocent pillows or relationships.

Scientific Counter-Evidence: Bushman's 2002 experiments are brutal for the venting crowd.[82] People who punched pillows to "release" anger? They got MORE aggressive afterward, not less. Lohr and his team reviewed the whole field and found the same thing. Expressing anger tends to amp it up, not calm it down.[77] It's like trying to put out a fire with gasoline. The catharsis theory is dead, folks. Has been for years.

Sadness Should Be Avoided

Why This Matters: Running from sadness creates this weird double whammy. You feel sad AND ashamed for feeling sad. It's exhausting. Accepting sadness as a normal part of being human lets you actually process tough stuff instead of making it worse by fighting it.

Scientific Counter-Evidence: Keltner and Gross showed that sadness evolved for good reasons. It signals loss and helps us conserve energy when we need to heal.[84] Bowlby's attachment research proved that grief and sadness are how healthy people respond to loss.[85] Fighting it just prolongs the pain. The ACT folks have mountains of data showing that accepting difficult emotions reduces suffering way more than trying to dodge them.[86] Turns out feeling your feelings is actually the shortcut.

I Can't Be Happy During Adversity

Why This Matters: Thinking you have to wait for all problems to disappear before feeling any joy is like waiting for perfect weather before leaving the house. You'll be waiting forever. People can and do experience happiness even in tough times. Knowing this changes everything.

Scientific Counter-Evidence: Bonanno's 2004 research blew my mind. 50-60% Of people who lose someone close show remarkable resilience.[87] They grieve, sure, but they also laugh, find moments of joy, and keep living. Tedeschi and Calhoun documented "post-traumatic growth". People who come through trauma reporting deeper relationships, more meaning, and greater appreciation for life.[88] The dual-process model shows resilient folks naturally swing between dealing with hard stuff and taking breaks for positive experiences. It's not either/or. It's both/and.

Avoiding Difficulties and Problems Increases Happiness

Why This Matters: Dodging problems feels good for about five minutes. Then they grow bigger, meaner, and harder to ignore. Plus you never develop the skills to handle life's inevitable crap. Facing challenges head-on, even when it sucks, builds real resilience.

Scientific Counter-Evidence: Hayes and his crew proved that "experiential avoidance", running from difficult thoughts and feelings, actually creates more distress, not less.[86] Aldao's massive analysis of 114 studies found avoidance strategies were the strongest predictors of anxiety, depression, and even addiction.[89] Meanwhile, people who face their challenges often report finding meaning, building stronger relationships, and appreciating life more.

Stress Must Be Eliminated

Why This Matters: Trying to live stress-free means avoiding everything interesting, challenging, or growth-inducing. That's not living, that's existing. Some stress is actually good for you, like exercise for your mind.

Scientific Counter-Evidence: Kelly McGonigal turned the stress world upside down. It's not stress that kills you. It's believing stress will kill you. Crum and Achor proved that seeing stress as enhancing rather than harmful actually improves performance and health.[90] The hormesis model shows that moderate challenges strengthen our psychological systems, in the same way lifting weights builds muscle. Zero stress equals zero growth. The goal isn't eliminating stress. It's getting better at it.

The grand irony of emotions? The more you try to control them, the more they control you. It's like trying to hold beach balls underwater. Exhausting and ultimately pointless. Your anger, sadness, and fear? They're not bugs in your operating system; they're features. The question isn't how to eliminate them but how to dance with them without stepping on your own feet. And speaking of dancing with life, let's talk about all those daily decisions we're convinced will lead us to happily ever after...

😊 EMOTION MYTHS - PLOT TWIST

✖ Negative emotions = something's wrong → They're useful information

✖ Vent anger to release it → Actually makes you angrier

✖ Avoid sadness at all costs → It helps process loss and heal

✖ Can't be happy during hard times → Joy and grief can coexist

✖ Dodge all problems → Facing challenges builds resilience

✖ Eliminate all stress → Some stress promotes growth

VI. DECISION-MAKING AND LIFE CHOICES

Ever stood in the cereal aisle having an existential crisis over Cheerios vs. Lucky Charms? Now multiply that by a thousand: that's modern life. Career changes, where to live, and how to spend our limited time on this rock. We're drowning in options while somehow feeling less satisfied than our grandparents, who had three choices for everything. I spent decades making decisions based on what I thought Future Me would want. Reality: I'm terrible at predicting what that guy likes.

These decision-making myths mess with everything from daily choices to life-altering crossroads. Like thinking more options equals more happiness (it doesn't) or that staying busy means you're winning at life (you're not). Once you understand how our brains actually handle decisions and what genuinely impacts happiness, you can start making choices that help instead of hurt. And that skill? Worth more than any degree hanging on your wall.

Having More Choices Makes You Happier

Why This Matters: Our "more is better" culture has us believing that infinite options equal infinite happiness. Wrong. Understanding that too many choices can paralyze and disappoint helps you appreciate what you have instead of constantly shopping for something better.

Scientific Counter-Evidence: Barry Schwartz nailed this with the "paradox of choice." Iyengar and Lepper's jam study is legendary. 24 jam options led to fewer sales and less satisfaction than just 6 options.[91] Too many choices create anxiety, paralysis, and regret. You second-guess yourself, wonder about the roads not taken, and blame yourself when things aren't perfect. Studies keep confirming: past a certain point, more options make us less happy, not more.

You Can Accurately Predict Future Happiness

Why This Matters: We make huge life decisions based on how we think we'll feel later. The problem is, we're terrible at this prediction game. Understanding our forecasting failures helps make better choices based on actual evidence, not imaginary future feelings.

Scientific Counter-Evidence: Gilbert and Wilson documented our spectacular failure at "affective forecasting." Their 1998 study showed we massively overestimate how long emotions will last. They called it "durability bias." [92] Think that promotion will make you happy forever? That breakup will destroy you? Both wrong. Their 2005 review found we consistently screw up predicting both intensity and duration of future feelings.[93] We're not fortune tellers, we're fortune guessers. And we're bad at it.

Thinking About the Future Will Make You Happy

Why This Matters: Living in tomorrow means missing today. Sure, some planning is necessary, but constant future focus steals the only happiness actually available. The kind happening right now.

Scientific Counter-Evidence: Killingsworth and Gilbert's smartphone study is mind-blowing.[94] Our minds wander 47% of the time, and we're less happy when wandering than when present. They tracked thousands of people in real-time. The data is clear. Mindfulness research backs this up: present-moment awareness correlates with well-being, while future-focused thinking often shows up as anxiety. The future's not where happiness lives. It's here. Now. While you're reading this.

Retirement Will Make You Happy

Why This Matters: The retirement fantasy sells us permanent vacation vibes. Reality check: Without purpose and structure, retirement can be surprisingly tough. Knowing this helps you prepare for the psychological shift, not just the financial one.

Scientific Counter-Evidence: Kim and Moen's 2002 research burst the retirement bubble.[95] Many retirees struggle, especially those whose identity was tied to work. Lose the structure, social connections, and sense of contribution? Well-being often tanks. The happiest retirees? They find new purpose through volunteering, part-time work, and serious hobbies. Retirement isn't a happiness destination. It's just another life phase that needs active engagement.

Keeping Busy Will Make You Happy

Why This Matters: Busyness as a status symbol is killing us. Understanding that "time affluence", feeling time-rich, matters more than packed schedules helps you protect empty space in your calendar like the treasure it is.

Scientific Counter-Evidence: Whillans and team proved in 2016 that people who value time over money report higher well-being.[96] Chronic busyness? It predicts stress, prevents savoring good moments, and damages relationships. The research on work-life balance is unanimous. Constant time pressure equals lower life satisfaction and worse health. Being busy isn't winning. Having time is.

Intelligence Leads to Greater Happiness

Why This Matters: Thinking smarter equals happier sets you up for disappointment. IQ can't hug you when you're sad. Understanding that emotional and social skills matter more for happiness helps you develop what actually counts.

Scientific Counter-Evidence: The IQ-happiness connection? Basically nonexistent. Penney's 2015 study found that high intelligence sometimes correlates with MORE rumination and existential worry.[97] Ouch.

Studies consistently show that emotional intelligence and relationships predict happiness way better than SAT scores. Smart people often overthink themselves miserable. Sometimes ignorance really is bliss.

Helping Yourself First Leads to Happiness

Why This Matters: The "put your oxygen mask on first" mentality, taken too far, misses a crucial point. Helping others IS helping yourself. Understanding this creates positive cycles benefiting everyone.

Scientific Counter-Evidence: Dunn, Aknin, and Norton's 2008 bombshell: spending money on others makes you happier than spending on yourself.[98] The "helper's high" is real. Volunteering, donating, random kindness all boost the giver's happiness, health, and even lifespan. Brain scans show helping others lights up reward centers just like personal pleasures. Turns out generosity is secretly selfish. In the best way.

Altruism Is Selfless

Why This Matters: Thinking you need pure, selfless motives to help others creates unnecessary guilt about feeling good when you give. Once you know helping is a two-way street, you can give freely without the weird guilt about enjoying it.

Scientific Counter-Evidence: That same Dunn study proved giving benefits to the giver.[98] Harbaugh's 2007 brain imaging showed voluntary giving activates our reward centers, we're wired to feel good about helping.[99] Stephen Post's 2005 review connected altruistic behavior to better mental and physical health for the helper.[100] It's not selfless, it's a beautiful win-win. And that's exactly how it should be.

So where does all this myth-busting leave us? Standing in that cereal aisle of life with a completely different shopping list. Truths: the secret to happiness isn't about having more choices, predicting the future, or putting yourself first until you're 'ready' to help others. **It's about making peace with less, staying present with what is, and discovering that the best way to fill your own cup is often by pouring into**

someone else's. The truth is, most of what we've been taught about happiness is backwards. The good news? Now you know better. And once you know better, you can do better. That's not just hope talking: that's science.

LIFE CHOICE MYTHS - WAKE-UP CALL

More options = more happiness → Too many choices create paralysis

You can predict future feelings → We're terrible at emotional fore-casting

Focus on the future for happiness → Present moment = where joy lives

Retirement = automatic happiness → Purpose matters more than leisure

Stay busy to stay happy → Time affluence beats packed schedules

High IQ = high happiness → Emotional intelligence matters more

Put yourself first → Helping others boosts your happiness

True altruism must be selfless → Feeling good about giving is natural

WITH DEEP GRATITUDE

To Suzy, my anchor and the person who taught me empathy by example. You believed in this crazy 2 a.m. project before I did.

To my five children. You've been my teachers in resilience and joy. Thanks for reading my happiness spreadsheets and somehow turning out amazing despite my imperfect parenting.

To Dr. Laurie Santos and The Happiness Lab. Your 200+ episodes transformed a desperate Google search into this book. You'll never know how your work changed one dog-walker's life on a New Jersey beach.

To my friend Chris Pridy. Thank you for proofreading an early draft and challenging me to be raw and real in my stories.

To all my friends and family scattered across different tribes. Knowing you wanted to read this simply because you care for me was an encouragement beyond measure.

To Yeti, who got me walking, listening, and discovering that beach + podcasts + belly laughs = transformation. Yes, I'm thanking my dog.

To every researcher whose work is scattered throughout this book. You're the real heroes. Your work is the linchpin of everything in this book.

To whatever it is in this universe that moves our hearts, encourages us, and leads us to go beyond ourselves in ways that we just don't understand.

And to you, the reader. Thank you for believing happiness is possible and for sharing these tools with others. You're part of this story now.

I'm grateful for every imperfect moment that led here. Because perfection isn't the goal. Our Connections are the goal.

With a full heart,
Billy

P.S. If I forgot you, blame my enthusiasm, not my heart. Consider yourself appreciated and probably owed a beer or coffee.

ABOUT THE AUTHOR

Billy Marshall's journey began at Pinelands Regional High School, where he first discovered that life's simple pleasures and strong community bonds matter more than achievements. An MBA in Finance from NYU and a successful career as an SVP of Reporting and Analytics honed his ability to decode complex data. But it was a desperate 2 a.m. Google search for 'how to be happy' that transformed his data-driven mind into a personal mission.

In pursuit of that mission, he distilled the lessons from his own gloriously imperfect life into a practical, real-world happiness toolbox. He has field-tested every science-backed principle in this book through decades of raising five remarkable children and building meaningful relationships.

Today, Billy and his wife Suzy try to live the principles they preach. Their Point Pleasant, NJ, home is a natural gathering place for family, friends, and neighbors. When not hosting cookouts or playing cornhole, they explore the country in their self-built camper van with Yeti, their white Golden Retriever. Whether he's analyzing spreadsheets, taking friends out on his boat, or crunching numbers, Billy shows every day that happiness isn't just measurable. It multiplies when shared.

A proud grandfather of five, Billy writes not as a guru but as a curious researcher and fellow traveler. He's learned that happiness isn't about perfection. It's about practicing what works and finding good people to share the journey.

Continue the journey with Billy and join a community of fellow travelers at **www.yourhappier.life**.

BIBLIOGRAPHY

1. Seligman, M. E. P., Steen, T. A., Park, N., & Peterson, C. (2005). *Positive Psychology Progress: Empirical Validation of Interventions.* American Psychologist

2. Lee, L. O., James, P., Zevon, E. S., Kim, E. S., Trudel-Fitzgerald, C., Spiro III, A., Grodstein, F., & Kubzansky, L. D. (2019). *Optimism is associated with exceptional longevity in 2 epidemiologic cohorts of men and women.* Proceedings of the National Academy of Sciences

3. Baumgartner, J. N., Schneider, T. R., & Capiola, A. (2018). *Investigating the relationship between optimism and stress responses: A biopsychosocial perspective..* Personality and Individual Differences, 129, 114-118.

4. Jamieson, J. P., Mendes, W. B., & Nock, M. K. (2013). *Improving Acute Stress Responses: The Power of Reappraisal.* Current Directions in Psychological Science

5. Jose, P. E., Lim, B. T., & Bryant, F. B. (2012). *Does savoring increase happiness? A daily diary study.* The Journal of Positive Psychology

6. Berk, L. S., Tan, S. A., Fry, W. F., Napier, B. J., Lee, J. W., Hubbard, R. W., Lewis, J. E., & Eby, W. C. (1989). *Neuroendocrine and stress hormone changes during mirthful laughter.* The American Journal of the Medical Sciences

7. Davidson, R. J., Kabat-Zinn, J., Schumacher, J., Rosenkranz, M., Muller, D., Santorelli, S. F., Urbanowski, F., Harrington, A., Bonus, K., & Sheridan, J. F. (2003). *Alterations in Brain and Immune Function Produced by Mindfulness Meditation.* Psychosomatic Medicine

8. Perciavalle, V., Blandini, M., Fecarotta, P., Buscemi, A., Di Corrado, D., Bertolo, L., Fichera, F., & Coco, M. (2017). *The role of deep breathing on stress.* Neurological Sciences

9. Lieberman, M. D., Eisenberger, N. I., Crockett, M. J., Tom, S. M., Pfeifer, J. H., & Way, B. M. (2007). *Putting Feelings Into Words: Affect Labeling Disrupts Amygdala Activity in Response to Affective Stimuli.* Psychological Science

10. Rudd, M., Vohs, K. D., & Aaker, J. (2012). *Awe Expands People's Perception of Time, Alters Decision Making, and Enhances Well-Being.* Psychological Science

11. Breines, J. G., & Chen, S. (2012). *Self-Compassion Increases Self-Improvement Motivation.* Personality and Social Psychology Bulletin

12. Schroder, H. S., Fisher, M. E., Lin, Y., Lo, S. L., Danovitch, J. H., & Moser, J. S. (2017). *Neural evidence for enhanced attention to mistakes among school-aged children with a growth mindset.* Developmental Cognitive Neuroscience

13. McCracken, L. M., & Eccleston, C. (2003). *Coping or acceptance: what to do about chronic pain?.* Pain

14. Koenig, H. G., McCullough, M. E., & Larson, D. B. (2001). *Handbook of Religion and Health.* Oxford University Press

15. Griffiths, R. R., Richards, W. A., McCann, U., & Jesse, R. (2006). *Psilocybin can occasion mystical-type experiences having substantial and sustained personal meaning and spiritual significance.* Psychopharmacology

16. Hopkins, N., Reicher, S. D., Khan, S. S., Tewari, S., Srinivasan, N., & Stevenson, C. (2015). *Explaining effervescence: Investigating the relationship between shared social identity and positive experience in crowds.* Cognition & Emotion.

17. Pargament, K. I. (1997). *The Psychology of Religion and Coping: Theory, Research, Practice.* Guilford Press

18. Ben Simon, E., Rossi, A., Harvey, A. G., & Walker, M. P. (2020). *Overanxious and underslept.* Nature Human Behaviour

19. Babyak, M., Blumenthal, J. A., Herman, S., et al. (2000). *Exercise treatment for major depression: maintenance of therapeutic effects at 10 months.* Psychosomatic Medicine

20. Kristeller, J. L., & Wolever, R. Q. (2011). *Mindfulness-based eating awareness training for treating binge eating disorder.* Eating Disorders

21. Wing, R. R., & Phelan, S. (2005). *Long-term weight loss maintenance.* The American Journal of Clinical Nutrition

22. Berman, M. G., Jonides, J., & Kaplan, S. (2008). *The cognitive benefits of interacting with nature.* Psychological Science

23. Hill, P. L., & Turiano, N. A. (2014). *Purpose in life as a predictor of mortality across adulthood.* Psychological Science

24. Amabile, T. M., & Kramer, S. J. (2011). *The Progress Principle: Using Small Wins to Ignite Joy, Engagement, and Creativity at Work.* Harvard Business Review Press

25. Stern, Y. (2009). *Cognitive reserve..* Neuropsychologia

26. Ridley, M., Rao, G., Schilbach, F., & Patel, V . (2020). *Poverty, depression, and anxiety: Causal evidence and mechanisms.* Science

27. Mogilner, C. (2010). *The Pursuit of Happiness: Time, Money, and Social Connection.* Psychological Science

28. Hunter, M. R., Gillespie, B. W., & Chen, S. Y.-P. (2019). *Urban Nature Experiences Reduce Stress in the Context of Daily Life Based on Salivary Cortisol.* Frontiers in Psychology

29. Ward, A. F., Duke, K., Gneezy, A., & Bos, M. W. (2017). *Brain Drain: The Mere Presence of One's Own Smartphone Reduces Available Cognitive Capacity.* Journal of the Association for Consumer Research

30. Gielan, M. (2015). *Broadcasting Happiness: The Science of Igniting and Sustaining Positive Change.* BenBella Books

31. Hunt, M. G., Marx, R., Lipson, C., & Young, J. (2018). *No More FOMO: Limiting Social Media Decreases Loneliness and Depression.* Journal of Social and Clinical Psychology

32. Conner, T. S., DeYoung, C. G., & Silvia, P. J. (2018). *Everyday creative activity as a path to flourishing.* The Journal of Positive Psychology

33. McMains, S., & Kastner, S. (2011). *Interactions of Top-Down and Bottom-Up Mechanisms in Human Visual Cortex.* The Journal of Neuroscience

34. Saxbe, D. E., & Repetti, R. L. (2010). *No Place Like Home: Home Tours Correlate With Daily Patterns of Mood and Cortisol.* Personality and Social Psychology Bulletin

35. Van Boven, L., & Gilovich, T. (2003). *To Do or to Have? That Is the Question.* Journal of Personality and Social Psychology

36. Waldinger, R. J., & Schulz, M. S. (2023). *The Good Life: Lessons from the World's Longest Scientific Study of Happiness.* Simon & Schuster

37. Algoe, S. B. (2012). *Find, remind, and bind: The functions of gratitude in everyday relationships.* Social and Personality Psychology Compass

38. Eslami, A. A., Rabiei, L., Afzali, S. M., Hamidizadeh, S., & Masoudi, R . (2016). *The effectiveness of assertiveness training on the levels of stress, anxiety, and depression of high school students.* Iranian Red Crescent Medical Journal

39. Gottman, J. M., & Levenson, R. W. (1992). *Marital Processes Predictive of Later Dissolution: Behavior, Physiology, and Health.* Journal of Personality and Social Psychology

40. Freedman, S. R., & Enright, R. D. (1996). *Forgiveness as an intervention goal with incest survivors.* Journal of Consulting and Clinical Psychology

41. Weger, H., Jr., Castle Bell, G., Minei, E. M., & Robinson, M. C. (2014). *The Relative Effectiveness of Active Listening in Initial Interactions.* International Journal of Listening

42. Mehrabian, A. & Ferris, S. R. (1967). *Inference of Attitudes from Nonverbal Communication in Two Channels.* Journal of Consulting Psychology

43. Hall, J. A., Horgan, T. G., & Murphy, N. A. (2019). *Nonverbal Communication.* Annual Review of Psychology

44. Galinsky, A. D., & Moskowitz, G. B. (2000). *Perspective-taking: decreasing stereotype expression, stereotype accessibility, and in-group favoritism.* Journal of Personality and Social Psychology

45. Bruk, A., Scholl, S. G., & Bless, H. (2018). *The beautiful mess effect: Self–other differences in judging vulnerability.* Journal of Personality and Social Psychology

46. Lyubomirsky, S., Sheldon, K. M., & Schkade, D. (2005). *Pursuing happiness: The architecture of sustainable change.* Review of General Psychology

47. Jenkinson, C. E., et al. (2013). *Is volunteering a public health intervention? A systematic review and meta-analysis.* BMC Public Health

48. Haslam, C. A., Jetten, J., Cruwys, T., Dingle, G. A., & Haslam, S. A. (2018). *The New Psychology of Health: Unlocking the Social Cure.* Routledge

49. Haslam, C., Jetten, J., Cruwys, T., Dingle, G. A., & Haslam, S. A. (2018). *The new psychology of health: Unlocking the social cure.* Routledge

50. Greenaway, K. H., Haslam, S. A., Cruwys, T., Branscombe, N. R., Dingle, G., & Tyreman, M. (2015). *From "we" to "me": Group identification enhances perceived personal control..* Personality and Social Psychology Bulletin

51. Fried, L. P., et al. (2004). *A social model for health promotion for an aging population: initial evidence on the Experience Corps model.* Journal of Urban Health

52. Lykken, D., & Tellegen, A. (1996). *Happiness Is a Stochastic Phenomenon.* Psychological Science

53. Ryff, C. D., & Singer, B. H. (1998). *The Contours of Positive Human Health.* Psychological Inquiry

54. Huta, V., & Ryan, R. M. (2010). *Pursuing pleasure or virtue: The differential and overlapping well-being benefits of hedonic and eudaimonic motives.* Journal of Happiness Studies

55. Davidson, R. J., & Begley, S. (2012). *The Emotional Life of Your Brain: How Its*

Unique Patterns Affect the Way You Think, Feel, and Live: and How You Can Change Them. Hudson Street Press

56. Kashdan, T. B., & Biswas-Diener, R. (2014). *The Upside of Your Dark Side.* Hudson Street Press

57. Bryant, F. B., & Veroff, J. (2007). *Savoring: A New Model of Positive Experience.* Lawrence Erlbaum Associates Publishers

58. Lyubomirsky, S., & Layous, K. (2013). *How Do Simple Positive Activities Increase Well-Being?.* Current Directions in Psychological Science

59. Mauss, I. B., Tamir, M., Anderson, C. L., & Savino, N. S. (2011). *Can Seeking Happiness Make People Unhappy? Paradoxical Effects of Valuing Happiness.* Emotion

60. Blanchflower, D. G., & Oswald, A. J. (2008). *Is Well-being U-Shaped over the Life Cycle?.* Social Science & Medicine

61. Kahneman, D., & Deaton, A. (2010). *High income improves evaluation of life but not emotional well-being.* Proceedings of the National Academy of Sciences

62. Schkade, D. A., & Kahneman, D. (1998). *Does Living in California Make People Happy? A Focusing Illusion in Judgments of Life Satisfaction.* Psychological Science

63. Brickman, P., Coates, D., & Janoff-Bulman, R. (1978). *Lottery winners and accident victims: Is happiness relative?.* Journal of Personality and Social Psychology

64. Sharif, M. A., Mogilner, C., & Hershfield, H. E. (2021). *Having Too Little or Too Much Time Is Linked to Lower Subjective Well-Being.* Journal of Personality and Social Psychology

65. Lyubomirsky, S., King, L., & Diener, E. (2005). *The benefits of frequent positive affect: Does happiness lead to success?.* Psychological Bulletin

66. O'Keefe, P. A., Dweck, C. S., & Walton, G. M. (2018). *Implicit Theories of Interest: Finding Your Passion or Developing It?.* Psychological Science

67. Tylka, T. L., & Wood-Barcalow, N. L. (2015). *What is and what is not positive body image? Conceptual foundations and construct definition.* Body Image

68. Kasser, T., & Ryan, R. M. (1996). *Further examining the American dream: Differential correlates of intrinsic and extrinsic goals.* Personality and Social Psychology Bulletin

69. Stoeber, J., & Otto, K. (2006). *Positive conceptions of perfectionism: Approaches, evidence, challenges.* Personality and Social Psychology Review

70. Hewitt, P. L., & Flett, G. L. (1991). *Perfectionism in the self and social contexts: Conceptualization, assessment, and association with psychopathology.* Journal of Personality and Social Psychology

71. Glass, J., Simon, R. W., & Andersson, M. A. (2016). *Parenthood and Happiness: Effects of Work-Family Reconciliation Policies in 22 OECD Countries.* American Journal of Sociology

72. Grover, S., & Helliwell, J. F. (2014). *How's Life at Home? New Evidence on Marriage and the Set Point for Happiness.* NBER Working Papers 20794, National Bureau of Economic Research, Inc.

73. Gottman, J. M., & Silver, N. (1999). *The Seven Principles for Making Marriage Work.* Crown Publishers

74. Kross, E., et al. (2013). *Facebook Use Predicts Declines in Subjective Well-Being in Young Adults*. PLoS ONE

75. Holt-Lunstad, J., Smith, T. B., & Layton, J. B. (2010). *Social Relationships and Mortality Risk: A Meta-analytic Review*. PLoS Medicine

76. Diener, E., & Seligman, M. E. P. (2002). *Very Happy People*. Psychological Science

77. Vogel, E. A., et al. (2014). *Social comparison, social media, and self-esteem*. Psychology of Popular Media Culture

78. Lyubomirsky, S., & Ross, L. (1997). *Hedonic consequences of social comparison: A contrast of happy and unhappy people*. Journal of Personality and Social Psychology

79. Diener, E., Wolsic, B., & Fujita, F. (1995). *Physical attractiveness and subjective well-being*. Journal of Personality and Social Psychology

80. Kashdan, T. B., & Biswas-Diener, R. (2014). *The Upside of Your Dark Side: Why Being Your Whole Self, Not Just Your "Good" Self, Drives Success and Fulfillment*. Hudson Street Press

81. Barrett, L. F. (2017). *How Emotions Are Made: The Secret Life of the Brain*. Houghton Mifflin Harcourt

82. Bushman, B. J. (2002). *Does Venting Anger Feed or Extinguish the Flame? Catharsis, Rumination, Distraction, Anger, and Aggressive Responding*. Personality and Social Psychology Bulletin

83. Lohr, J. M., et al. (2007). *The psychology of anger venting and empirically supported alternatives that do no harm*. The Scientific Review of Mental Health Practice

84. Keltner, D., & Gross, J. J. (1999). *Functional accounts of emotions*. Cognition and Emotion

85. Bowlby, J. (1980). *Attachment and Loss, Vol. 3: Loss: Sadness and Depression*. Basic Books

86. Hayes, S. C., Strosahl, K. D., & Wilson, K. G. (2012). *Acceptance and Commitment Therapy: The Process and Practice of Mindful Change (2nd ed.)*. The Guilford Press

87. Bonanno, G. A. (2004). *Loss, Trauma, and Human Resilience: Have We Underestimated the Human Capacity to Thrive After Extremely Aversive Events?*. American Psychologist

88. Tedeschi, R. G., & Calhoun, L. G. (1996). *The Posttraumatic Growth Inventory: Measuring the positive legacy of trauma*. Journal of Traumatic Stress

89. Aldao, A., Nolen-Hoeksema, S., & Schweizer, S. (2010). *Emotion-regulation strategies across psychopathology: A meta-analytic review*. Clinical Psychology Review

90. Crum, A. J., Salovey, P., & Achor, S. (2013). *Rethinking stress: The role of mindsets in determining the stress response*. Journal of Personality and Social Psychology

91. Iyengar, S. S., & Lepper, M. R. (2000). *When choice is demotivating: Can one desire too much of a good thing?*. Journal of Personality and Social Psychology

92. Gilbert, D. T., et al. (1998). *Immune neglect: A source of durability bias in affective forecasting*. Journal of Personality and Social Psychology

93. Wilson, T. D., & Gilbert, D. T. (2005). *Affective Forecasting: Knowing What to Want*. Current Directions in Psychological Science

94. Killingsworth, M. A., & Gilbert, D. T. (2010). *A wandering mind is an unhappy mind*. Science

95. Kim, J. E., & Moen, P. (2002). *Retirement transitions, gender, and psychological well-being: A life-course, ecological model.* Journal of Gerontology: Social Sciences

96. Whillans, A. V., Weidman, A. C., & Dunn, E. W. (2016). *Valuing time over money is associated with greater happiness.* Social Psychological and Personality Science

97. Penney, A. M., Miedema, V. C., & Mazmanian, D. (2015). *Intelligence and emotional disorders: Is the worrying and ruminating mind a more intelligent mind?.* Personality and Individual Differences

98. Dunn, E. W., Aknin, L. B., & Norton, M. I. (2008). *Spending money on others promotes happiness.* Science

99. Harbaugh, W. T., Mayr, U., & Burghart, D. R. (2007). *Neural responses to taxation and voluntary giving reveal motives for charitable donations.* Science

100. Post, S. G. (2005). *Altruism, happiness, and health: It's good to be good.* International Journal of Behavioral Medicine

www.ingramcontent.com/pod-product-compliance
Lightning Source LLC
Chambersburg PA
CBHW060407130626
46555CB00005B/1998